Founder of
FLEETWOOD MAC

First published in the United Kingdom by Sanctuary Publishing
This edition published by Omnibus Press
(A division of the Wise Music Group
14–15 Berners Street, London, WIT 3LJ)

'Closing My Eyes', 'Before the Beginning' & 'Little Dreamer'
Written by Peter Green
Published by Mute Song Limited

Cover designed by Simon Goggin

ISBN: 978-1-915841-59-9

Martin Celmins hereby asserts his right to be identified as the author
of this work in accordance with Sections 77 to 78 of the
Copyright, Designs and Patents Act 1988.

Every effort has been made to trace the copyright holders
of the photographs in this book but one or two were unreachable.
We would be grateful if the photographers concerned would contact us.

A catalogue record for this book is available from the British Library.
Printed in the Czech Republic.

www.omnibuspress.com

Peter Green

Founder of
FLEETWOOD MAC

OMNIBUS PRESS

London / New York / Paris / Sydney / Copenhagen / Berlin / Madrid / Tokyo

Contents

Foreword
by BB King

Back in the 1960s, Peter Green was one of a new breed of great guitar players, and during that time I spent a week touring with him and Fleetwood Mac. Sure, he was a very fine person, in fact he was the same person no matter who you were. Now that sort of guy is hard to find in this business.

It's funny, but I kind of remember him more after he left Fleetwood Mac, like when he played on my *In London* album. It was around that time, I know, he became disillusioned, but it was also then that our friendship grew.

I could sympathise with him because there had been times for me too when I felt the same – sometimes maybe it seems like everyone else is doing better than you, looks happier, got the best ideas. But then things change – it's hard to know how, but they do. Years later when I played concerts in London, Peter would still sometimes come backstage and say hello – and that meant something to me. It didn't matter that he didn't want to say much, I was real glad that he bothered to come along at all.

People have told me that in his early years my guitar playing influenced Peter a lot. Now that's something I take as a great compliment, but I have to tell you when I hear Peter Green...I hear Peter Green.

I'm happy to see Peter is back and playing, and I know his many friends back home are very happy about it too. Peter is the kind of guy who doesn't say much and lets the guitar do all his talking for him. Well, it's great to hear that voice again.

You know, I can understand his silence all these years. There are many times too when I feel disgusted by the music I'm playing because I can't find the right notes and play the way I really want to. But that's a cancer I'll have to live with for the rest of my life, because if you want to punish me for anything, then take away my guitar. I don't have to touch it, but let it sit in the room so that I can just look at it and daydream.

Peter is back with a guitar in his hands and is trying. That's a big thing for me.

BB King
Glasgow, October 1997

Foreword
by Andy Fairweather Low

One True Voice

BB King, Albert King, Freddie King – they all played Gibson guitars. Each one was blessed with their own unique and instantly identifiable sound. Their very own...

One True Voice.

You can add Peter to that list. It seems obvious to me that Peter didn't think about what he was playing, he wasn't copying, mimicking or reinventing anything. He was just using his very own...

One True Voice.

Amen Corner, Peter Green's Fleetwood Mac – both appeared at the National Jazz & Blues Festival in Windsor in 1967. Peter in 1967 was where I want to be now.

In the late 1960s, Peter's phenomenal songwriting was taking the blues by the scruff of the neck and showing us all what could be done and where we should go. We should all still be listening – but I'm not so sure. 'Oh Well', 'Man Of The World', 'Albatross', 'Green Manalishi', 'Black Magic Woman', 'Love That Burns' – man, what a solo on that song.

For me, Peter wrote the book – one chapter, one edition. He spoke with…

One True Voice.

There's no pretender to that throne. A memory is what all of us will ever be if we're lucky. I hear you, Peter, I will always hear you.

P.S. I own and use Peter's Fender Bandmaster Reverb.
Well, you never know, do you?

Andy Fairweather Low
October 2021

Acknowledgements

By the time this revised edition of *Peter Green* is published it will be 30 years since my research on the original book began.

The first list of useful names and numbers was provided by guitarist and artist Top Topham. Thanks always, Top. That initial research was all speculative because, 'Thank you – but no thank you...too specialist' was the general response I got when seeking a publishing deal.

One commissioning editor thought differently. Thanks always, Phil Scott.

In January 1994 Peter agreed to do a series of interviews, mostly at a café in the Arches at Westcliff near Southend-on-Sea. Then in summer 2008 I interviewed him at Canvey Island for a *Record Collector* magazine career retrospective (November 2008, issue no. 355). I have included other extracts from that interview in this revised edition.

For this edition it was my pleasure to interview or receive written contributions from: Nick Buck, Danny Da Costa, Jeremy Spencer, Nick Pickett, John Altman, Andy Silvester, Andy Fairweather Low, Daliah Sherrington, Pete Brown, Pete Stroud, Mike Dodd, Peter Illingworth, Snowy White, Colin Allen, Peter Vernon-Kell, Clifford Chewaluza/Mataya, Bruno Ducourant, Alfred Bannerman, Gregg Kofi Brown, Willie Bath, Emmanuel Rentzos, Gus Isadore, Michael Shrieve, Andrew Flude, Rob Spragg, Julian Swainson, Paul Hoenderkamp,

Rainer Langhans, John Weinzierl, Margret Greenman and Maria Zantkuijl. The Steve Thompson interview is from 2005 – sadly he passed in 2007.

For reference works, my thanks go to Christopher Hjort and his indispensable *Strange Brew: Eric Clapton & The British Blues Boom 1965–1970* (Jawbone 2007). Gigs and session date timelines and many news items are taken from that book. Thanks also go to Richard J Orlando and *A Love That Burns* and essays on the www.smilingcorgipress.com website.

Colin Allen's *From Bournemouth To Beverly Hills: Tales Of A Tub-Thumper*, Bruce Thomas's *Rough Notes…And Grainy Images*, *Out Of Reach* by Anthony Smith & Morten Strand (with Don Brown) and John Mayall with Joel McIver's *Blues From Laurel Canyon: My Life As A Bluesman* have been useful. So too, Dinky Dawson's *Life On The Road*, and Rufus Publications' *The Albatross Man*.

Thanks also go to Ben Lazarus for constructive critique and proofing of drafts of the text. And to Bela Swardmark Stephens of The Blue Pearls – a band imbued with the spirit of the original Fleetwood Mac; Daniel Svendsen, Tony Smith, Misa Drezgic of the Peter Green Blues Society on Facebook, Andrew Kastner, Al Gold, Don Brown and Christa Ritter.

Very special thanks indeed go to Green devotee and expert Mario Pirrone for tireless additional research and always helpful opinions, and to him and RJ Greaves for the updated discography.

For the original 1995 edition, in addition to Peter's family, the following kindly contributed or helped: Peter Anderton, Peter Bardens, Lynn and Adrian Boot, Jenny Boyd, Bob Brunning, Cliff Cooper, Alex Dmochowski, Dinky Dawson, Sandra Elsdon-Vigon, Mick Fleetwood, Kris Gray, John Hammond Jnr, Jane Honeycombe, John Holmes, Madge Jones, Andrew Kastner, BB King, Dennis Keane, Dave Kelly, Danny Kirwan, Harry Lee, Paul Jones, Bernie Marsden, Beryl Marsden,

John Mayall, Phil McDonnell, John McVie, Neil Murray, Zoot Money, Paul Morrison, John Moorshead, Roger Pearce, Huw Pryce, Cozy Powell, Keith Randall, Mich Reynolds, Andy Silvester, Ed Spevock, Cliff Stewart, Bobby Tench, Stuart Taylor, Mike Vernon, Peter Vernon-Kell, Charlie Watkins, Stan Webb, Nigel Watson, Chris Welch, Snowy White, Charlie Watkins, Jeff and Dee Whittaker, Kevin Winlove-Smith and Judy Wong.

Thanks also to managing editor at Wise Music, David Barraclough, who commissioned this book, and this edition's editor Lucy Beevor, who edited the revisions.

Introduction

To set the tone for this revised edition, several musicians recall how they themselves experienced the musical genius of Peter Green.

Bassist Bruce Thomas auditioned for the original Fleetwood Mac in summer 1967, and would go on to play with Elvis Costello And The Attractions, and once shared the stage with Pete Townshend and Paul McCartney. Bruce was in Peter Bardens' band, The Village, when Mac's leader joined them on stage at the Marquee for a blues-shuffle jam one Saturday night in August 1969: 'If I were forced to pick one musical highpoint from my entire life, then this is it,' he wrote in 1994, and in his 2017 autobiography *Rough Notes* added: 'Neither before, nor since, have I heard anyone play with such tenderness, passion, purpose, precision, intelligence, lyricism, tone, taste, soul and power – with such fire in his belly and authority under his fingers.'

Alto saxophonist and composer John Altman would go on to be Van Morrison's musical director, conduct the Royal Philharmonic Orchestra and write film scores (he also conducted all the brass for the Bond movie *No Time To Die*). But as a student at Sussex University in Brighton he too had an unforgettable jam there in early June 1970, very soon after Peter left Mac: 'What I remember is that Peter and I were on completely the same wavelength – we could go from playing blues to freer things, then to Coltrane. I had never met anyone at that time who I felt was doing what I wanted to do. Playing with him was a truly transcendent experience.'

Musician and songwriter Nick Pickett had never even heard of Fleetwood Mac before first seeing them at Glastonbury Town Hall on 6 April 1968. And yet his reaction was unexpected and intense: 'I took my new girlfriend to see them and soon after Peter began to play suddenly there were tears running down my cheeks...that day changed my life forever.' Nick became and remained a good friend of Peter and his parents in the years to come.

Much more recently, Mike Dodd, who gradually assembled Peter's last band Peter Green And Friends starting in 2007, remembers first hearing his electric guitar playing during rehearsals in Spain: 'Up until then we'd played on acoustic guitars but when Peter was playing "The Thrill Is Gone" and I heard some of those notes that he can do on an electric, I just...my eyes started watering...I don't mind saying it. For the first time, I was there in the room to hear the way he could make the simplest phrase – the timing and delivery of it – a thing of total beauty.'

Add to Peter's musicianship his charisma as a performer – expressed succinctly by ex-Chicken Shack/Savoy Brown/Big Town Playboys bassist Andy Silvester: 'You just couldn't take your eyes off the guy.'

The Yardbirds' guitarist Chris Dreja, in the 2004 rock-doc *Unbroken Chain*, rated Peter's stage presence above that of Eric Clapton: 'I mean, his voice was an incredible, incredible voice and he had that charisma...he actually had more charisma than Eric had...and Eric had a lot of charisma. But Peter Green had a presence on stage that was quite extraordinary.'

And then add to that his innovation and originality as a songwriter, and you have a portrait of a unique artist, musician and legend.

After Peter's sudden and untimely passing on Saturday 25 July 2020, Mark Knopfler's tribute highlighted his lasting legacy: 'I loved Peter Green's playing from the moment I first heard him. He was one of the few greats. There's hardly a month goes by when I don't play a Peter Green recording on my jukebox. He will be idolised by guitar players forever.'

Simon Rocker's tribute in the *Jewish Chronicle* the following week recalled Peter's generosity of spirit, and how back in 1970 Melvyn Carlowe, then head of the Jewish Welfare Board, was met with a surprise when he visited one of its homes for the elderly in Highbury, north London. Carlowe: 'I saw this guy in the dining room serving lunches to the residents. The typical volunteer at the time was a middle-class Jewish lady or a retired Jewish tailor. And he was a youngish man.' Mr Carlowe was then informed by staff that the young helper was one of Britain's most acclaimed guitarists who had not long before suddenly left Fleetwood Mac. He then added: 'They told me he'd been there several times. He may have lived nearby and I think he re-indentified with his Jewish faith. Maybe he had a relative there.'

Naturally, Peter mostly will be remembered for the songs he wrote while leader of Fleetwood Mac, and for his deep and unique interpretation of blues guitar at such a young age. Most tributes reflected that. However, Ed Vulliamy, writing his tribute in *The Observer* on 26 July 2020, highlighted a Peter Green And Friends gig at the Cheese & Grain, Frome, on 30 May 2010: '...later that evening, when he gave his signature instrumental 'Albatross', Green's musicianship had progressed from the technical and emotional cogency of his earlier work to something bordering, frankly, on sublime. As though the agony and ecstasy he had long abandoned formulating into words or conventional communication could be spoken more articulately than ever through music.'

From boyhood onwards, Peter enjoyed listening to a wide

range of music including traditional Jewish songs and tuneful classical music like Prokofiev's *Peter And The Wolf*. The first tune he ever ventured to learn on acoustic guitar was the Spanish guitar solo in the theme from *Gunsmoke*, the American Western TV series first aired in 1955 and titled *Gun Law* in the UK. Then he heard the subtle vibrato of Hank Marvin and soon would play The Shadows' 'Apache' with brother Michael on rhythm guitar. He also loved 1950s rock 'n' roll, skiffle, Mersey Beat and The Beatles.

He played guitar in a school band, The Strangers, and switched to bass for covers bands The Ken Cats, Bobby Dennis And The Dominoes, The Tridents, The Didlos, and Richmond R&B outfit The Muskrats. Very briefly, he was guitarist with professional band Errol Dixon And The Honeydrippers and joined Peter B's Looners in late 1965.

By then, the British blues boom was gaining momentum with bands such as The Rolling Stones, Them, The Yardbirds, The Animals and John Mayall's Bluesbreakers all playing their take on the blues of Muddy Waters, Robert Johnson, Howlin' Wolf, John Lee Hooker, The Three Kings, Jimmy Reed, Chuck Berry, Otis Rush and many others.

Peter had observed closely, listened intently and then practised intensively. When, in July 1966, he joined John Mayall's Bluesbreakers, the young guitarist was on his way.

In this revised edition there is a new Author's Note and then at the back of the book the update begins at Chapter 17 with the Splinter Group era and Peter's return to the stage in 1996. In Chapter 18, Mike Dodd recalls Peter Green And Friends' genesis, and gigging in 2009–10. That chapter ends by describing Peter Green's final years – a happy time for him, living in Canvey Island. Chapter 19 takes a look at his songwriting and Chapter 20 looks back at the guitarist's late 1960s/early 1970s spiritual quest and interest in Buddhism and Christianity.

Sadly, in too many tributes to Peter, the 'Munich Incident' was recycled and embellished. So in Chapter 21 there is an alternative perspective, partly based on interviews with three artists who were at that infamous acid party in March 1970.

Then 1970–75, the late 1970s *In The Skies* and *Little Dreamer* era, and 1981–85 *White Sky* and *Kolors* years are all revisited, plus the February 2020 Tribute to Peter Green London Palladium concert. A tribute from singer and writer Daliah Sherrington published in the *Jewish Chronicle* follows a personal Epilogue.

The book ends with an updated discography by Mario Pirrone and RJ Greaves.

Author's Note

The Author's Note in the first two editions included two stories illustrating Peter Green's fearlessness. One had him driving a Jensen sports saloon at death-defying high speed in London; in the second, seemingly he was unfazed when knocked to the ground on his motorbike in a collision.

This edition's fearlessness anecdote is a ghost story Peter recalled in 2008, which goes back to his 1966 Peter B's Looners' days and the band driving back to London from a gig: 'Do you know that story about the ghost in Cobham? We were all sitting in the front of the van with all the gear in the back, on the A3 road which goes down to Guildford. And we saw what seemed to be, what appeared to be a ghost one night. Someone walking along – around the Cobham bend. And they all went, "Aaarggh!... Did you see that?" Peter Bardens was driving and he goes, "Hey...we gotta get out of here, man!" and I said, "No! Let's go back – that wasn't a ghost, that was someone walking alone at night," and Peter Bardens says, "No...no!" and then Mick Fleetwood goes, "No!...it's a ghost!" [laughs]. They [ghosthunters] had investigated around Cobham and a number of ghosts have been seen around there. And one is a retired colonel or retired military man and this could have been this, and to this day I don't know – I wouldn't like to say what that was. But he did look our way and did seem to be aware of us, and was swinging his arms like this [marching]. But they all thought it was a ghost. Yeah, we had lots of laughs like that.'

So, he wanted to go back to the spot that freaked out the others. Who knows, the sighting may even have inspired Bardens' 1969 song 'Don't Goof With A Spook', on which Peter played suitably eerie guitar. Interestingly, Bardens' father, Dennis, was a journalist and author who reportedly moved in London social circles linked to occultist Aleister Crowley. His book *Ghosts And Hauntings* was first published in 1963: 'Mr Bardens has made a strong case for the existence of ghosts,' wrote the *Sunday Express*.

Looners' bassist Dave Ambrose also recalled a fun-loving band (*MOJO* May 1994): '[Peter] was a straightforward person, no nonsense, never said much – but me, Fleetwood and Bardens were much more kind of wild and debonair. It was a good mix. In those days everything was just healthy, naive, good fun, like hiding from each other in cupboards. Peter would always turn up wearing these baggy dungarees which I think was all part of trying to be a bluesman.'

At Peter's audition, Bardens overruled his rhythm section and gave him the gig, with one proviso, as Peter recalled: 'Pete [Bardens] said, 'You've got to do bendy strings like Steve Cropper'. He said the other guitarist [Mick Parker] didn't do bendy strings and had more of a clean jazz style.' And bendy strings he duly gave on his studio debut solo on Bardens' 'Jodrell Blues', the B-side to 'If You Wanna Be Happy', released 11 March 1966 by the Peter B's.

The Booker T-style instrumentals band then morphed into soul music revue Shotgun Express in late April 1966, adding singers Rod Stewart and Liverpudlian Beryl Marsden. Beryl and Peter became an item.

Peter: 'I was kind of hooked on the Liverpool scene.' Especially so, drummers who, he felt, had their very own stylisation. 'Aynsley Dunbar was good fun...a modern jazz and modern rock player, and he was Liverpudlian as well.'

The Yardbirds' Paul Samwell-Smith and Bill Wyman influenced young bassist Peter but Paul McCartney's playing also inspired him, especially on 'I Saw Her Standing There'.

When asked by *Guitar* magazine (September 1981) if he felt he was in anybody's shadow he replied: 'Tony Crane of The Merseybeats.' *His guitar playing?* 'Him and his interpretations – his way. I was very impressed with The Merseybeats. But I'm not really in his shadow. People would have said I was in Eric Clapton's shadow because I followed him into John Mayall's band, but it wasn't true; I was just doing my own thing.'

His romance with Beryl ended and caused him to leave the band, and also inspired the first blues he said he wrote – 'Evil Woman Blues', recorded with John Mayall accompanying him on piano. Peter: 'I wrote some of that song about her...but only loosely though.' So from the start his songwriting, while always based on personal experience, may have also included some poetic licence (see Chapter 19).

Having been a Bluesbreaker for a couple of days in late October 1965 (see Chapter 3) Peter said yes again to John Mayall in early July 1966, just ahead of the *Blues Breakers With Eric Clapton* 'Beano' album's release on 22 July.

Aynsley Dunbar joined just in time for the *A Hard Road* album sessions, which began in October 1966. The album featured Peter's first signature instrumental, 'The Supernatural', in which he declared his unique bluesman's calling card – mystical, eerie electric blues. 'The Stumble' was John Mayall's choice. Peter: 'John told me I had to play a Freddie King instrumental, maybe because Eric had played 'Hideaway' and so he chose 'The Stumble' for me. I didn't think I was ready to do that...in fact I didn't complete my learning of that now-famous instrumental until I was in Splinter Group.' This shows just how modest and self-critical he was about his playing. He once told the author that 'Greeny' – a classy instrumental taped on 16 February 1967 with Aynsley Dunbar and John McVie – and on which he is already a master of dynamics – should not have been released. It was 'only a jam' he said.

On Willie Cobbs' 'You Don't Love Me' – the main riff and first words of which are rooted in Bo Diddley's 1955 'She's Fine, She's Mine' – his vocal phrasing is already rhythmic in the Junior Wells style. 'The Same Way' is about his and Sandra Elsdon's devoted young love for each other.

For five weeks beginning April 1967, Green, Fleetwood and McVie were together as Bluesbreakers before Mayall fired the drummer for excessive boozing. In Fleetwood Mac, Peter also disapproved of drinking, though in his very early days with Mayall he did have a tipple or two before going on, but soon realised that his playing suffered. Peter in 2008: 'It's only recently that I learned to try and chase the intoxication – the lodger, the new tenant in your head taking over...helping or hindering – a bit of each. In those days I couldn't do it – I get intoxicated very easily.'

Ever free-spirited, he became a restless Bluesbreaker in less than a year. Peter: 'There seemed to be something buzzing around saying that John's direction was going in jazz.' He had decided against checking out the South Side Chicago blues scene, but travel still appealed: 'I was going to go to Ibiza...beatniks...I liked beatniks...that sort of thing. I wanted to do that... When I was in The Muskrats I learned all about that – the Richmond scene. In England they go to Richmond and in Spain they go to Ibiza.' Looking back on his time with Mayall he told *Disc* in August 1969: 'I was awful in the days I was with him – very snappy and a bit bitter, but he put up with me.'

He met Jeremy Spencer at his last Mayall gig in Birmingham's Metro venue on 11 June 1967. Peter: 'Mike Vernon got me to pick Jeremy. He said, "I know this guy in Lichfield up Birmingham way who plays guitar like Elmore James and JB Hutto. Why don't you try and get him for your group? You're going to need someone before you go out and play..."'

Initially, he thought about asking asking ex-Muskrat, Dave Bidwell, to be his drummer. Dave later joined Chicken Shack, Savoy Brown and Steve Peregrin Took's supergroup, acid rockers Shagrat. Peter: 'I played bass in The Muskrats so I was going along with the tempos and Dave could keep consecutivity – he seemed to be all right.' But he then chose Mick Fleetwood instead: 'He came around and sat on the stairs and he had his curly hair – because Jimi Hendrix was around the scene, and Mick had a sort of bubble-cut. I was on the telephone to somebody and he said, "Jenny's left me...". I'd never seen him look sad before...'. Peter thought that starting a band would give him something to do and help him to get over his heartache. Rehearsals began in July with Bob Brunning as temporary bassist ahead of the band's Sunday 13 August 7.30–7.50pm debut at the Windsor Jazz & Blues Festival. John McVie then finally decided to join the band partly named after him, making his debut on 9 September.

Signed to Blue Horizon that autumn, Mac's debut 45, 'I Believe My Time Ain't Long', was released on 3 November, followed by the debut album *Peter Green's Fleetwood Mac*, which became known as the 'Dog and Dustbin' album, on 18 February 1968, which rose to Number Four in July. The album cover, though, was not to Peter's liking: 'I don't know why they put a dustbin on the front of an album. You can put a shaggy dog on if you like – but a dustbin? Why Mike Vernon thinks that's something to do with whatever he thought it was...I'd like to put it on his album – dustbins and things. I don't know why it was dustbins and alleyways.' The standout Green composition is 'I Loved Another Woman' – a true story – with its Latin-bluesy feel auguring Mac's second single 'Black Magic Woman', released on 29 March. 'Looking For Somebody' highlights his blues harp playing – in the 1990s he wanted that song in Splinter Group's set.

Mick Fleetwood's theatricality took over for the follow-up *Mr. Wonderful*'s cover, released in 1968, and he posed as a drag queen on 1969's *English Rose* compilation cover. On the *Mr. Wonderful* standout, 'Love That Burns', Peter's guitar phrasing in places is right on the beat, then sometimes free of the pulse altogether – uniquely free-form. Single three, 'Need Your Love So Bad' – released on 5 July – showcased his unmistakeable voice. Then Mick Fleetwood's idea to recruit 18-year-old Danny Kirwan as Peter's blues-rock foil was a masterstroke. He debuted on 19 August 1968.

Chart-topping 'Albatross', of course, was the game changer in many ways. In the 14 June 1969 issue of *Rolling Stone* Peter explained to Rick Sanders: 'What I am after is atmosphere… well…and I've had ideas in me for a long time that are starting to really come out now…stuff like 'Albatross'. When we recorded that I knew it had to be a single, though the others needed a bit of persuading.' Peter has described 'Albatross' as the first 'work' by the band, referring to the studio time spent on it – two bass parts and dubbing. 'Man Of The World' was even more of a 'work'. Sound engineer/co-producer Martin Birch in 1998 recalled them dubbing some 20 guitars onto the basic track.

Three weeks after the 6 October 1968 'Albatross' studio session Peter, talking to Kate Joseph for *Rave*, mentioned The Beatles' studio inventiveness: 'My first real introduction to the blues was when I heard a Muddy Waters record. I was probably influenced primarily by Robert Johnson, Elmore James and BB King – they really got me going. But The Beatles are my only influence at the moment. Probably mostly in the way they can keep creating different sounds.' Creating sounds can take time and after 'Albatross', surprisingly, studio time became an issue, as he told Sanders for *Rolling Stone*: 'We simply couldn't get enough studio time when we were with Blue Horizon. When I asked for a session to finish off a track they were shocked that we should ask for so long just to do that. But it's a bit bloody stupid if you've just had a million-selling record to quibble about eight hours' studio time.' That said, he then decided he didn't want to leave the label but was outvoted by the others.

The *Blues Jam At Chess* double album was recorded on 4 January 1969, then four days later, 'Man Of The World' began as a Blue Horizon single in a New York studio, and was completed in London in mid-February and released 4 April on the Immediate label, reaching Number Two in the charts. In early August the band signed to Warner Bros. Reprise.

Seemingly, Peter already had mixed feelings about the fame that came with chart success, as he explained to Sanders: 'When we play a gig now we have to stay in the dressing room. We can't go out into the bar or dance because we've become people on the other side of the television screen. You get girls playing the "ooh I touched him" game, which is a bit depressing.'

The interview ends with Peter declaring his priorities that summer: 'We're doing more work now than ever, I think John and Mick would like to take it a bit easier, but as far as I'm concerned, it's a case of really getting down to it. I don't want to concentrate on gigs for ever – I'm more concerned about composing and recording – but now is the time to do a lot of hard work... But in the past I've had a lot of ideas for songs which I never bothered to put down because they occurred to me when I was driving to a gig or something.' This might have happened with his Spanish guitar solo on 'Part 2' of Mac's next single 'Oh Well', released on 26 September 1969. Peter: 'The guitar solo part came to me at Marble Arch. I thought, "I must try and remember this – it's really good". Yeah, that came to me and I got it home and it was still there so I thought I'd try to see what I can make out of it.'

Not concentrating on gigs forever is relevant when weighing up reasons why he left Mac – he first thought about quitting in late summer 1969. After releasing *Then Play On* on 19 September, the band's tour and gig diary would basically be full until the autumn of 1970.

Speaking from Dublin to *Melody Maker*'s Tony Wilson in October 1969 – by then he'd been persuaded to stay – he talked about touring, audiences, solo albums, and then added: 'But the next LP is a Fleetwood Mac LP, very much a group album, everyone is on it a hundred per cent.' He told *Disc* he wanted each writer to contribute four numbers. But, of course, that next Mac studio album never happened. Christopher Hjort's *Strange Brew* details a De Lane Lea session on 24 October when a potential single – Danny's 'Love It Seems' – and two very promising work-in-progress instrumentals were taped and finally released in 1998 on *The Vaudeville Years* outtakes album, titled 'October Jams 1 & 2'. Was that session one of the first for the next album? Possibly…but sadly between then and him leaving in late May 1970 only a few days here and there were set aside for recording original material. Mac toured the USA from 20 November 1969 until mid-February 1970. By early January a road-weary, stressed-out Danny Kirwan was rumoured to be leaving, and other 'personnel and policy changes' might be on the cards (*NME* 17 January).

Back from the USA in mid-February, after a week off, Mac then gigged in the UK, Ireland and Europe until April, then the UK again and, had Peter not left, an early June UK concert hall tour was planned, after which the band would have left for America again on 19 June for a four-month coast-to-coast concert hall tour – but without a new studio album to promote.

And so, strong stage numbers like 'Sandy Mary', and Danny's 'Loving Kind' and 'Only You', were never completed as full Mac studio productions. 'Sandy Mary''s main twin-guitars riff and its fast/slow build/fast arrangement, produced by Martin Birch and Peter, surely would have been another classic Mac cut. 'The October Jams', and Danny's haunting instrumental duet with

Peter taped on 8 June 1969 – titled 'The Madge Sessions – 2' on *The Vaudeville Years* – plus, Danny's 'Love It Seems' and 'Tell Me From The Start', all should have made it onto vinyl. Thanks must go to Receiver Records for *The Vaudeville Years* release which gives at least some idea of what might have been.

Plentiful studio time for *Then Play On* had yielded a breakthrough album. But from 1970, evidently touring was prioritised: the 31 January 1970 issue of *NME* reported Mac's next single – 'The Green Manalishi (With The Two Prong Crown)' – would be recorded immediately after they got back from the USA for release probably in early April. But a two-month delay followed, by which time the leader had announced his departure. Maybe heavy touring was a contractual obligation from the record company or booking agents. A *Disc* interview with Christine McVie on 5 August 1972 mentioned that by then Mac was contracted to spend at least five months a year touring the USA.

Reasons cited for Peter quitting have include his charity band idea, Munich, new free-form direction, and not enough creative input from the others, Danny excepted. But in a 26 June 1970 *NME* article, Jeremy Spencer distilled into one sentence the many words written about why he left: 'A creative person like him needs time to create and he didn't have it. I can see that.'

Shortly before he left, Peter told BBC DJ Brian Matthew about his post-Mac plans: 'So I'll earn money from records, which is the main thing, to make lots of LPs. I've got lots of ideas for that...' He then spoke about being eager to cut his first solo album, and that 'Sandy Mary' might be one track on it. And then the *NME* reported that 'it's likely to end up a double set'.

That solo album turned out to the 1970 free-form instrumental *The End Of The Game*. But then there would not be another from him until 1979's *In The Skies*. Chapter 24 1971: Turning Points considers why that was so.

Peter Green changed direction and playing styles during his career but his calling card *blue feel* – as Mike Vernon described it – was a constant. 'Albatross', 'Underway' and then 'Timeless Time' from *The End Of The Game* album...then ten years on, the *Little Dreamer* album's title track and *White Sky*'s 'Just Another Guy (Blues For Dhyana)', 'The Supernatural' in 1967 and 'The Apostle' in 1979...different styles but all posses that blue feel – sometimes mystical or even eerie. And with Peter Green And Friends it was also right there in phrases and the solo of, say, Bobby Parker's 'Blues Get Off My Shoulder', performed at Dublin in 2010 (posted on YouTube).

And that is the subtext of this revised edition – that after the legendary Bluesbreakers and Fleetwood Mac era his music-making may have been lower profile and sporadic, but throughout his musical journey Peter Green's blue feel remained intense and unmistakeable.

1 Before The Beginning
Roots And Early Days

It runs in the family: go-for-it Jewish *chutzpah*, a keen sense of survival and humour that shines through hard times. Generations of warm-hearted east Europeans ready to help anyone in trouble – except, that is, those with any airs and graces. They soon freeze.

Peter Green's grandfather on his mother's side, Mark Rachman, was by all accounts an accomplished self-taught violinist, while on the other side of the family Grandfather Greenbaum was an impulsive and restless man who appears to have felt settled only when contemplating his next move. His son, Peter's father, Joe, could pick up any musical instrument and make sense of it in no time. And Peter's mother? Well, when 80-year-old Anne Green speaks, she still modulates her voice like a trained actress; she commands attention easily and laughs at everything. She always did.

So, the Peter Green pedigree consists of two natural musicians: one a free spirit and the other a homespun communicator. Not forgetting, of course, the Ukrainian, Polish and Jewish mix of blood – hardly the average Anglo-Saxon Protestant.

Mark Rachman arrived in England from Ukraine with his wife and daughter in 1913, just as the Great War was looming. Here were three Jewish *emigrés en route* to a new life in America, leaving behind quite recent memories of pogroms and the instability of pre-Revolution Russia to start a new life under the watchful eye of Liberty.

In fact, the Rachmans' original intention was to visit friends in London's East End for only a couple of weeks, but during that time Mark was offered work and they stayed for good. He was conscripted into the British Army as Private Richmond and Peter's mother, Anne, was born in 1916. After the war, Mark started his own hairdressing business. Anne still has fond and vivid early memories of her father the musician: 'When he came home from work each evening, the first thing he would do was go to his room, pick up the violin and play his heart out. It was like a ritual in which he would forget all his cares.'

As one set of Peter Green's forebears were laying down roots within earshot of Bow's church bells, his father's father had decided that the time had come to move. Of Polish Jewish descent, Grandfather Greenbaum left wife Rachel, son Joseph (then aged four) and daughter Maory, and returned to his fatherland in 1920. This would have been around the time that the Polish Army were vowing to fight to the last man in order to beat back Trotsky's Red Army (the Bolsheviks) from the gates of Warsaw. Joe and the others never saw or heard from him again.

Anne and Joe were married in 1934, and the first pair of tiny feet to patter around the couple's home were Len's in 1935. They lived in Bullen House in Bethnal Green's Collingford Street. Singer Georgia Brown (then known as Lily Klotz) lived in the same block and was a childhood playmate of Len's in what was a predominantly Jewish part of the East End.

Then came the late 1930s and some awful, awful times. As Jewish communities came increasingly under threat in Germany and Poland, many in London were taunted and worse by Hitler clone Sir Oswald Mosley and his British Union of Fascists. Decked out as paramilitary stormtroopers, the Blackshirts flaunted their thuggery and anti-Semitic prejudice through the streets of Bethnal Green and Whitechapel.

No great surprise, then, that Len's early memories include nasty incidents such as bricks being thrown through neighbours' windows and anti-Semitic slogans and graffiti daubed on buildings in Jewish housing estates: 'When I was a kid, the Mosley mob were marching around the streets. I remember a mate of mine, Danny Del Monte – he became an auctioneer – and two friends of his, Vidal Sassoon, the hairdresser, and a guy called Marksovich, who was a tailor. When these three were about 12 or 13, they used to go down the East End, down the streets, wait for the mob to come along and then get into them and fight. Danny was only a couple of years older than me.

'Off the Commercial Road somewhere there were some blocks of flats, and Mosley's lot knew there were old Jewish girls living there, so they'd come marching up at night and just throw bottles and bricks through the windows and paint "Go Home Jew" on the walls.

'At school, kids used to blame us for starting the war because of Hitler. But now, looking back, I think the real trouble was jealousy – even English people couldn't stand the fact that Jews were good at business. The English people were used to working in factories and going home at five. Jewish immigrants – a bit like Pakistanis today – would come over and in no time be starting their own businesses and be working 12, 15 hours a day.

'English working-class people just wanted to do their job, come home, get washed and dressed up and then go down the pub. They lived for pub life. All my mates' mothers and fathers would be in the pub Friday, Saturday and Sunday dinner, always singing. Kids would stand outside waiting for one of their parents to come out with a bottle of lemonade and a bag of crisps. And for half the English Christian boys, that was their life every weekend – they just got used to it.

'My mother and father were never in the pub; they stayed at home. They were ordinary indoor people but, I tell you, we were the first family to have a television and first in the flats with a phone. We were Jewish business-minded people. Neighbours would want to drop by and use our phone to place bets at the bookies!'

Today, Len, in his early 60s and happily retired, looks back to those hard times with a resilient cock-sparrow's humour. From the word go, he'll tell you, he has survived mostly by 'ducking and diving', but all of it 'strictly legit…if you know what I mean'. He's not even sure that they were the hard times many have made them out to be.

Peter's mother, Anne, agrees: 'Looking back, I've never had any really hard times; we've always managed to get by. The children never really went without anything because life was a lot simpler in those days. I don't think that the working class expected so much out of life as they do now. I mean, it was only really the business person who needed and had a car – I don't think more than one in ten ordinary working men had a car to use for pleasure. It was mainly if it was a necessity for their work.'

Peter's middle brother, Michael, arrived in August 1940, to the sound of ack-ack guns. He was born during an air-raid in the Blitz, as his mother well remembers: 'We were evacuated from the East End Maternity Hospital – about 20 of us – down to a country house near Epping Forest. This place, Hill Hall, had been turned into a maternity hospital; I think it's a women's prison now, so I can say I've been in a women's prison!'

Peter's only sister, Linda (now a successful civil servant), came along in 1942, and Peter Alan Greenbaum was born on 29 October 1946, at home, which was still 27 Bullen House, off the Mile End Road. 'Because Peter's birth was just after the war,' Anne Green points out, 'all the soldiers were coming home and being demobbed, and so the birth rate was very high that year. There were no beds in the hospitals for all us ladies, so if it wasn't your first baby you stayed at home.'

Some two years later, in 1948, Joe decided to change the family name by Deed Poll from Greenbaum to Green. He'd had enough. Michael now remembers some of the background to this decision: 'I think my father in all probability did encounter some discrimination. Remember, he'd been in Bethnal Green quite a long time and at the beginning lived in the rough end, around Brady Street and Whitechapel. He may have decided enough was enough when he heard some kids shouting "Green bum" or something like that.'

Fast-forward some 20 years to 1968, to a Lightnin' Hopkins-inspired Peter Green blues on Fleetwood Mac's second album, *Mr. Wonderful*. On the track in question, 'Trying So Hard To Forget', Peter mournfully recalls childhood days when he was 'nothing but a downtrodden kid'. He refuses to talk about it nowadays, or makes light of it, joking that 'I grew up to the sound of gunshots around my ears.'

Fast-forward a further ten years to 1978, when Peter told a journalist, 'When you're Jewish, you can still create a lot of feel of your own. I was always a sad person – I don't really know why – and I suppose I felt a deep sadness with my heritage.'

In the early 1950s in Bethnal Green, Peter was outwardly an ordinary and likeable lad with no hang-ups and no problems. Even so, opinions differ as to what he really felt inside. Was he himself ever the butt of anti-Jewish sentiment? Michael Green thinks not: 'Because he was the youngest, Peter was protected from all of that. He went to Lawrence Road Primary, which was a decent school – especially compared to Daniel Street Secondary, which is where Len and I went; I only recently discovered the Kray twins were there, too.

'I think those kinds of sad, troubled feelings that he was later to write songs about came out of sympathy He was always very, very bright and aware of everything that was going on around him – he always kept his eyes open. I can vaguely remember a couple of times in my early teens when local kids would throw stones at the window and then shout 'Yid'. But it never got to me because I don't think they actually knew what they were saying. Perhaps this did leave an impression on Peter because he was so very sensitive."

Sandra Vigon (*née* Elsdon) was a model and Peter's steady

girlfriend from the John Mayall days. Her recollections leave little room for doubt that Peter was all too aware of those ugly incidents: 'I think a lot of Peter's pain comes from his early childhood. Being Jewish, his parents and his family really had a terrible time. I remember one time, when he and I were all alone and talking, he burst into tears. He sobbed as he talked about how painful it was as a little boy being Jewish. He was teased and taunted, and quite obviously the scars were still there. I could see then and there how he had absorbed the resentment shown towards his family. And to me, those are Peter's blues; the blues for him are Jewish blues.'

Michael Green distinctly remembers one instance of Peter's sensitivity. He had taken the seven-year-old Peter to see *Bambi* and they had both found the film moving. Later, at home, when Michael started to hum the tune Peter burst into tears. He burst into tears because he loved animals.

Peter's sensitivity and awareness reached a peak when he was 11 or 12, about the time he started to learn to play the guitar: 'You just couldn't pull the wool over his eyes about anything. He would ask questions and keep asking questions until he completely understood what you were talking about.'

In the late 1940s, their father, Joe, changed his job as well as the family name, leaving tailoring to begin a 20-year career with the Post Office, at first working as a postman in Bethnal Green.

Despite persistent health problems, Joe Green, who died in 1990, was a colourful extrovert and prototype 'looner', always looking for the funny side of life. Whenever there was a Kodak Brownie camera in someone's hands, there was Joe pulling off some silly stunt just for a laugh. However, it was partly because of Joe's health problems that, in 1956, the family moved into a larger council maisonette in Lytton Avenue, Putney. As far as Peter Green, the embryonic guitar hero, was concerned (then aged nine, and yet to pick up his first Spanish acoustic), this most definitely was a move in the right direction.

Putney is just a short bus ride from Kingston and Richmond, and during the early 1960s the music-making in the art colleges and pubs of these two deceptively sedate London suburbs would shape the rock sound of the '60s – Jagger, Clapton, Beck and Page, to name just a few, were all rumbling and about to erupt from this unlikely epicentre. However, in 1956, young Peter was perhaps more preoccupied with making sure his pets were happy in their new home and settling himself in at Elliot Comprehensive, situated on Putney Hill.

The school was a whole new scene, and not just for Peter but for post-war Britain in general. Its futuristic building was equipped with every imaginable facility and was sited alongside a council estate made up of smart flats that some home-owners would have killed for. This blueprint for the socially classless 1960s would in time dispense with the 11-plus exam, which brought with it the humiliation of failure and rejection at a tender age. Instead there was a labyrinth of streams and grades that attempted to demarcate tactfully the bright from the not so bright. Peter Green, although maybe reluctant and stubborn, was unquestionably bright.

Ed Spevock was in the same year as Peter at the Elliot. After a brief spell in advertising, he went on to drum for soul band The Amboy Dukes in the late 1960s, followed by gigs throughout the 1970s with the likes of Babe Ruth, Chicken Shack and The Peddlers.

Both schoolboys were Jewish, both would-be pro musicians and both the same age, but even so they weren't good friends, as Ed explains: 'I was in the sporty fraternity and Pete wasn't. The school was one of the first experiments of the 1950s and 1960s comprehensives. It was a huge school with 1,500 kids and lots of sports facilities: five gyms opening out into a full-size pitch with an assembly hall that doesn't look like anything you can imagine – like a tank's wheels, an ellipsis – and it was virtually on stilts because right underneath there were piano practice rooms.'

Pupils were graded using the name of a nearby council estate, Ashburton. A-S-H were the top three grammar school streams, B-

U-R were sort of central and T-O-N were the secondary modern equivalents, to use old parlance.

Ed recalls how, 'despite being shy, I think [Peter] was well liked. You know, at school there were loud kids who you liked, loud kids who you hated, quiet swots who you didn't like and quiet blokes who you liked, but they always kept to themselves. Pete was like that.'

Peter Anderton, another contemporary of Peter's at the Elliot, remembers a more extrovert Peter Green. Anderton, then a fledgling drummer, was in the same class in the third and fourth years and played in a Shadows-type school band with Peter on lead and Michael Green on rhythm guitar. 'We rehearsed,' Anderton recalls, 'at a flat in Walham Grove, Fulham, and at Peter's parents' flat in Putney. This would have been a bit before The Beatles broke through. I remember Peter playing "Perfidia" by The Ventures, and even as a skinny kid of 14 he was obviously a naturally talented guitarist. I recorded a school concert we played at in that enormous assembly hall on this Elizabethan reel-to-reel tape recorder. There we were, the three of us, on this vast stage where you struck a chord and then heard it come back a second and a half later!'

Anderton stresses that Peter wasn't at all shy in his own social group: 'He was a very popular guy, very laid back, with not a care in the world. He actually stood out because he was always courteous. I remember thinking that he was Italian Jewish because he had dark black hair and a very slim face.'

Whereas Anderton's sensitivity and artistic character meant that he hated his time at that school, he remembers thinking how Peter was better at mixing: 'Elliot was too big a school for me... There was an awful lot of bullying and some really tough guys who would regularly have fights with their teachers. Then there was the Mods-and-Rockers thing, so the school was split. Peter most definitely was a Mod, in the Parka-and-Lambretta brigade. He was fairly streetwise, but not a hood or a toughie.'

Despite being slim and about average height, other boys soon discovered that it was best not to pick fights with Peter, as Ed Spevock points out: 'He knew how to handle himself. I can say that because I remember once I walked into the toilets where Pete was having a fight with a guy called Jim Bryant. Jim was a big, stocky fellow, the school's reserve goalie, and Pete was skinny. But I remember looking at Pete in action and thinking, "I wouldn't like to get on the wrong side of him." Nobody won, and nobody went down, but Pete definitely held his own and word soon got round the school.'

Today Peter himself remembers several occasions when he got into an argument with somebody, wouldn't back down and ended up challenging his opponent to a sort of schoolyard duel: 'If you wanted to fight, you could go to the headteacher, ask for boxing gloves and he would act as referee. I guess I had about half a dozen fights and won them all. I learnt how to move around and get the other bloke to open his guard, then get straight in there with a quick punch.'

It was only years later (well after Fleetwood Mac) that an astonished Ed discovered that Peter was Jewish. It was something he would never have guessed while they were both at the Elliot. Spevock now emphasises widely differing attitudes to their faith at school: 'I came from what I call a "convenient orthodox" background and never cared whether or not people knew I was Jewish. Because of this, I used to take a lot of flak. I remember playing football and a guy from Pete's class saying, "Pass the ball." I wanted to take it on my own, and he then shouted, "Pass the ball, Jew!" It used to hurt, but I never thought it was worth getting in a fight over. I remember after Fleetwood Mac Pete once said that the thing he admired about me at the Elliot was that I didn't care that people knew. I don't think the fact he was Jewish worried him at school, you know, being exposed or found out or anything like that. Somehow, then in his teens, he just didn't have a Jewish identity.'

Even so, Peter appeared to be uneasy about his background during an interview that took place at the height of his fame with

Nick Logan of the *NME*. Logan asked him what his real surname was: '"Greenski?" I inquired, but Peter just smiled and wasn't telling.'

So Peter apparently repressed his Jewish identity during his youth, and certainly Sandra Elsdon-Vigon (now a psychotherapist) felt that there was a lot of pain hidden deep down. But his faith appears not to have really bothered him until after rock stardom.

During the 1970s, Peter over-compensated. First he worked on a kibbutz in Israel for a couple of months, then he wanted to form an all-Jewish band with Ed Spevock. Ed fondly remembers how he told Peter he was going about it the wrong way: 'We don't need any more confrontation; we need integration!' He then found a nice Jewish girl to marry, but instead of religion being a cause of inner peace, as it had been for him with girlfriend Sandra when he explored Eastern mysticism, it became a cause in itself.

Sandra's assertion that Peter's uniqueness is to be found in the Jewishness of his blues playing is an interesting one. Take the beat away from the soloing in 'Fool No More', for instance, or the brooding 'Love That Burns', and it might just be a troubled soul wailing in a synagogue. Those blue notes and trademark trills could just as well be coming from a cantor.

Back at the Elliot in around 1960, though, homework was the thing that was beginning to make Peter wail. Being in the top stream, he was obviously potential college material (like his sister, Linda, a grammar-school girl who went on to university), but after about two terms he began to lose interest in his studies. Academia's dull, repetitive process of retaining facts to show off at a later date by committing them to paper bored him witless, as would playing the same songs night after night in a hugely successful rock band some ten years later.

But there would be times later on when he regretted his lack of formal education, as he explained to Nick Logan of the *NME* in late 1969. Referring to the life-swap that resulted in him leaving Fleetwood Mac, Peter emphasised, 'I'm not going to do anything until I've done some reading. There are a lot of books I want to read – history, general knowledge. I want to put something in my head because there's nothing there. I wasted all my schooldays, really, and it's a nuisance.'

Despite good intentions, Peter never did get to be a 'book person'; his education has always come from the street, meeting people from all walks of life and listening to what they have to say. An offbeat and typical example of this comes from Peter Vernon-Kell, his second manager during the late 1970s, who remembers Peter gleefully recounting the time he spent in Brixton prison in the mid-1970s. He was there for so-called 'psychiatric tests' after the notorious shotgun incident (see Chapter 14). 'He told me how he actually enjoyed his time inside,' Vernon-Kell smiles, 'and was just as happy talking to a rapist or murderer as a millionaire fraud. He had, and probably still has, a totally open mind.'

Back in Putney in the late 1950s, though, he had more of a two-track mind: rock 'n' roll and girls, and in that order. The first single he ever bought was Jerry Lee Lewis's 'Whole Lotta Shakin' Going On', and his first steady girlfriend, according to brother Michael, was a young lady called Patsy Gregory. Once young Patsy was on the scene, he forgot the homework.

Peter liked the teddy-boy Edwardian-drape-jacket look, fashionable just before Mods and Rockers were invented as a stylistic device enabling adolescent hyperactivity to kick the hell out of itself. So, during the mid-1950s, Saturdays saw the budding teddy boy on his own outside British Home Stores in Putney High Street, listening to hit singles being played 'on approval' by pop-pickers inside. The lad even cried his eyes out because his mother wouldn't take him to see the film *Don't Knock The Rock*, featuring kiss-curled Bill Haley.

Peter Green first picked up a guitar as a ten-year-old, but it wasn't really obsessive love at first sight. Learning chords proved something of a problem and, being bright, he had no time for problems. Brother Len had left home by then and got married, but on one family visit to Lytton Avenue he brought a Spanish guitar for young Pete to look over. Michael was there as well: 'Len turned up one day to come and see Mother and Father and all of us, with a guitar under his arm. Apparently he'd had some lessons – about half a dozen – and could play some chords. Pete was obviously interested and Len showed him the three-chord trick – E, A and B7. Soon after that, Pete and I got a guitar each and we started learning to play. Peter picked it up straight away, but what he was good at were the single notes; chords he found difficult to remember.

'So gradually, after that we would learn to sing and play Elvis Presley and Pat Boone numbers. I used to play the rhythm and Pete used to play lead. The first instrumental we learned to play like that was The Shadows' 'Apache'. Pete must have been about 13. There were no books around then to learn from; he played it all by ear, and to me he was already sounding as good as the record, even though he was playing on an acoustic guitar with steel strings and no tremolo arm.'

Michael and Peter then started to write songs together. One of them, 'Bandit', was recorded 20 years later for the *Little Dreamer* album.

Peter's solo playing improved rapidly, even though he never had a single lesson, and it was immediately evident that Peter had a very sensitive ear. He and Michael were ambitious right from the start: Michael wrote songs, Pete did the instrumental bits and they'd send them to Norrie Paramor at EMI Records. None were accepted.

'We also used to sing Everly Brothers stuff and would sometimes entertain the neighbours,' recalls Michael. 'Pete had a terrific voice, especially before it broke. I remember he used to sing Laurie Landon's "He's Got The Whole World In His Hands", and again it sounded just like on the record.' Peter's parents even organised a spot for him on Carroll Levis's *Discoveries* television show, but he 'chickened out'.

Peter left school without any formal qualifications at 15 after his fourth year. Peter Anderton went on to do O and A levels and couldn't understand why Peter was in such a hurry to ditch schoolwork. At the time, Peter just said he was keen to go out to work and chip in with some money for his parents. But he was clueless about how to get a job, even though these were the full-employment early 1960s, when apprenticeships, labouring and casual work were there for the taking.

Len encouraged Peter to try trainee butchering. Len himself was in the fish market and was doing quite well. He believed that the future was going to be computers and automation, and that the only thing computers or robots couldn't do was fillet fish or bone out a side of beef.

So Peter got a job as an apprentice butcher, earning £5 a week, at David Gregg's in Fulham High Street, and he did really well. Within a year he could break down a side of beef into cuts. He stayed there for two years and then he got his music idea. The manager of the butcher's was disappointed about Peter's decision and predicted that he would only end up struggling like the rest of the many young people entering that field. 'You're a good butcher,' he said. 'You've learnt really well and I don't want to lose you.' But Peter's mind was made up and he left.

Some 20 years later, during a mid-1980s interview with Richard Newman published in *Guitarist* magazine in September 1993, Peter recalled his butcher's apprentice days: 'In the end, I didn't serve an apprenticeship; I just went as another member of the shop. I wasn't good at it at all. I couldn't master it. There's a feeling you had when you had mastered it, but I never got anything.'

February 1994 and Peter's present recollections of his butchering days are hazy: 'I think I left because the manager died – I may have handed my notice in before he died but I can't really remember.' What's more, he is quick to correct a myth according to which he quit his apprenticeship because of an incident where the manager sliced his own thumb off whilst demonstrating some finer aspect of the art of butchering to Peter. The story continues with Peter, looking on, being stuck for words, only managing to deliver a well-meant but ultimately insolent inquiry as to whether it hurt or not. (In reality, it wasn't the manager who hurt his thumb but one of the other lads.)

And so Peter, the future vegetarian, replaced brute force and the bloodied meat cleaver with a job requiring dexterity more akin to guitar chops. He found slightly more gainful employment as a trainee French polisher, working for the television rental company DER, restoring and refurbishing television cabinets: 'There's a great skill to it. I had to clean up old telly cabinets, fill in the chips and scratches, then polish it all over and spray it with lacquer.' Peter hated it; he even had nightmares in which the skies were filled with old tellies and maintains that the only good bits of the job were the 'tea breaks spent talking to this deaf and dumb bloke who use to load up the vans'. Eventually, after about a year, his mostly successful attempts to converse with his handicapped colleague met with the foreman's disapproval, and Peter the semi-pro bassist was sent 'up the road'.

Peter recalls walking out: 'The foreman came wandering over to us and said, "Come on, get on with your work and stop wasting your time. If you don't want your job, don't have it!" So I said, "I won't have it, then." I'd already made up my mind that I wanted to leave and see what else was on the cards for me.'

He now thinks this might have been some kind of divine providence guiding him towards a career as a full-time professional musician. His semi-pro days had begun soon after he left school, playing as bassist for a local dance band called The Ken Cats, who later became Bobby Dennis And The Dominoes. 'I switched to bass guitar,' Peter explains, 'because I loved the look of the thing. I was round at a friend's and he showed me this bass – I think it was a Gibson – and I really liked its solid, meaty look. So my brother Michael lent me the deposit for a Star bass – not a Framus Star; it was just called Star. It cost me £40 and it was a really beautiful thing to play, with lovely action.'

Peter started playing music by The Beatles, The Hollies and

similar as a semi-pro in pop groups. After Bobby Dennis's band broke up, the drummer played for another band called The Tridents. They already had a string-bass player, although to Peter's mind he didn't play too well, and so Peter was asked to join. 'I'll never know why I got in,' he comments, 'because they were a very professional group.'

After The Tridents, Peter joined a band from Battersea called The Didlos, a Kinks-style group, and then, in spring 1965, a rhythm-and-blues band from Richmond called The Muskrats: 'I went along to see them play. The bass player looked good, but he couldn't play a note, so I got the job.' Quite soon after Peter joined, he painted the name 'Muskrats' on the side of his van in blue and yellow.

During his six months or so with The Muskrats, Peter must have started to realise his place in the overall scheme of things. He'd been listening to bits of blues for three or four years by now, having been initiated around at a friend's place with a scratchy 78rpm pressing of Muddy Waters' 'Honey Bee', which he described as 'very spare and together'. Along with fellow Muskrat, guitarist Roger Pearce, he would go to local R&B clubs like the Zodiac and Crawdaddy, eye up the competition and then set himself what most would regard as immodestly high standards to work towards. This competition included The Yardbirds (featuring Eric Clapton) and even The Rolling Stones.

It's quite clear that from the word go Peter was able to discern what it takes to make it in the music business. He admired Eric Clapton as the English innovator of the guitar solo – as a song-within-a-song approach to playing – and he liked The Stones' Bill Wyman for his unusual image, earnest and serious, adopting a serious, upright bass pose.

Roger Pearce saw Peter's talent surge during the time they played together: 'Although he played bass in our group, he was already contemplating a move back to lead guitar. We used to go along to see Eric at a gig, and Peter often went up to him afterwards for a chat. Eric freely gave us advice and playing tips. I was a bit in awe, but I think Peter was quite able to take it all in, go home and get stuck in to some very serious practising.'

It runs in the family. Just as brother Len had mastered the difficult art of butchering by strolling around Smithfield and using his eyes, so as a fledgling guitar star Peter thought nothing of going straight to the summit of modern blues guitar playing, knowing that there he would find out how the land lies. *Chutzpah*.

Roger often visited the maisonette where the Greens lived, in Putney, and he remembers how Peter's parents' devotion and support for their son's musical efforts impressed him more than anything else: 'Peter's mum and dad encouraged him at a time when most parents were praying that pop music was just a stage that junior was going through. Sometimes there'd be a hit playing on the radio and Pete's father would be going, "That's a terrible guitar solo. Hey, Pete, you can do much better than that, can't you?" I really envied him for that.'

During Peter's time with The Muskrats, Roger remembers how Peter worked on developing strength in his fingers by playing intricate solos on bass. It was around this time that he began to realise that Peter was something special: 'On one song, The Yardbirds' "I Ain't Got You", we played a guitar solo and a bass solo. I always used to make a complete mess of the solo break on guitar, and yet he could get it right...on bass.' The writing was on the wall.

2 Seriously, A Looner

In those semi-pro days, Peter could always – apparently – take the knocks, of which there were many. Progressing in leaps and bounds as a guitarist throughout the summer of 1965, Roger Pearce recalls Peter being much in demand as a ringer in other Richmond bands, as well as being The Muskrats' bassist. It was obvious, though, that his days with them were numbered, and Pearce saw Peter's decision to play lead guitar as an early sign that he was determined to go pro: 'He certainly had the right attitude: he was like a cocky barrow-boy who wouldn't take no for an answer. I remember one very rare instance when someone did manage to shut him up. It was during that summer just before he left, and we drove into town in a friend's sky blue open-top Ford Consul. We were driving along the Strand – you know, on a real lads' night out – and Peter spotted these dolly-birds walking along. As we drove up to them, Pete yelled out "Oi! Do you drop 'em?" and one of them instantly shouted back, "No, I move 'em to one side." Pete blushed and didn't know what to say. I think at that point he used to talk about doing it rather than actually doing it!'

Although Eric Clapton had already left The Bluesbreakers for his 'Magic Bus' Greek odyssey at the end of August, Peter didn't get his chance to play with John Mayall until the end of October, which, as luck would have it, was just a week before Clapton returned, although that was still enough to help Peter decide to turn professional. Among the unsuitables that Mayall had hired and then fired were John Weider (of Tony Meehan and Johnny Kidd And The Pirates) and Jeff Kribett (later in Dr K's Blues Band). Had it not been for Clapton's untimely return, Peter would have upstaged these other hopefuls and landed the Bluesbreakers gig, and this must have given him the boost to go for it, even though he was bitterly disappointed at the time (see Chapter 3).

Peter's first pro experience after this was with a band called Errol Dixon And The Honeydrippers. It was a total disaster for him: 'I got that gig because I'd told them I was a blues guitarist and they said they played blues, but at my one and only gig with them I couldn't really play anything. They were into jazzy blues, with all these jazz chord progressions, and I just stood there on stage not being able to play a note.' After that little fiasco came a couple of months as an out-of-work pro who, on anxious Thursday mornings, would go through classified ads on the jobs page of the *Melody Maker*. He would also hang around the Gunnell brothers' agency in the hope that something might turn up. In February 1966, it finally did.

To all intents and purposes, Rik and Johnny Gunnell were the London music scene in the mid-1960s: they owned the Flamingo Club in Wardour Street, an all-nighter venue at weekends which attracted American GIs, who loved their R&B and blow. The Gunnells also owned the Bag O' Nails and the Ram Jam club in Brixton, and they had a big slice of any half-decent live act going. They were very good at their job, commanding – and demanding – respect. Just as the Stax/Atlantic soul-music invasion was being talked about, they put an instrumentals band together styled on Booker T And The MG's – as in 'Green Onions'. This me-too outfit was called Peter B's Looners – masters of 'cool blue pop', according to the agency blurb – and at the start of 1966 they were looking for a new guitarist.

Mick Parker had left to join a palais dance band and Peter duly turned up at the Gunnells' agency to apply for his job. Judy Wong, who ten years later ran the Fleetwood Mac office in Los Angeles, was then friendly with Peter Bardens and remembers seeing this shy, rather serious-looking young man waiting outside the office with long muttonchop sideburns and a Liberty print shirt. 'The first thing Peter Bardens said to him was, "So you wanna be our new guitarist, do you? Well, those sideburns will have to come off right away." Peter was speechless.' But interestingly, on subsequent publicity shots, the muttonchops had survived.

The other Looners at that point were Dave Ambrose on bass and Mick Fleetwood on drums. It beggars belief that, when Peter did the audition, The Looners' rhythm section was unimpressed with his playing. Mick Fleetwood admits, 'I just felt that he was too restricted as a guitar player, which is my biggest screw-up, probably, of all time. And to be perfectly honest, if it wasn't for Peter Bardens, he certainly wouldn't have joined that band. He had a great sound and repeated certain phrases which were pretty cool, but then I thought, "What else can he do?" So I took the cheap way out and said, "Well, he's not good enough." I remember Peter Bardens came straight back saying, "You're both wrong. This guy's got a great talent. He's going to be great." I was into John McLaughlin at the time and I just didn't think Peter had enough fire. Of course, that misjudgment has been a great lesson in life for me: Peter remains my favourite guitar player, so when I listen to anyone now I tend not to be so hasty.'

Peter Bardens explains: 'Pete played that very simplified, incisive, clean style perfectly. In a short space of time he changed from hacking out a few clichés to developing a style and playing with a lot of power, becoming a real contender. He had a raw talent, and because we played so much in those days – too much, if anything – he really honed it.' Each weekend, The Peter B's played around six gigs: a Friday night evening session (7:30pm 'til 11pm), followed by a Friday all-nighter (midnight 'til 6am), Saturday evening (throughout the night) and Sunday afternoon (3pm 'til 6pm). All this intensive playing was mostly on the London circuit – the Marquee, the Ram Jam and the Flamingo.

Before growing into Shotgun Express, the band recorded one single, 'If You Wanna Be Happy' b/w 'Jodrell Blues', which was also Peter's first time in a studio. The B-side draws on a Ramsey Lewis jazz-piano groove and features more guitar than the A-side. According to Peter B, Peter G apparently took to the studio situation with no problems: 'He was a very easy-going guy then who would take things as they came. He didn't try to take over or anything like that. He was very retiring in a way, never got in your face and could take a joke. We used to take the mickey out him a lot in those days, but it was never malicious. I used to call him "pleb" because I was a bit of a middle-class snob, and he didn't take offence in the slightest.'

Peter had a taste of how the other half lived when The Peter B's were together supporting American stars The Lovin' Spoonful at Tara Brown's 21st birthday party, held at a grand house in Ireland. Brown, heir to the Guinness brewing family fortune, was later to be another in a long line of Guinness family tragedies: he was killed in a car crash before he reached the age of 22.

Despite Johnny Gunnell's hunch, the instrumentals-only idea didn't land them too much work outside London, so in May the brothers decided to expand the group's appeal by adding two powerful singers: Rod Stewart (fresh from Long John Baldry's Steampacket) and Beryl Marsden, who was already Liverpool's answer to Lulu and presently Peter's first real love interest. Soon, this new band, Shotgun Express, were very visible, sitting in Peter Bardens' black 1956 Cadillac limo, which according to Peter G was too often to be found broken down on the hard shoulder of the M1, with Peter and Beryl snogging on the back seat. 'We used to get a lot of stick,' Beryl laughs, 'because it is difficult, especially when you're starting a band, to he rehearsing and keeping that head on…and then the personal thing gets into it – playing on the same stage and giving your best when one of you has upset the other earlier that day.' Then also 19, Beryl was already four years a pro when she joined Shotgun, and all this experience in one so young impressed Peter.

Beryl began her career in Liverpool in 1963, when Merseyside was the centre of the pop universe and Beatlemania had broken out. As the 15-year-old singer with The Undertakers, a band who as a publicity stunt would drive around town with a coffin not too securely fixed to the roof of their van, she was too young to go with them on their first trip to the Hamburg Star-Club. But she'd already had a deal with Decca and a hit record, 'Who You Gonna Hurt?', which sort of got to Number 29. 'I never classed that as being a hit,' Beryl points out. It was a bit dodgy. My manager, I think, had paid a few backhanders to a music weekly to place it in the chart, which went on all the time then, you know. The journalist just kind of dropped it into the Top 30! I didn't even know that at the time, and only got to know when the *News Of The World* did an exposé a few years later.'

When Beryl arrived for Shotgun's first rehearsals, above a pub in London's Tottenham Court Road, Peter didn't make a huge first impression on her: 'He was a little spotty-faced 19-year-old... It took a month or so before I got to know him and found out he was such a very gentle and deep soul. He'd come round to this house I shared with Jenny Boyd [Mick Fleetwood's future wife], and he nearly always brought me flowers. We'd have long talks about quite deep subjects – the planets, stuff like that – which was quite a change for me, as I was a bit of a butterfly...a scousie-scallywag!'

Beryl was immediately taken by Peter's guitar playing and, looking back, she could foresee something new breaking through, not just with Peter but also the others: 'I thought Peter was very talented but in a very different sort of way. We were all a good four years younger than many of the people who'd already made it doing soul, pop and R&B – people like Georgie Fame, Alan Price and Geno Washington. What Peter G, Peter B and Rod did was to bring something a bit more poppy to the blues-orientated stuff that was already out. On nights when Rod and I were on target doing Sam And Dave numbers, I thought we sounded good together and a bit different. The trouble in the end was that we were gigging every night and it just got to be too much. We got a flat wage of £50 a week, which wasn't bad, but we were going out for £200 a night, and eventually I think somebody started asking the Gunnells questions. It ended soon after that.'

Amidst all this pressure of work, it quickly became clear that the romance between Peter and Beryl was not evenly balanced. She recalls, 'I was young and up the wall then, and he was very serious about me, but I wasn't that serious about him.'

Peter now remembers, 'It soon felt right to get married, and so I asked Beryl and she said, "Oh, so it's all or nothing, is it?" A bit later she turned me down.'

By this time, summer 1966, Peter was living in Bayswater's Porchester Road, in the same block as John Mayall. He'd already received at least one interesting offer from a name band to tour with them in the States. Together with Mayall, he was also listening to a lot of straight blues and was probably quite ready for a change. Following the break-up with Beryl, there wasn't a lot holding him to Shotgun Express, apart from his good friendship with both Mick Fleetwood and Peter B. Indeed, over the following ten years, he would record and gig with the keyboardist on several occasions. But there was someone else on Peter's mind: Eric Clapton. Inwardly, he was still priming himself for the challenge he knew would inevitably present itself: 'Somehow, to come alongside him [Clapton],' as Peter later put it.

Judy Wong clearly remembers one rather revealing incident during the Peter B days: she and Peter bumped into Eric at a bus stop at London's Notting Hill Gate as the Bluesbreaker was *en route* to Decca's West Hampstead studios to do some recording for Mayall's 'Beano' album. Judy and Peter accompanied Eric to the session, at which he put the vocals on a Robert Johnson track the band had recorded called 'Ramblin' On My Mind'. As Judy and Peter returned home afterwards, Peter was silent and, Judy thought, put out by something. Eventually he spilled the beans: 'Oh, shit. He can sing, too,' groaned Peter.

Then, as luck would have it, Eric Clapton left The Bluesbreakers to form Cream in July 1966, which presented Peter with the opportunity to walk away from gnawing heartache and throw himself into another all-consuming love affair: playing the blues. He remained fond of Beryl for years to come, although the next time she saw him the scenario was very different from their young and quite innocent romance. Peter had by then formed Fleetwood Mac and was outwardly basking in the success of his first hit, 'Albatross'. Peter wrote to Beryl (who by then was back in Liverpool), saying that he was losing it, that he didn't like what was going on and that he was desperate to see her: 'So I actually travelled down and when I got to London I phoned his parents' place. They said they hadn't seen him for a day or two. I thought he might be hanging out at the Speakeasy nightclub, so that's where I went. He was there and totally off his face, with girls hanging around him. It wasn't the Peter I knew. I went up to him very briefly to tell him that I'd got his letter and was worried. He said, "Oh, that! No, don't worry. I'm fine." I could see it was a cover-up job, but it was awkward with all those girls crowding round him. So I just left.' Beryl caught the next train back to Liverpool and didn't hear from Peter again.

Early July 1966 saw a bruised Peter hand in his notice to his boss of five months, after which Peter B brought in John Morshead. This replacement, formerly of Johnny Kidd And The Pirates, would go on to admire Peter greatly and play with him in the late 1960s and early 1970s.

Once away from Shotgun and Beryl, Peter didn't stay forlorn for long. About a year earlier, he'd met a blonde model called Sandra Elsdon, and once he was installed in The Bluesbreakers he gave her a call to ask her out. She accepted. Romance blossomed on their first date, spent at London Zoo in Regent's Park.

3 A Hard Road To Easy Street
The Mayall Spell

When John Mayall returned to Manchester in the mid-1950s, after a three-year army stint spent mostly in Korea, he chose to live in a treehouse. Later on, as travelling bandleader, he would make the most of what little sun Britain's summers offered, by sunbathing morning to night on the roof of the group's van – as it motored along highways and byways to the next gig, that is.

An expatriate domiciled in Los Angeles since the 1970s, John Mayall was – and now, in his 60s, happily still is – a shining example of an almost extinct breed: the great British eccentric. More than anyone else, it was Mayall who helped to form the character of Peter Green, bluesman. Discipline, taste and songwriting skills were all things that a forceful 19-year-old absorbed from this equally forceful, sometimes dour artist from the North, already in his early 30s. For a year or so they lived in the same house in Paddington's Porchester Road, a strange huddle of rooms on the top floor of a seedy block of flats. Daily the blues fell down one storey from John's flat to Peter's: old 78s from John's wall-to-wall record collection, impromptu jam sessions and caffeine-fuelled conversations at all hours. Neither musician had the time to squander on alcohol.

On the face of it, theirs was an unusual friendship: an ex-art student of arty/bohemian stock and a butcher's lad always a little wary of 'college boys'. Still, they hit it off in spades. The blues was a mutual and all-consuming passion: 'While he lived at Porchester Road,' John reflects, 'we got very close. It was one of those instant things when you recognise your own kind. I guess from a musical point of view I was a kind of father figure, but it wasn't like a schoolteacher – you know, "Write a 500-word essay on JB Lenoir and the civil-rights movement." We just spent a lot of our free time talking and listening to blues.

'He'd just as often listen to stuff and play me records. You have to remember that records were nowhere near as accessible then as they are now, with the advent of CDs and everything being available. So if you'd got a 45 and nobody else had it, then that was something really special and people would go out of their way to hear it. That's the way it was with musicians back then. I'd been collecting for about 10 or 15 years prior to that – 78s and stuff – and Peter more or less wanted to hear everything!'

Peter's first contact with John was over the phone, when Peter answered an advert for a guitarist in a blues band. The ad didn't say whose band it was: 'The guy on the other end of the phone asked me who I liked on the English blues scene and I said, "John Mayall and Graham Bond,"' recalls Peter. 'Then the guy said, "Well, this is John Mayall." He then told me he was looking for a replacement for Eric Clapton, who'd gone to Greece.' Mayall told Peter where he was playing that night and asked him to come along.

John recalls meeting Peter first during the interval of that Bluesbreakers gig in August 1965. Mayall was desperately looking for a reasonable replacement, and by the time Peter approached him he'd already been through six or so unsuitable contenders. Jeff Kribett was featured guitarist for the night: 'Peter got up from the audience between sets and came up to me, angling for the job, saying, "You let me play, because I'm better than he is." He kept on doing this, each time getting a bit more forceful. My first impression of him was that he sounded very believable. I was pretty much open to hearing anybody. I hadn't a thing to lose, really. But when Eric went off, I'd told him that the job was there for him when he came back. Just before that, he'd been getting very, very unreliable – not showing up, things like that.

'Peter was the last of about half a dozen replacements. As soon as I gave him a shot at it, that was it. He just sounded great and everything was all right again. But unfortunately less than a week later Eric came back and Peter's last gig was at the Mojo, up in Sheffield. By the end of his week, Peter had really got into it and so he was bitterly disappointed that he didn't have the gig any more.'

This was to put John in a difficult position with Peter when Eric finally did leave The Bluesbreakers about a year later and John had to ask Peter back. However, by this time John had got the flat below his own for Peter and the two of them were friends, which made things easier: 'But right at the time I needed him back, he'd also got an offer from Eric Burdon to join The Animals – or rather Eric Burdon And The New Animals because Alan Price had left – and go to America with them.' This meant Peter had to make a decision: should he go to the States, the home of the blues, which he had always wanted to do, or should he stay in the UK and play the music he wanted to play?

Close friends or not, Peter force-fed John with dollops of humble pie before reaching a decision. 'When I asked him back,' John remembers with amusement, 'It was no surprise that he played games with me, like I'd played games with him when Eric was away. He definitely wanted to keep me on the hook and make me have a hard time getting him back, so there was a bit of revenge there. He made me sweat for about a week before he accepted the offer!'

History has it that, in his first few weeks as a Bluesbreaker, Peter was frequently heckled at gigs with 'Where's Eric?', and 'He ain't as good as Clapton!' However, neither John, Peter, nor Roger Pearce, for that matter, who went along to many of those first performances, remember this being the case: 'I was at a Marquee gig,' Roger points out, "a couple of weeks after he'd joined, and there was nothing like that. Peter already had a following of his own and I remember a group of girls right at the front by the stage. What I can still see vividly is Peter's beaming face when I went round to visit him just after he'd been asked to join. He was very excited; he had this advance copy of the "Beano" album and was learning Eric's solos as well as working out his own ideas.'

Peter doesn't remember ever actually learning Eric Clapton's parts: 'I didn't learn Eric's parts; I just enjoyed them. And then, when I joined John, I played things my own way.' In the short term, the main effect of Clapton leaving The Bluesbreakers was a financial one: Mayall was out of pocket. As a bandleader who paid his musicians a fixed weekly wage no matter how few – or many – gigs they got, what John remembers most about the Clapton-to-Green switch was an immediate and noticeable fall in audience sizes: 'When Eric left, all the die-hard Clapton fans left with him anyway, so in other words the audiences went down by at least a third, but then quite quickly – in a couple of months, really – we built up a following for Peter. I don't remember any jeering; I think all that's a myth. Maybe very occasionally one or two people may have said something, but as I say, Eric's contingent left with him, so they weren't even there at the gigs any more.'

Even so, in an interview with Norman Joplin for *Record Mirror* shortly after quitting Mayall in June 1967, Peter conceded that things had got to him when he first joined: '[Verbal taunts] weren't the kind of things which made me play better; they would just bring me down. For a long time with John, I wasn't playing at my best. Only in the last few months with him could I really feel uninhibited.' Whilst still settling in as a Bluesbreaker he told another journalist, 'I just wish people would stop comparing me to Eric: I'd like them to accept me as Pete Green, not "Clapton's replacement". I've felt terribly conscious of this on stage. I can feel them listening for special phrases. It makes my job tougher, and sometimes I try too hard and overplay. If I make a mistake when I'm doing this, I'm spoiled for the rest of the evening.' So at this stage, Peter's sensitivity as a performer often could work against him, but then again just a few years on he would berate himself for not trying hard enough on stage and simply going through the motions.

There was always this keen self-critical tendency which could verge on the destructive and can only have been exacerbated by finding himself in a situation where he was forced to be a guitar hero. Without a doubt, it was the mid-1960s that saw the creation of featured soloists – guitar heroes. Until then, the guitar solo in pop singles was usually a perfunctory token gesture, slotted in after the middle-eight just for the record, as it were. Then John Mayall discovered a new market.

An astute judge of crowd reaction, Mayall noticed, first with Clapton and then with Green, how extended guitar solos got punters – men, especially – hooked. As Peter recalled in an interview with Richard Newman, published in *Guitarist* magazine in 1993, 'I was jumping the gun a bit, trying to play as well as Eric Clapton; I had to try because I had to fill his place. In The Yardbirds, when there was a solo break, they all went in there and they all came out the other end. It was nice, the proper thing. But then Eric started taking too many solos. Maybe John pushed him into it, I don't know. John tried to push me forward. But I was just coming out of work, so I was pretty cold about going to the front if I couldn't handle it.'

Pretty soon, however, he did learn to handle it, and then, if audiences were so-so, he would do what was expected of him: namely, scorch the fretboard in time-honoured Clapton tradition. This most definitely was a compromise, as Peter explained at the time: 'The applause I get when playing fast, this is nothing; it is something I used to do with John when things weren't going too well, but it isn't any good. I like to play slowly and feel every note – it comes from every part of my body.' This kind of restraint and minimalism, back in 1966/7, went against the grain: guitarists had learnt that flash, if nothing else, meant cash. It was Eric Clapton who first discovered this, quite by accident, and there were soon expectations which Peter did his best to ignore.

The improvisational, solo-orientated style with which Cream made their mark (most of which left Peter cold) was rooted more in panic and a dire need to pad out the length of their set than in any grand musical vision. During a Radio 1 interview in the late

1980s, Eric chuckled as he recalled how Cream had a rather limited repertoire, in terms of quantity, with just days to go until the debut gig at Manchester's Twisted Wheel club in summer 1966 – they had about half of what the contract specified. Lengthy improvising was the band's hastily construed solution, and as accomplished musicians they pulled it off, necessity, as ever, being the mother of invention. Thus they unearthed a hit formula which also lent itself to studio albums at the time.

So, in effect, Cream's unique selling proposition at the time of their launch was that they were a rock band with the attitude of a modern jazz trio – out to impress each other, and only then (almost begrudgingly) the audience. It was updated and highly marketable British *sang froid* and snootiness.

Fleetwood Mac came from a totally different place. Where Cream emerged as a new strain, Fleetwood Mac was an offshoot. Peter had been a Bluesbreaker for only a couple of months when Mayall could already see something new forming, a groove and style perhaps best typified by Peter's swing instrumental 'Greeny' (or, as Peter liked to call it, 'A Million Knobs'). As a bandleader, Mayall was understandably equivocal to such musical developments unfolding before him – on the one hand, it was satisfying to stage-manage new and fruitful empathies between musicians, but on the other it was something of a pain, because almost inevitably they would up sticks and move on.

Mick Fleetwood's thoughts on John Mayall also articulate the fostering role of bandleaders in general, and the fact that truly gifted ones are about as abundant as rocking-horse manure: 'John had a natural authority – he was like a schoolteacher, and there were certain things you did do and certain things you didn't. In the short time I was a Bluesbreaker, I was aware of Peter being extremely grateful to John and respecting him a great deal. Obviously, as a bandleader he had an acute ear for talent, but what makes him really special is his generosity of spirit. Here you have a frontman who, if he admired somebody's ability, was quite happy to step back and almost become a backdrop for that talent.' What often happened was that Eric, Peter or Mick Taylor outshone or 'outfronted' the frontman, and yet John didn't mind at all. Now, that's a rare quality and one to be admired.' True enough; Little Richard and Jimi Hendrix, Diana Ross And The Supremes, Brian Jones and Mick Jagger, Bryan Ferry and Brian Eno, even Take That are just a few examples of there being room for only one ego of size in a group.

John Mayall had an objective view with regard to the extent of his own talents, an ego which allowed him to see that musically the whole is almost always far bigger than the sum of the individual parts. This enabled him to make the best of each line-up he brought together. 'He knew and certainly taught me that, in a good band, it's as if each musician plays vicariously through the others,' remembered Mick Fleetwood. 'In the short time John McVie and me were together in The Bluesbreakers, that's exactly the attitude he encouraged in us: to be a solid backdrop.'

When Peter replaced Eric Clapton, John soon changed the repertoire to suit the new arrival's talents, and for some six months this worked out fine. *A Hard Road* sold as well as *Blues Breakers*, the so-called 'Beano' album. 'As soon as Peter joined, we wouldn't play things that Peter didn't feel comfortable with. There's no point in trying to make one person fit someone else's mould. There were some favourites that we didn't carry on from one to another, like Freddie King's "Hideaway", which was the guitar solo at gigs with Eric. I don't think Peter ever played "Hideaway". We just picked another Freddie King instrumental, so Peter did "The Stumble".'

By April 1967, when three-quarters of what would be Fleetwood Mac were assembled, John, as bandleader, perceived potential drawbacks as well as strengths. 'When Mick came in the band,' he reflects, 'something did click: on certain numbers and certain types of rhythms, all three of them obviously felt very much at home. But that posed a problem for me because the variety of what they could do wasn't really wide enough for The Bluesbreakers as

I saw the band. Mick's drumming style was more the basic things, like shuffles, rock 'n' roll and some slightly Latin rhythms which ultimately became the Fleetwood Mac trademark.'

So, for Peter, the Bluesbreakers era was something of a baptism of fire. 'Practising and developing technique, and delivering the required product and performance on the night, are two different things,' he explains. 'Delivering the product comes from experience, and John Mayall gave me a lot of experience: he used to let me play three choruses of a solo, if a number was going well, instead of one.' John recognised these two apparently contradictory qualities in Peter – self-criticism and a deep-seated confidence – within weeks of him joining, and until they went badly out of kilter some three years later these qualities actually fuelled his talent.

But Peter was sometimes just as quick to turn that aggression inwards, like the time he did his first Bluesbreakers studio session at the end of September ('Looking Back' b/w 'So Many Roads'). Experienced pro John was very happy with the outcome, yet newcomer Peter was not. 'We recorded that single very quickly after he'd joined,' John points out, 'and he felt that he could do a better job. The blues boom was on and things were coming through thick and fast, so I wanted a single with Peter on it out as soon as possible. After it was released he told me how he wished we'd waited until he'd been in the band a little longer. But I didn't think so… It's got all the fire and intensity that was what Peter was all about right then.'

Decca producer Mike Vernon, who subsequently set up the Blue Horizon label, was similarly and instantly impressed when he first met Peter at the 'Looking Back' session: 'When John booked the studio some weeks earlier, he hadn't told engineer Gus Dudgeon and me that Eric had left the band. So when Peter walked into the studio with that big black-and-red-chequered lumber jacket and curly hair, I remember Gus was a bit put out. When John casually walked over, told us who Peter was and that there was no problem about him replacing Eric, we were still put out! Once he'd set up his amp and guitar – similar gear to Eric's – within about five minutes we realised, to our absolute amazement, that John was right. His style was very different from Eric's but he had the same touch and conviction. What's more, he was affable and friendly, quietly confident and easy to work with.' 'Looking Back' was, in effect, Peter's second time in a recording studio.

A couple of weeks later, the band began to make *A Hard Road* and the new Bluesbreaker recorded his songwriting debut, 'The Same Way'. In the months before Peter joined, John shared his ideas about songwriting with Peter. 'We had a lot of fun writing songs,' John recalls, 'and I taught him my way of doing it. If I write a song, there's usually some memory-bank reference that will give me a mood that I'm looking for. And then I have to know what the story is going to be all about. It's usually a personal experience which is more in the abstract, or it could be a specific incident in life. You've got those two elements: you've got the story to tell, which tells you what mood it should be in and that will help you figure out the most suitable key. Then, somewhere along the line from your vast memory bank of blues references, you get a starting point. Peter did that with "Black Magic Woman"; he started with a few notes and the feel of Otis Rush's "All Your Love". Everything in the blues is a borrowed thing: in its essence, it's just a very basic and simple music but one that lends itself to so many different offshoots and interpretations. It's really limitless.'

Around the time of the *A Hard Road* sessions, in mid-October 1966, the Mayall schedule was gruelling. 'It was very exciting,' John recalls, 'to be in the scene at that time because there was so much work. With Peter in, it didn't take long before we'd built our audiences back. A lot of the time we were doing eight, nine, even ten gigs a week – you know, afternoons and evenings at weekends. The Flamingo was still the mainstay, because we were being booked by Rik Gunnell, and so on a Friday night we'd play a ballroom somewhere and then come back to the Flamingo and do an all-nighter. Same routine on Saturdays, too!'

The *A Hard Road* line-up (John McVie, Aynsley Dunbar and Peter) got on well with two provisos: Aynsley's love of the spotlight and John's love-like devotion to Scotch. Aynsley saw himself as a featured drummer in the jazz tradition and so would forever be hankering for solos, often to Peter's and McVie's annoyance. 'Aynsley was a very wild drummer with a jazz and rock 'n' roll background, and he started taking too many solos,' John explains. 'That was a case where giving a musician his freedom backfired. Peter and John, who were not from a jazz background, really didn't like just standing there on stage, arms folded across instruments and doing nothing! "Don't like that…" Peter would say disdainfully. "Too jazzy!"' the bandleader chuckles.

John McVie's reputation for boozing through the years has been engraved on stone tablets and remains an endearing part of British blues mythology. Yet the fact that Mayall rehired him more times than firing him speaks volumes about his bass playing. The firings were variously for lapses or impromptu displays of amateur gymnastics on stage (the alcohol-induced forward somersault into a bank of speakers was, for a time, McVie's speciality) and John McVie remembers them with wry amusement: 'When I joined Mayall, the drinking was a part of the scene. I never drank for pleasure; it was more an environment thing in The Bluesbreakers that started it off. I met a lot of people who drank, and it snowballed until I'd be drinking half a bottle of spirits a gig.' But Mayall was loath to let him go because 'his playing was simple, not a front-line Jack Bruce thing; he had a good tone and could really swing, which is what blues bass-playing is all about, really'. What's more, the tale that ruthless disciplinarian Mayall once, when returning from a gig, left a loaded McVie on a roadside in the middle of the night to make his own way back is somewhat exaggerated: 'I left him on the Old Kent Road by a bus stop. He was just totally out of control,' Mayall laughs, 'so we had to do something drastic before he threw up!'

McVie's aversion to sobriety was matched only by his dislike of brass sections in blues bands. 'To me back then, brass equalled jazz,' the bassist remembers. It may seem such a trifling point now, but back amongst the blinkered blues purism of the mid-1960s, the fact that Mayall used horns on *A Hard Road* was perceived by some as the most significant thing about the album – more important, almost, than Peter's contributions.

The four tracks he did during the sessions drew from a wide range of styles, from protest singer JB Lenoir ('Alabama Blues', which was not included on the album) to showman Freddie King ('The Stumble'). Peter's own instrumental, 'The Supernatural', uses extremely controlled feedback to spooky effect. 'That [composition] was Mike Vernon's idea,' Peter now points out. 'We were in the studio and he was playing this chord sequence on the organ which was really good. I did some guitar and the piece developed from there. Really, it should have been Mike's, but he just said, "Have it. It's yours."' Peter's rendition of 'The Stumble' goes out on the English airwaves every week 30 years on as the introductory music to Paul Jones's *R&B Show* on BBC's Radio 2.

It was through John, during his time as a Bluesbreaker, that Peter met and backed visiting bluesmen like Chicagoan pianist Eddie Boyd ('He came round to my parents' house...got on well with my dad') and white harp player Paul 'Bunky' Butterfield, with whom the Mayall band recorded an EP. It was Butterfield and guitarist Mike Bloomfield who together gave John Belushi the idea for *The Blues Brothers*, and Butterfield may also have first given Peter the idea to live in Chicago and play alongside local black musicians (something he thought about doing when he left The Bluesbreakers in mid-1967). By 1966, this white-American college boy had already achieved the very thing every white blues boy wanted to achieve: he was accepted in black clubs on Chicago's South Side as a musical equal.

Recording sessions took place at monthly intervals with Mayall. Although he never had anything approaching a hit single, as a former adman John could see the publicity value of issuing 45s regularly and at least having them reviewed in the music press. After the *A Hard Road* and Paul Butterfield sessions in October and November, the band were back in the studio in January to record a sweet country blues, 'Sitting In The Rain'. Primitive, with gentle swing, it perhaps marks the four musicians at their tightest. However, Aynsley was getting very busy (witness that chunk of ego rhythm 'Rubber Duck', in which manic Scot Dunbar gives his kit some real *laldie*), John Mayall was increasingly into jazzy horns, and all this served to make Peter rather restless.

Ironically, just as *A Hard Road* came out and went into the album Top Ten, in March, things began to fall apart for this line-up of The Bluesbreakers and began to come together for Fleetwood Mac. In early April, Mayall decided that Dunbar was out, and after briefly rebounding into The Jeff Beck Group (at that point also featuring Rod Stewart, hot-foot from the defunct Shotgun Express) Aynsley formed his own band, Retaliation. The name is thought to have some bearing on how he felt about being dumped by The Bluesbreakers for being too flash. It was Peter who suggested Mick Fleetwood as a replacement and, after Mayall agreed to give him a try, phoned him up and asked him to come along to a gig. At this point, Aynsley was still in the band, so it was all a bit sticky.

'It was a strange situation,' Mick reflects quizzically, 'because I basically had no idea why I was being invited in to John Mayall's Bluesbreakers. I drove down to this gig the night [Aynsley] was fired. The thought of taking over from Aynsley, who to this day is an incredibly capable drummer technically and has played with everybody from Frank Zappa to The Mahavishnu Orchestra, was awesome. He was a great performing drummer who had his own following at gigs. I never even remotely thought of myself like that. I thought of myself as a guy that has a lot of fun banging the drums: mine was a naive animal approach, really. I think that's why Peter and John wanted me in, because Aynsley was getting too clever, playing a format of music which didn't warrant paradiddles every three seconds or drum rudiments during a blues shuffle. Even so, at the time I didn't understand and said, "Why do you want to get rid of him? He's great!" So I went into it, and came out of it about a month later with a sense of humour, to be quite blunt. I even had a graph in the van – a datesheet, like a calendar – and I remember one time ticking off the gigs: "That gig drunk; that gig drunk; that gig fairly good – good drum solo," and then at the bottom it said, "Fired for drunk and disorderly behaviour." I showed it to John Mayall and everyone had a laugh, but practically that same day I was actually given my marching orders. In a way, I was almost willing it to happen, often saying, "I won't be upset if you fire me," so it was very above-board and lighthearted.'

London drummer Mickey Waller (formerly with Cyril Davies, Joe Brown, Marty Wilde, Brian Auger, Georgie Fame, Steampacket and others) stood in for a couple of gigs before Mick joined in early April, and almost straight away the band was back in the studio to record their third single of that year, Otis Rush's 'Double Trouble' b/w Elmore James's 'It Hurts Me Too'. By the time this was released, in June, the drummer and featured guitarist would be halfway to forming their own band, named after another track recorded by the three 'April '67' Bluesbreakers, minus Mayall: Fleetwood Mac.

Could Mayall sense dissent rising within the ranks? 'I think as a bandleader you always do. Peter had certainly expressed dissatisfaction with the more jazzy things and was quite open about wanting to do things that were more basic. Then, on his birthday, I gave him some recording time to use as and when he wanted, and a bit later he got together with Mick and John and did that Fleetwood Mac thing. From then on, I guess it was just a matter of time.'

Even so, John's recollections about Mick's departure from The Bluesbreakers differ somewhat from those of the giant drummer himself: 'The main thing I remember is not the drinking part of it, although he did get totally wasted here and there along with McVie, and not necessarily at the same time! I remember that there were limitations. There were other songs that I needed to be able to do which required different rhythms. It was probably a bit of both – you know, the drink limited what he could play proficiently.'

A no-nonsense pro, John wasn't upset by Peter's departure. Peter didn't defect when he left at the beginning of June; he left ostensibly to do nothing but go with the flow, possibly to Chicago. The bond between mentor and protégé remained strong as ever: 'The rapport that brought me into contact with him in the first place and that made us so close – once you get that kind of friendship, you never lose it,' John proudly points out. 'It's always there: you look into that person's eyes and it's all there, right to this day.'

At the end of 1967, Peter was up to his neck in getting Fleetwood Mac's first album finished and gigging virtually every night of the week, yet he still found time to do a session for his former boss. The product included Mayall's all-time favourite with his former guitarist, 'Picture On The Wall', the B-side of 'Jenny'. 'It was about a girlfriend of mine, Rosalyn, a very sad love affair. It was just Peter and I who recorded that together. He was playing that beautiful Dobro slide guitar and I was playing normal guitar. It turned out a sublime piece. Every time I hear it, it tells me everything about Peter's music that I loved. The thing with Peter's playing, and people like Eric and BB King, is that they have that touch – they can pick up a guitar and play just two notes and you know who it is. Now that's a very rare thing.'

In mid-July 1966, when Peter joined The Bluesbreakers, Mayall was effusive about the abilities of Clapton's replacement and told one interviewer how, in his opinion, Peter was 'a young genius who will grow into something better than Eric'. Reminded of this sonic 30 years later, and of Mike Vernon's generous praise, Peter now remains completely unflattered: 'They had to say something, didn't they? Especially as they were expecting a disaster.'

4 Fleetwood Mac Rolls Onto The Tracks

Blues harp wailing like an express, cymbals clicking like steel wheels on rails and a percussive steam-engine bass: that was 'Fleetwood Mac' the instrumental, the studio debut of Messrs Green, Fleetwood and McVie as a unit. The roots of Fleetwood Mac the band, though, take a little longer to trace. 'The name just came to me,' says Peter. 'I thought "Fleetwood" sounded like an express train, and groups were starting to call themselves after musicians. Then, we were in the studio recording an instrumental that sounded like a train.'

Fleetwood Mac were haphazard, flukey and in complete contrast to the kind of world-domination vibe that surrounded, say, the launch of Cream a year earlier, in 1966. Some maintain that Peter formed Fleetwood Mac because there was nothing else to do. Others, like Mick Fleetwood, say he had no choice. After leaving Mayall, he was toying with the idea of an extended pilgrimage to Chicago, but came to the conclusion that life for a white boy might prove rather dangerous in a place once torn apart by race riots. So for a couple of weeks in mid-1967 (after his 15 June swansong with Mayall), Peter was gigless and, according to Mick, being pestered by producer Mike Vernon, who was hungry to establish one of his three independent blues labels, Blue Horizon, as Blighty's answer to Chicago's ultra-hip Chess Records.

Mike Vernon now insists that Peter was not coerced into forming Fleetwood Mac; it was something he wanted to do, initially as a threepiece in the Buddy Guy, Jimi Hendrix and Cream format of lead, bass and drums. 'Being involved with John Mayall,' Mike points out, 'Peter was being pushed in one direction, because John did tend to rule the roost, give commands, and people would jump. That's how The Bluesbreakers worked.'

The original plan for Fleetwood Mac was a trio, but Peter always thought it would be great to have a guitar player who nobody had heard of and who was completely different from himself. Six months beforehand, Mike had done some demo tapes at Decca with a trio from Lichfield. He had thought the drummer and the bass player absolutely dire but the guitarist, Jeremy Spencer, sensational, the nearest thing he'd ever heard to Elmore James. Mike gave Peter Jeremy's phone number and also called Jeremy to tell him that Peter Green was sniffing around for a guitar player and was possibly leaving The Bluesbreakers. Mike suggested that Jeremy should go to a gig to introduce himself to Peter. The next thing Mike knew was that Peter and Jeremy were talking and that the idea of a trio was completely wiped out.

Peter got out of The Bluesbreakers because he thought John Mayall was getting too jazzy. 'John's material,' Peter said at the time, 'was less and less the blues. We'd do the same thing night after night. John would say something to the audience, count us in and I'd groan inwardly.' One of the last times Peter had to take orders and suppress the groan was up at the Birmingham club Le Metro, where The Bluesbreakers played on Sunday 11 June 1967, the same week that Mayall placed an advertisement in the situations vacant pages of *Melody Maker* for Peter's replacement: 'John Mayall requires lead guitarist to match the brilliant blues standards set by Eric Clapton and Peter Green (BB King, Otis Rush-style). Also, tenor player, preferably doubling baritone, for section work only. Both candidates must have an unswerving dedication to the blues.' The successful respondent to the advertisement was future Rolling Stone, 18-year-old Mick Taylor.

Keith Randall, who later became a close friend of one-man blues band Duster Bennett, was in the audience that night at Le

Metro and remembers how an informal audition took place afterwards between Peter and 'a local Elmore James nut called Jeremy Spencer': 'After the gig, when the bar had closed, we hung around for a bit and saw Peter and Jeremy jam for a couple of numbers – just the two of them without a band.'

Peter's recollections of that first meeting with Jeremy are twofold: 'I thought he played slide with conviction, and looking at him, I could see he was a villain.' So Jeremy Spencer was in.

What Jeremy couldn't have known was the role that Peter had in mind for him at the time. In effect, he was to be the warm-up man, something Peter had explained to Tony 'The Duster' Bennett at the time, as Keith Randall recalls: 'Tony said Peter had once told him that Jeremy was brought into the band as a foil for Peter Green, somebody to start the show off, do some up-tempo rock 'n' roll numbers – although what Peter called rock 'n' roll included Elmore James – and warm up the audience. So, after he'd done three or four things, he'd go off stage not to be seen again for about an hour. Then he'd come back on, not very pleased, because Peter had hogged the stage all that time. A few times I heard him say, very sarcastically, "Thanks for bringing me back on stage." Then they'd end the set with a rock 'n' roll finale.'

Mick Fleetwood's involuntary rest from the music business (after being kicked out of The Bluesbreakers that April) was to last all of six weeks. Having just obtained a loan from his father to buy ladders so he might earn a living as a window-cleaner and decorator, Mick got a phone call from Peter, so he too was in. 'At the time, I didn't have a lot of musical confidence,' Mick recalls. 'Peter knew that, but he also knew from the John Mayall days that he enjoyed playing with me. And from what he was planning to do with Fleetwood Mac, he realised that I was the guy for the job. He didn't want to be Cream; he wanted to play the real stuff.

'To be quite blunt, that was the way I played naturally. I didn't learn that shuffling especially for Fleetwood Mac. A lot of it was just luck. The insight that Peter had was that he saw how he could utilise my style of playing and give me the encouragement. He would say, "Mick, just stay as you are. You swing like the clappers, so just stay on the groove, and that's all you have to do." I used to be very insecure about it, and I'd say, "I'm not that good, Pete," and he'd say, "Yes you are – you're great!"

'He went immediately for the human touch with me, and that's what Peter's playing has represented to millions of people: he played with the human – not the superstar – touch. And so I always listened to what he had to say, even if he was beating me up a bit.'

In mid-1967, amidst the Summer of Love and celebrity drug busts, the blues in Britain were beginning to boom. They continued to do so for a further 18 months, until the novelty of raunchy, repetitive 12-bars and lightning pentatonics began to fall on somewhat jaded, not to mention aching, ears.

While it lasted, though, there were literally hundreds of blues trios and quartets pounding the country's newly built motorways in ridiculously broken-down old vans. (This was before MOT tests were introduced to try and keep certain death off the roads.) Happy to play gigs at the countless Hoochie Coochie blues clubs that had sprung up, most of these bands were appallingly bad, as Peter himself then observed: 'There were a million groups making a mockery of the blues and a million guitarists playing as fast as they could and calling it blues. I didn't want the music messed around with; I suppose I was possessive about it.' Their leader was going to make sure that his band was a cut above, not only in ability but also in attitude. Despite the laddish, insouciant image they affected, Fleetwood Mac were really purists on a mission, not just artisans on an outing.

By 1967, 20-year-old Peter's blues guitar had already earned him a reputation that reached as far as Chicago's South Side. In March, whilst still in The Bluesbreakers, he had gone into the studio with veteran blues pianist Eddie Boyd, who praised him as a great blues man, later remarking, 'He's a negro turned inside-out.'

There is something in every sense funny, upside-down and

inside-out about that whole 1960s UK/US musical exchange. In the United States, negroes increasingly wanted to move on from their blues heritage. Ever since the 1940s, migrations from the rural South to northern cities like Chicago had produced a black urban underclass. By the 1960s, successful blacks wanted to leave all this behind and be assimilated – something reflected in the visual style of artists on Tamla-Motown's roster. With their western-style wigs or shiny mohair suits, the fashion statement of acts like The Supremes and The Four Tops was 'We too can dream the American dream.'

Meanwhile, in England the reverse was true: any snobbery amongst the young was radically inverted as cool, middle-class musicians – some with double-barrelled surnames – adopted for a while the Barbecue Bill style of the Mississippi cotton plantation. Dressing up entailed studiously dressing down in old jeans and hobo hairdos. The outcome of these bizarre transatlantic games of sociological snakes and ladders? Blues music prospered as never before, first in England and then later as it was re-imported back into America. This is in part why Eddie Boyd, BB King and Otis Spann were so grateful to Eric Clapton and Peter Green in the late 1960s: in America, English guys represented the acceptable face of the blues to sons and daughters of Republican apple-pie mommahood.

What Fleetwood Mac did, then, was to draw unwittingly from the music in three ways: they parodied it, they developed it and they actually performed it. The result was a unique rhythm and blues, rock 'n' roll vaudeville show. Anybody who hammed up Elmore James today to the extent that Jeremy Spencer did then (he was, in effect, a blues Al Jolson without the greasepaint) might be dismissed as bad, politically incorrect and out of order, but in 1968/9 the illusion of a tiny white boy impersonating a big black man and his music was great entertainment.

In fact, one of the more ironic incidents of that decade relating to the transatlantic crossover of blues did actually involve a bunch of white boys and a black man: The Rolling Stones and Muddy Waters, the man who gave that group their name. The Stones were in Chicago in June 1964 and were booked in for a two-day session at the famous Chess Studios to record a cover version of The Valentinos' R&B hit 'It's All Over Now'. (Some five years later, Fleetwood Mac themselves would record there.) 'We were unloading the van, taking the equipment in, amps, guitars, mike stands, etc,' recalls Bill Wyman, 'when this big black guy comes in and says, "Want some help?" We look round and it's Muddy Waters. He starts helping us carry in the guitars and all that! As kids, we would have given our right arms just to say hello to him, and here's the great Muddy Waters helping to carry my guitar into the studio.'

Alas, the American blues legend was not at Chess cutting a new disc; he was redecorating the studios because he needed to earn some extra dollars. Over time, it was this kind of incongruity that gave English fans the blues about the blues and a cool cause to fight for. (After all, what was on offer in the English folk tradition? Morris dancing?) And in the right hands, the blues about the blues moved the music forward, beyond faithful or even outlandish pastiche to the new black-and-white blues which surprises nobody today. Back then, John Mayall's blues about the blues related in particular to JB Lenoir: Mayall would later champion the late Lenoir's music so that his family would get any royalties due.

So by 1967, in Britain, it was all rather earnest. Before that, in the mid-1960s, The Yardbirds, The Pretty Things, The Animals and The Stones somehow managed to juggle pop with rhythm and blues, and to do so in a way that was quaint and very English, but presentation was still often rather straight-faced and moody. When Fleetwood Mac was being formed, it was precisely because the blues pose was one of angst that Mac set themselves apart: they would openly enjoy themselves on stage, shout obscenities, enjoy whatever the musician's life had to offer and then laugh all the way to the VD clinic.

Combine this image with guitar playing that was outstanding in its authenticity and they soon became mavericks well ahead of the herd. Peter chose Mick Fleetwood as a drummer because his style was both simple and strong and his sheer strength as a shuffler – shi-boom...shi-boom – was really the band's calling card in those very early days. There were blues bands and there was Fleetwood Mac – or 'Fleetwood Mack', as the *Melody Maker* first called them; or 'Fleetwood Wing', as they were christened by *Record Mirror*. That June, in 1967, the music press got other things wrong.

The announcement of this new band, 'Fleetwood Mack', took all of two and a half column inches in *Melody Maker*. In an article entitled 'More Cream?', the text read, 'A new Cream-type group is being formed by ex-John Mayall guitarist Peter Green, and they will make their debut at Windsor Jazz Festival next month. The group includes Mick Fleetwood (drums), Gerry Spence (bottle-neck guitar, vibes and piano) and a bass player yet to be enrolled.'

Jeremy Spencer – 'on vibes' – was prescient: the guitarist's ribald humour would dominate the group on and off stage, often to outrageous effect. But the hack who wrote the piece couldn't have known how wide of the mark he was in comparing this new band to Cream, a 'progressive' supergroup whose very name spoke volumes about the testosterone-on-acid swagger of its members. A part of Eric Clapton's musical vision when he formed Cream was to adapt Robert Johnson's legacy to the second half of the 20th century, something he did with the heavy-rock version of Johnson's 'Crossroads', amongst other things. But in direct contrast, Peter Green was a bluesman who wanted to preserve blues music like a cherished antique.

Peter's Jewishness helped him identify with the political roots of the blues – field hollers, persecution and oppression – whereas 'motherless son' Eric Clapton went more for notions of the bluesman as an artist, stud and achiever against all odds, despite a painful childhood.

'I would try to picture,' Eric once said, 'what an ideal bluesman would live like. I would picture what kind of car he drove, what it would smell like inside. Me and Jeff [Beck] had this idea of one day owning a black Cadillac or Stingray that smelled of sex inside and had tinted windows and a great sound system.'

Peter explains how his early blues aspirations at that time were somewhat less hedonistic: 'JB Lenoir was a symbol for me of African slavery. That high voice said something to me. And Sister Rosetta Tharp – I first saw her on telly when I was about 14, just this woman with a guitar, her voice and the gospel – marvellous.'

JB Lenoir and Sister Rosetta Tharp were both politically and spiritually aware musicians and perfect role models. Small wonder then that, in around that time, in 1967, blues 'traddie' Peter even berated Eric for his modernity: 'Eric sat in with us the other week and he isn't the same. He's lost the feeling. He could get it back but he's so easily influenced. He sees Hendrix and thinks, "I can do that. Why don't I?" But I'll always play the blues.'

Peter's launch plans for Fleetwood Mac ran up against a problem when John McVie, his first-choice bass player, refused to budge from what was a financially secure gig with John Mayall. McVie had been with Mayall for many years, and it was a very, very good job. What's more, Mayall put up with McVie's taste for drink – after all, he always put in the business and played very well. So Peter placed an ad in *Melody Maker*.

Bob Brunning replied to the ad: 'It read something like, "Bass player wanted for Chicago-type blues band." But it had the wrong phone number because of a misprint. The *Melody Maker* gave me the right one and I got through and arranged to audition. When I arrived at a council flat in Putney, I made a complete fool of myself: this guy introduced himself as Peter Green and I said, "You've certainly got the right name for a blues guitarist. Do you know about your namesake who plays with John Mayall?"' Somehow, the bass player recovered from this gaffe, did the audition and got the gig. So Bob Brunning was in.

The band began rehearsals in July at the Black Bull pub on the

Fulham Road, during which time Peter naturally established himself as leader. 'Peter formed Fleetwood Mac,' Bob reflects, 'because he wanted a successful band to play his own music. He did have a clear idea of what he wanted, but he didn't turn round to everybody and say, "Here is the song: you do this, and you do that." Instead, he would explain the structure of the thing and then we'd play it and see how it sounded. The first time we rehearsed at the Black Bull, I remember I went over to buy a pint and then about an hour or so later I went over to buy another pint and Pete said, "Oh, Bob, you're not having another one of those, are you?" He was very strict on people not being remotely drunk at gigs. He just wouldn't allow Mick to do that.'

As Mick recalls, Peter had made his stance about booze and blues quite clear during the Mayall days: 'He would find my drinking amusing, but only up to a certain point, and then he'd turn round and say gruffly, "Mick, you're pissed as a newt!" There was a cut-off point, which did happen more than once or twice in the Mayall days, where he felt compromised because John and me weren't playing properly. He most definitely wasn't amused by that and he would let us know. But still there were those moments, unfortunately, with me and John where the whole rhythm section was pissed as a newt, and it was not right. Peter would then choose an appropriate moment to coldly say, "You just don't do that when I'm on stage."'

In the run-up to their Windsor debut, Peter and Mick looked after the practicalities of getting a band on the road. Although Peter was only 18 months a pro, you couldn't put one over on him, and in the four years since Mick first went on the road with The Cheynes he too had seen it all, relatively speaking. Both were wise to the dubious ways of Tin Pan Alley crooks and wide boys who were all so adept at promising the world and then delivering little more than ultimata and the odd threat to sue. 'What we were trying to do,' Mick explains, 'with very little money, was to get to a situation where we didn't owe our souls to our booking agents, the Gunnell brothers, because what they seemed to do was get everyone in debt and then, for some strange reason, you'd never seem to be able to get out. So you were basically working for a small wage and yet were unable to leave when things appeared to be getting better. Peter had the savvy, being an East End lad, to call their bluff.'

Peter decided that the band would have their own van and equipment, so he and Mick went scratching around answering ads to buy old Reslo microphones and, a few weeks before Windsor, even went to an outdoor music festival near Alexandra Palace for the sole purpose of hustling amps and mic stands from the various roadies. 'In that sense,' recalls Mick, 'it was stressful because we were getting in quite deep. I think my parents had even signed for some equipment.' So determined were they not to be in debt to anyone that Peter and girlfriend Sandra Elsdon moved out of their flat in Porchester Road and he went back to live with his parents at Putney to save on rent.

Sandra, meanwhile, got a flat with some girlfriends and Peter would spend a lot of time there. Although they talked about getting married and both going to Chicago so Peter could play with the blues guys there, Sandra remembers there was always something inside him that was restless. Getting the group together and developing was Peter's main focus. Their relationship was always important, but his biggest love was the guitar. 'Peter's music was an expression of his emotional and spiritual being,' reflects Sandra. 'He is a deeply spiritual person and that was his main driving force – to express that spirituality. He wasn't out to be famous, and the responsibility of the power that goes along with that kind of position was not something he wanted. Like any performing artist, he needed recognition, but he didn't have a big ego in that sense. Purity is a word that springs to mind – he came from a solid working-class background, and there was a certain refinement which came across in his music.'

On the big day of the Windsor debut, Sunday 13 August, two

small things happened which, though insignificant at the time, would prove prophetic for Peter Green and Fleetwood Mac. Bob Brunning well remembers that, while they were driving along in the van, Mick suddenly started to talk about investing money in property, initially buying a cottage in Wales, once the band started to earn a few bob. 'Now, for people like me who'd just been to college, this was something I'd never even vaguely thought about. Even at that point Mick didn't care what material was being played; his aim was always success.' However, in less than three years' time, and right in the middle of a headlining European tour, it would be a more heated version of the same brief exchange between founders and bosom pals Peter and Mick, one which would prompt the leader's departure.

The second incident of 13 August is recalled by Chicken Shack's Stan Webb, whose group was also part of that Sunday's programme at the seventh Windsor National Jazz, Pop, Ballads and Blues Festival (forerunner of the Reading Festival). Stan was privy to a chat backstage between Peter and Eric Clapton which neatly illustrates the two musicians' somewhat different style and aspirations: 'Peter and me were talking about the price of beer – Peter was wearing a white T-shirt and blue jeans – then Eric turned up and came over to us wearing a bedspread, rings on every finger, his frizzy hair sticking out six inches, and said to Peter, "Pete, you'll never be a star if you dress like that." Peter just smiled. And that sums it up.'

Fleetwood Mac were given an encouraging reception from the 40,000 *bona fide* and weekend hippies assembled on Balloon Meadow at the Royal Windsor race course, even though the sound quality of every band on the bill was by all accounts patchy. In today's age of 1,500,000W outdoor public-address systems, it's unbelievable that, during that weekend in 1967, sound engineer Charlie Watkins (of WEM PAs) had all of 1kW at his disposal. With this – a whisper by today's standards – Watkins manfully tried to project the music, theatre and egos of acts like Pink Floyd and Arthur 'although my hair's on fire there's a mile high angel watching over me' Brown.

According to Chris Welch of *Melody Maker*, every single performance featured technical hitches and embarrassing unplanned silences, and even at 1kW the noise levels were enough to drive some crusty locals to despair: 'A host of guitarists,' wrote Welch in his review, 'like Peter Green, Eric Clapton, Jeff Beck and David O'List had their sound reduced to a near pathetic level. Peter Green's Fleetwood Mac made an impressive debut, while John Mayall was received with fervent enthusiasm. But Eric Clapton is still 240 miles ahead of other guitarists in his field.'

Fleetwood Mac also played at a fringe blues event on the Sunday evening. The only person who had a bad word to say about their performance there was the musician who would join them three weeks later: John McVie is reported to have found them 'boring'.

Huw Pryce, the band's first roadie, who has since worked for Pink Floyd and Paul McCartney, amongst many others, was then not long out of Goldsmith's teacher-training college in south London. Seeing Fleetwood Mac at Windsor sealed a lifelong fate: 'I got the job,' Huw remembers, 'through Stan Webb and Chicken Shack, really. I went down to the festival from Kidderminster in Shack's J2 van and got introduced to Peter and the band backstage. They offered me a job there and then, basically. Peter was a straightforward, sincere guy, but someone you obviously wouldn't want to mess about.'

Being a roadie in those days wasn't very sophisticated; the roadie was usually the guy who had a van and was often better paid than the band itself. When Huw started working for them, they had already bought a van – a brand-new, light-blue, short-wheelbase Ford Transit. (This was pre-Clifford Davis, who at that point was a booker for the Gunnell brothers.)

After the Windsor gig, Fleetwood Mac went straight onto the pub-rock circuit. With four or more gigs a week, up and down the country, this 'new and increasingly successful combo', as they were sometimes billed, had a strong following from the very start. Huw wryly recalls one gig where Peter was actually described on the flysheet as 'the world's third-greatest guitarist'. The promoter presumably gave Hendrix and Clapton gold and silver. 'A typical pub gig would see us arriving about seven, setting up the gear, which didn't take long, a bit of a soundcheck, then off to the bar until start-time at nine,' remembers Huw. 'Everyone was deadly serious about their careers, but while Bob was all right playing in a blues band, what he really wanted to do was be a teacher – you know, get a proper job!'

Nonetheless, in the short time he was with them, Bob recorded four tracks with the band, two of which – 'I Believe My Time Ain't Long' and 'Rambling Pony' – were released as the first single. These recordings were respectful tributes to Elmore James, and Hambone Willie Newbern's 'Rollin' And Tumblin'', plain and simple roots music at a time when psychedelic trimmings – wah-wah, fuzz and prototype phasers – were the order of the day. The single went nowhere with a bullet.

Then *Melody Maker* announced in its 9 September issue that 'former Zoot Money bass guitarist Paul Williams had joined John Mayall's Bluesbreakers, replacing John McVie, who is joining Peter Green's Fleetwood Mac. Tenorist Dick Heckstall-Smith has also joined Mayall.' Brass instruments in a blues group was more than John McVie could bear. He now remembers, 'In those times, I was very blinkered, and horns equalled jazz. Of course, in retrospect, that wasn't the case, but there was this Bluesbreakers gig in Norwich or somewhere and during the soundcheck one of the horn players asked John what kind of solo he wanted in a section. John Mayall told him to play free-form. That was it. I phoned Peter that night.' So, after a three-week dither, John McVie was in.

In that same issue, *Melody Maker* ran a feature on 'The Magnificent Seven'. Nothing to do with Hollywood gunslingers, this article gushed on and reminded readers who needed no reminding that this was the age of the guitar hero. The seven were, in fact, Eric Clapton, Jimi Hendrix, Pete Townshend, Jeff Beck, Jimmy Page, Stevie Winwood – and Peter Green, 'the newest, toughest, and meanest of the guitar heroes'.

Some time after this, another article in music weekly *Disc* nominated 'Britain's new Fab Four' as being Eric Clapton, Alvin Lee, Peter Green and Stan Webb. But, as Stan now points out, this was all over-the-top media hype: 'We were all ordinary blokes who, when we met up, talked about ordinary things. We didn't rush up to each other saying, "I'm Number Two! You're only Number Three!" or whatever. Playing guitar was something we just did. To us it wasn't this big precious thing that lots of people wanted to make it into.'

Even in those early days, Peter would become less able to shrug off all this attention. As he rose to fame, people began to treat him differently, and where others may have lapped it up, he grew suspicious: 'Why am I now so attractive when, just a couple of years ago as a butcher, nobody wanted to know? Why all that applause just for playing guitar?'

What Huw Pryce remembers more than anything else about that first autumn that the band was on the road was the sheer enthusiasm coming from everybody in Fleetwood Mac: 'Jeremy was absolutely fastidious about getting his Elmore James and Homesick James right down to a tee, and they'd sing their hearts out every night. They'd sometimes practise backstage and Peter always took his guitar back to his room. I honestly don't remember a single bad gig, or a poorly attended gig.'

In the final weeks of 1967, the band turned its attention to recording their first album for Mike Vernon's Blue Horizon label. They were to quit the label early in 1969, which Peter later regretted, but in 1967 Blue Horizon was exactly the right label for the band.

It was a prototype independent label that oozed integrity, rootsiness and every other wholesome non-capitalist quality, as its head Mike Vernon explains: 'It had been set up as an independent, limited-edition label, the product of which was sold directly through a blues fanzine called *R&B Monthly*. We had a limited-edition single of Hubert Sumlin which I recorded in my bedroom at my parents' house with Neil Slaven playing second guitar. If you pressed just 99 copies, you avoided paying MCPS royalties, so all we had to pay out was for the pressing and a fee for the artist. We sold the lot in just ten days with one small ad. We did a couple of other limited editions on Blue Horizon which also sold out. Then we gallantly ventured into the world of MCPS by pressing 1,000 copies of "Lonely Years" by John Mayall and Eric Clapton on the Purdah label, another indie venture of ours. We could have sold ten times that amount.'

So, in classic cottage-industry style, studio producer Mike learned about the record industry by operating on a scale where novices' mistakes didn't break the bank: 'I released a terrible thing by Jimmy McCracklin called "Christmas Time, Parts One And Two" and also tested the market with another label called Outa-Site. In all, we brought out about a dozen singles before we concluded a deal with the major record company CBS, who would release and distribute material on Blue Horizon. Fleetwood Mac was our first signing, a one-year deal with the option on our side of a further year.'

Fleetwood Mac's first album, *Peter Green's Fleetwood Mac* (the sleeve for which featured a Soho back alley aspiring to be a Chicago slum), was recorded as part of a frenetic schedule. Huw Pryce remembers one gig up in the Midlands on 26 November 1967: 'We did the Union Boat Club gig at Nottingham and then drove straight back down to London to the CBS studios in Bond Street and started recording at three in the morning. As I remember it, the first and second album was an ongoing project, and it was Jeremy who had the idea to play through the PA to get a live blues sound in the studio. The first album was mostly DI'd [direct input into the tape deck], but for *Mr. Wonderful* we had speakers and amps all over the studio and Mike Vernon positioning microphones.'

...ter in contemplative mood. June 1969.
...LTON/GETTY IMAGES

Michael, Linda and Peter, Clacton-on-Sea, circa 1950.

Peter, aged 12, with the hand-me-down acoustic guitar.

Michael Green – Buddy Holly glasses with pla[i]n lenses for onstage posing only, circa 1960.

Early 1966: The Peter B's. Promo ad for *If You Wanna Be Happy/Jodrell Blues*.
Peter, Peter Bardens, Mick Fleetwood and Dave Ambrose.

John Mayall & Peter. Decca's West Hampstead Studios. Autumn 1966.

Peter in hippy stage attire – Putney 1967.

Spring 1968. Peter with his '59 Les Paul going into a Vox AC100 stack.

March 1968: Serious young bluesmen – John McVie, Jeremy Spencer, Mick Fleetwood and Peter.

FLEETWOOD MAC

AVAILABLE RELEASES

SINGLES
BLUE HORIZON 57-3051   I Believe My Time Ain't Long
   Rambling Pony

BLUE HORIZON 57-3138   Black Magic Woman
   The Sun Is Shining

BLUE HORIZON 57-3139   Need Your Love So Bad
   Stop Messin' Round

ALBUMS
BLUE HORIZON 7-63200   FLEETWOOD MAC

BLUE HORIZON 7-63205   MR. WONDERFUL

MANAGEMENT
CLIFFORD DAVIS 01-405 0943

Tel:
01-242 9000

Manufactured and distributed by CBS   c AUG 1968

ue Horizon promo postcard flags Danny Kirwan
ining. August 1968.

Reverse side of postcard.

FLEETWOOD MAC
FINDING THE TRUE BLUE HORIZON

ter with one of the first Orange Matamp
)0 watt stacks. Orebro Sweden. 23 November
'68. BELA STEPHENS

John McVie with Peter and without inhibitions.
Blue Horizon promo poster from late-1968.

Spring 1969: Peter with Alexis Korner, Father of British Blues and founder of the seminal Blues Incorporated in 1961. PICTORIAL PRESS LTD/ALAMY STOCK PHOTO

Joe, Ann & Peter. Proud parents with their gifted son in the garden of 'Albatross' New Malden. Summer 1969.

The mansion known as The Castle at Kronwinkl, near Landshut. ARCHIV RAINER LANGHANS

...eter backstage at Munich Circus Krone-Bau,
...arch 22 1970. LU PACHOTTA/ARCHIV RAINER LANGHANS

...ainer Langhans & Peter, central Munich. Rainer's friend Christa Ritter has described this
...oto as a 'double image' taken by Lu Pachotta the day after the party, March 23 1970.
PACHOTTA/ARCHIV RAINER LANGHANS

The End Of The Game sessions July 25 1970 De Lane Lea Studio. BRUNO DUCOURANT

'They must have been some of the strangest, weirdest recording sessions of the 1960s,' Mike laughs. 'To get an authentic feel of Chess Studios in the 1940s, Mike Ross, the engineer, and I spent a lot of time manoeuvring amplifiers and speakers around the studio to get a muddy, murky sound.'

For the first month or so, Fleetwood Mac had no manager. Mick Fleetwood naturally slotted into this role: a born diplomat with what Huw calls a 'posh services background'. His sisters, Sally and Susan Fleetwood (the acclaimed Royal Shakespeare Company actress), would occasionally go to the London gigs, and Huw remembers them as 'charming daughters of the Raj'. So, although Peter was the leader, it was Mick who right from the start organised the musicians, informed them of what was happening the following week and suggested doing certain radio shows and interviews.

The band did a lot of recording for the BBC at various studios around London: Maida Vale, Regent Street, the BBC Playhouse on the Embankment just by Charing Cross, and the Paris Theatre at Shepherd's Bush. The BBC of the 1960s was a far cry from the more streamlined enterprise of the Parons era of the 21st century, which contracts out programmes to really slick production companies. It was then a musty, slightly decadent and very overmanned civil service, employing jobsworths who had little else to do all day long but affect an officious manner.

So the average BBC studio engineer was hardly your hip freak with flares and attitude. More likely he was a pipe smoker in grey-flannel bags and brown suede brogues, and with a fondness for the Gang Show and Vera Lynn. These engineers were also particularly adept at putting Jeremy's nose out of joint.

Most of the sessions the band recorded were either for Alexis Korner or for John Peel's *Top Gear* on Radio 1, which had just been launched as the BBC's version of the pirate stations. For one session at the Playhouse Theatre, the band even did a couple of numbers for The Joe Loss Bandshow. For their *Top Gear* debut on 16/17 January 1968, the band received a fee of £30.

Over the following two years, these BBC sessions would include some rare Peter Green gems like 'Sandy Mary', a track featuring him in rock 'n' roll mode on a song which was shortlisted for possible release as a single. But at that time rock 'n' roll meant something quite different to Peter than to most people, whose definition was 1950s modern dance music. 'For me,' Peter said, 'all faster tunes are rock 'n' roll songs. The blues has always been the slower tunes, and I put all my life and emotions in while I'm playing. Blues unchains all my emotions, but with rock 'n' roll I'm back on this Earth again.'

Journalist Chris Welch first met Peter that autumn. At the time the *Melody Maker* office was right in the middle of Fleet Street, a convenient place for musicians and artists – The Beatles, The Stones, The Kinks, David Bowie, Marc Bolan, Rod Stewart and even Bob Dylan – to call in whenever they were visiting the papers. Chris recalls, 'The Red Lion pub in Fleet Street was where musicians would hang out because they knew they'd meet lots of journalists, and that's where I met Peter. He came with this god-like reputation – you know, a successor to Eric Clapton – and I wasn't sure how he would be, but he surprised me. He was trying to shake off this tag of being King of the Blues: he felt that blues was black music, and he didn't want to give himself too many airs and graces; he just wanted to downgrade his position. I liked him for that: he was a bit shy and down to earth when most musicians at that time tended to be quite full of themselves!'

The Gunnell Brothers agency, based in Soho's Gerrard Street, looked after the band's bookings from day one. Clifford Davis, who once worked for The Beatles' Brian Epstein, had recently joined Gunnells as a hooker, although initially he didn't look after Fleetwood Mac, or rather 'Peter Green's Fleetwood Mac Featuring Jeremy Spencer', which was the perfectly democratic mouthful the leader originally had in mind as the group's name. Not long after Davis arrived, Peter went to see him at the office to complain that Mac's hooker wasn't getting them enough work. The problem was sorted.

Once he knew Clifford a little better, Peter told him how Rik Gunnell was leaning on him to sign an exclusive management deal. Either that, Gunnell warned, or Fleetwood Mac would find themselves looking for a new agency. Davis was a martial-arts instructor and reacted swiftly, decisively and in a way that must have impressed and reassured a vulnerable Peter. He confronted Rik about the matter in a West End club that same night, and just to show that he meant what he said, he reportedly floored Johnny Gunnell before leaving.

According to Huw, Clifford Davis made the first move to become Fleetwood Mac's manager as they were travelling to a gig at Guildford Civic Hall a month or so after their Windsor debut. Clifford put the question to Peter about managing them and, although reluctant, Peter agreed he would sign, although he didn't sign then and there. Huw vividly recalls to this day how Peter later confessed to not trusting Clifford Davis, but he knew he had to sign for the band to get on and further their career.

Clifford Davis's reputation as Fleetwood Mac's 'big bad manager' is apocryphal, but this, it must be said, has more to do with bitter disputes that took place between him and the band after Peter left. Without a doubt, he was a crucial part of the band's early success, booking them into much larger venues as soon as the hits started to come.

What no one could have known at that stage is that the job Clifford was there to do and was best at doing – making money for himself and for the band – would eventually become such a contentious point in Peter's eyes. Lots of bands have fallen out with managers who turned into devious money syphons, but few managers found themselves reprimanded for making money in the first place.

Len Green at one point suggested that he should run his brother's group, but Peter had his doubts about this. 'When Pete cracked it and they'd suddenly become popular,' Len says laughing, 'I said to him, "Want a manager? This is going to be a moneyspinner."

Pete said, "Len, I wouldn't have you as a manager. You're too dishonest."' Looking back, Len now freely admits that, working in London's Smithfield market, everybody had to be a 'tea leaf' to some extent just to get by. Still, he was a bit hurt by his younger brother's attitudel; he'd taught Peter to play. 'So what I'm saying,' continues Len, 'is that, when he took over, Pete really liked Clifford.'

In addition to their new manager, there was another crucial player who, for the time being, was waiting in the wings, a young guitarist blessed with perfect pitch who would spur Peter on to some of his best work.

In the autumn of 1967, Danny Kirwan was 17 going on 12. Not long out of school and armed with six O levels, he worked as an insurance clerk in the City. Danny set his heart on joining Fleetwood Mac the first time he saw them, and he eventually did so in classic fairy-tale fashion.

The ending, however, was far from happy. Back in 1994, 45-year-old Danny was to all intents and purposes a homeless alcoholic. Divorced and with a son he hardly ever saw, he lived in a men's hostel near London's Covent Garden. The experience of stardom at such a young age left him with a very tenuous grip on reality. As Mick Fleetwood achingly reflects, 'Danny just wasn't cut out for the world of showbiz.' Peter himself adds, 'It was Mick who asked Danny to join, not me. I preferred his playing before he joined us – he should have stayed with Boilerhouse. Then he started to overplay… I think Mick and I are responsible for where he is now.'

In the late 1960s, Danny's wild, precocious talent made him a catalyst for the band's rockier music. However, in 1967, a year before joining, he was a Clapton/Green fan who loved it all and fronted Boilerhouse, his own three-piece blues band. Peter first spotted Danny ('he had a marvellous finger vibrato') when Boilerhouse supported Fleetwood Mac at the Blue Horizon club at Battersea's Nag's Head pub. Following that, Danny's band – with David Terry and Trevor Stevens on drums and bass, respectively – often supported Mac at London's Marquee. It was clear to Huw Pryce that Danny was angling: 'When we had gigs in London, Danny would often turn up in the afternoon, hang around and offer to help me carry the gear in. He and Peter would jam after the soundcheck and before the doors were opened. Peter really enjoyed that.' Danny's subsequent fate is the most cruel blow that the Mac story dealt anyone.

Back then, the music press often busied itself in defining 'the blues' – that is, when it wasn't arguing the toss about who was the world's third-greatest guitarist. In typically brusque form during one interview, Peter remarked, 'There is such a sick thing about "What is blues?" Some people think that it is just a way of playing guitar, but it isn't. The blues really is having the blues, and if you haven't got the blues, forget it – you cannot play or sing the blues.'

Fast-forward to October 1993 and a chilling snapshot of what he meant. In a Soho pub where downwardly mobile bohemians kill time and liver tissue as they rub shoulders with low-lifers and smacked-out aristos, Danny Kirwan is being interviewed by a reporter from *The Independent* newspaper: 'Yesterday, looking cheerful but dishevelled, [Danny] told of five years' living as a hermit in a dark basement flat in Brixton, south London, and his time with Fleetwood Mac: "I was lucky to have played for the band at all. I just started off following them, but I could play the guitar a bit and Mick felt sorry for me and put me in. I did it for about four years, to about 1972, but...I couldn't handle the lifestyle and the women and the travelling."'

This is the story of the blues as told by Kirwan, a hobo who, thanks to substance abuse, has strayed a million miles too far. But in 1967, at a Christmas gig at the Marquee, as Peter Green, Mac and Boilerhouse saw 1968 fast approaching, things couldn't have looked brighter. Their mission, musically, was to bask in the light of that blues horizon.

5 Finding A New, True Blues Horizon

In early 1968, Peter Green had a very low boredom threshold. Just six months into Fleetwood Mac, he already felt that the band musically was marking time, even though they were playing to packed houses each gig. The size of their following was reflected by the debut album's sales that year: released on 24 February, *Peter Green's Fleetwood Mac* sold an estimated 1,000 copies per day in the United Kingdom during the first few months, stayed in the Top Ten for 15 weeks and in the album charts for a year. Commercially, they were marking big time – for a blues band, that is.

Jeremy's wah-dah-dah-ing, Mick's high energy shi-boom, McVie's beefy bass playing, reverential crowds and a hit album. Who could ask for more? Peter Green, for one: 'I had two parts to play because Jeremy wasn't going to make the effort to learn my things, to play properly on the piano. I was told he could play properly, but I never saw him do that.'

Although these were undoubtedly happy, carefree times for the four-piece band, Peter is still often quick to criticise now, as then, according to Ed Spevock and Andy Silvester. 'I remember Pete at his strongest,' Ed recalls, 'around the 1968 "Need Your Love So Bad" period. Two of Amboy Dukes' brass section, sax player Steve Gregory and Buddy Beadle on baritone sax, were doing some sessions for the *Mr. Wonderful* album, and we had to pick them up from CBS's New Bond Street Studios before a gig. When I got there, they were recording "Need Your Love" and I was sitting on

86

the floor in the middle of the recording studio. I was amazed because they did it live in a single take, and I think Pete was singing through two PA speakers. The only thing that was put on afterwards were the strings. What really impressed me about him, and I only realise it now, is that he knew what he wanted. I remember him saying to Mick Fleetwood, "Lay on that beat more!" or something like that. It definitely made me think he'd be hard to work with. I sometimes had run-ins with our sax player about my drumming, but Pete struck me as even more critical.'

Mick Fleetwood has already mentioned how he could stand being 'beaten up a bit' by Peter, and this is something that Andy Silvester well remembers: 'Peter was a perfectionist and wasn't always happy about Mick's drumming. Pete and I used to talk a lot about other musicians, and he once asked me to play Mick lots of Jimmy Reed. There was one track I remember in particular, "My Bitter Seed", which just had this amazing groove to it: the tempo was really slow and yet it shuffled along with a lot of swing…it just flowed. Anyway, I played that to Mick and, simple as it was, he just sat there in disbelief. What he didn't realise was that he himself already had that. Having had bands of my own, you always think the grass is greener on the other side, [that] musicians in other bands are better.

'Pete also sometimes had quite a cruel sense of humour, and I think this was under Jeremy's influence. The whole band could be really wicked at times. I had a tape once of Mac recorded live at a club near the Oval cricket ground. Christine was in the wings at the side of the stage, watching the show. They did one number during which Peter introduced the band individually. When it came to John, Pete mentioned how his bass player was a really shy person, and John dipped his head as if to lay it on a bit. Pete then said something like, "You know, it took John six months before he could even summon up the gall to hold Christine Perfect's hand…" Then there was a big silence before Peter said, "…let alone fuck the arse off her!" John was really annoyed by this. He went up to the microphone and shouted, "You fuckin' Jew!" He managed to control himself, but it was close. I'm sure Peter only said that for Jeremy's benefit. It was the kind of thing that [Jeremy] loved to do.'

To describe Peter's relationship with Mick as a marriage of sorts is not at all far-fetched. Mick openly admits that he was basically in love with his leader and more or less worshipped the ground he stood on. But there were also times when Peter's directness rubbed Mick up the wrong way. Another occasion recalled by Andy Silvester was after a gig at the Toby Jug in Tolworth: 'Mick was really depressed saying, "Shuffles... I'm sick to death of fuckin' shuffles!", whacking his hand against the roof so hard he could quite easily have broken some bones.' His intensity left Peter obviously quite devastated, and he knew he could say nothing to calm him.

Peter was the only member of the band who had a problem with Jeremy Spencer's refusal, or inability, to extend his musical contribution beyond recreating Elmore James and parodies of 1950s American rock 'n' roll teen idols. John McVie still regards Jeremy as the supreme exponent of Chicago blues slide guitar: 'In my opinion, he was the best around at the time, and nobody has come near him ever since.' Mick Fleetwood liked him for his onstage theatricality: 'He was a real performer.' But Peter now says he found him 'quite hard to get on with', and Bob Brunning didn't get on with him: 'Jeremy was a weak person. He used to do these impersonations of John Mayall, and John didn't like it. Mick used to laugh at him, but I couldn't see what was funny.'

Andy Silvester is convinced that Jeremy's humour influenced the band more than anything else, and not always to good effect: 'I remember Fleetwood Mac as a happy band, but one with a bizarre humour. They used to take things too far really, and Jeremy seemed to be the instigator. He used to do these really explicit drawings of women's private parts. On their first tour of the United States in the summer of 1968, a lady called Judy Wong had them stay at her place in Los Angeles. Jeremy used to do these horribly explicit drawings of women with their legs wide open, stick them on a shelf in her fridge and close the door so that, when she went to the fridge to get some milk for a cup of tea, that's the first thing she'd see. I think all of that must have had an effect on Peter, because Jeremy was so perverse.'

In early 1971, though, and after nearly four years in the group, Jeremy suddenly left the band midway through the tour, decamping to a Los Angeles religious cult called the Children of God.

The son of an RSPCA officer, Jeremy and his childhood sweetheart Fiona got married when she was 15 and Jeremy was not long in Fleetwood Mac, and they had their first child, Dickon, very soon after. Bob Brunning well remembers congratulating on fatherhood: 'When his first child was born, I expressed great interest and offered my sincere congratulations to him and his wife Fiona. I was simply amazed when he couldn't remember the name of his brand-new baby!'

Dennis Keen, Fleetwood Mac's road manager in the late 1960s, has some less tasteful memories of Jeremy's weird ways: 'His wife used to wank him off on the plane and on coaches, and he'd think it was funny. I remember on one tour they were both sitting at the back of the coach. He'd be touching her up, then he'd put his hand under your nose and think it was a joke. His hotel room when we were in the States was thick with dope fumes. For days on end, when they didn't have gig, he'd be holed up in his room all by himself, smoking and reading the Bible!'

During that year Mike Vernon began to share Peter's views about Jeremy, that musically he was very limited and had no intention of being otherwise: 'There's no doubt about it, he was amusing, but when all's said and done, his talent was to copy Elmore James, and once you'd heard him for half an hour, you'd heard it all. He was, though, a great novelty to have when the band first started.'

Between 4 and 12 May 1968, the band, plus roadie Huw Pryce, toured Denmark, Sweden and Norway, appearing on television for the first time on a show made in Copenhagen. Jeremy's mega-swing version of Elmore James's 'Shake Your Money Maker' was released as a single (to promote their debut album in Scandinavia) and actually went to the top of the charts there, a complete anomaly for conservative Nordic tastes in pop music.

Meanwhile, Mick and had spotted a new member for the band. Harold, as it came to he called, was a 15" dildo – or 'false penis', as Peter now refers to it – that was incorporated into the band's act when they returned to England. As Huw remembers, 'Some nights I used to come on stage carrying a tray of drinks for the band and they'd introduce me, lark about and point out Harold lying on the tray. Other times we'd attach Harold to Mick's bass-drum head so it could spend the whole gig erect and staring at some very shocked young ladies. Mick Fleetwood loved to shock audiences – he used to wear those wooden balls dangling from his belt – and, as I say, could go far too far sometimes by throwing condoms filled with beer or milk out into the crowd. He got his come-uppance once from John Gee, manager at the Marquee, for wearing the dildo sticking out from the flies of his jeans whilst they did their set. It got them banned from one of London's most prestigious venues, but nobody in the band could give a damn. I remember Pete just said, "There are lots of other good places left to play." That's how it was back then, very carefree and very vulgar.'

During this, the band's most boisterous phase, Peter was quite renowned for his bad language on stage. 'If I use the work "fuck" in normal speech,' he said defiantly at the time, 'then I'm gonna use it on stage as well – at least until I get arrested for it.' Eventually, though, manager Clifford Davis had to persuade them to tone things down somewhat because their ribald humour and attitude were upsetting promoters and actually losing them work.

It's ironic that it was Jeremy, the band's least adventurous musician, who gave them their first taste of success in the singles charts that spring, when 'Shake Your Money Maker' was a hit in Scandinavia. It was a case of third time lucky: it's no great surprise that the studiously uncommercial and rootsy debut single, 'I Believe My Time Ain't Long', bombed out, but the lack of success of 'Black Magic Woman' (released at the end of March, it briefly nudged the bottom reaches of the Top 50) must have hurt Peter a bit. Looking back, though, he is characteristically abrupt and matter-of-fact about it all: 'Although it was a good song, I guess it wasn't good enough or commercial enough to be a hit. The first really commercial thing we did was "Albatross". I knew that would be a hit.'

The inspiration for 'Black Magic Woman' – subsequently a worldwide million-seller for Carlos Santana – was two-fold: his girlfriend at the time, model Sandra Elsdon, and Otis Rush's classic 'All Your Love'. Peter liked to call Sandra his 'magic mama' and, as she now recalls bluntly and with fond amusement, when he wrote the lyrics, Peter wasn't getting his oats: 'I had decided to be celibate as part of some lofty spiritual quest I was pursuing at the time, and so in that second verse, when Peter sings "Don't turn your back on me, baby," his blues are all about frustration!'

The melody line Peter developed from the opening notes of 'All Your Love'. 'When I was in The Bluesbreakers,' he explains, 'John got me started with songwriting, and one of the things he said was that, if you really like something, you should take the first lines and make up another song from them. So that's what I did with "Black Magic Woman". But then it turned out sounding more like BB King's "Help The Poor".'

Even with Mick Taylor – now a Bluesbreaker – it was Peter whom John Mayall asked back in December 1967 to guest on both sides of his next single, 'Jenny' and 'Picture On The Wall', two country-blues tracks featuring Mayall on piano and vocals, Peter on guitar and Keef Hartley on drums. In August 1968, Peter would also make one strong contribution to Mayall's *Blues From Laurel Canyon* album, on a talking blues by Mayall called 'First Time Alone'. If anything, it was around this time, 1967/8, that Peter's taste and interpretation of all the blues he had listened to over the past five years began to develop into something wholly original; although some of his subsequently best-known work may have strayed from a strict blues structure and form, all of it retained a blues feel. At the time, Peter gave some indication of the more panoramic blues horizon he was looking to when he described The Beatles' 'Eleanor Rigby' and Tim Hardin's 'Hang On To A Dream' as 'contemporary blues'.

Chicken Shack's Stan Webb emphasises Peter's unique taste: 'Peter always acknowledged where he came from, but what happened in the end is that Peter's style came from himself. He's the only white player I've ever heard that has come from himself. He first did everything and everyone, like we all did with Robert Johnson, Mississippi Fred McDowell, Big Mama Thornton, Buddy Guy, BB King and Freddie King; but then Peter developed into the only white player that ended up totally original. That's not praise; it's a fact. Eric Clapton's another matter: back in the early days, Eric was far more selfish and self-centred. A few years ago, me and Eric bumped into each other at some cricket do and started talking about the old days. He said to me, "Do you know, I'm really selfish?" I said, "Yeah, Eric, I know. You never acknowledged Matt Murphy [Memphis Slim's regular guitarist], did you?" And there was nothing Eric could say because he knew I was right. I've got old 1950s records in my collection of Matt Murphy which has stuff that is note for note what Eric played on John Mayall's Bluesbreakers' "Beano" album.'

This point illustrates well the hand-me-down nature of blues. One of Peter's early inspirations for 'Albatross' was 'a group of notes from an Eric Clapton solo played slower'. So who knows? perhaps Matt Murphy should get some remote credit for the hit instrumental.

At the end of June 1968, Fleetwood Mac set off for a six-week exploratory tour of America. Everyone, apart from John McVie, approached the trip with some trepidation, mainly because of the many stories of violence and racial tension they'd heard about. When asked by *Melody Maker* on the eve of the tour whether Peter would like to perform his blues for an all-negro audience, he replied,

'I would like to, but at the moment it's so violent there you have to be known, anyway. We will be playing in New York and Detroit, and I hope that there the audiences will he mixed.'

In most respects, Fleetwood Mac's first American tour was something of a sodden squib, although perhaps this was less so on the West Coast, where they were gigging only on alternate weekends in Los Angeles and San Francisco, which meant that they could socialise during the week with musicians like Jerry Garcia of The Grateful Dead and Carlos Santana, and generally soak up the very tail end of San Francisco's Haight-Ashbury scene before the rip-off merchants moved in and cleaned up.

When they flew across, the single 'Black Magic Woman' and the debut album were out in America on the Epic label but made no impact at all on the charts. What's more, feeble tour management and promotion meant that attendances were extremely thin for any gigs where they were the main act. Peter still remembers, 'On our first visit to New York, we went to play a gig at this club on Broadway called the Space, and there was no one there...no audience at all! So we cancelled the gig and went to another place called the Scene and played there. Then they changed the name to Ungano's, and that's where I met Jimi Hendrix. He was just standing on stage, playing about with his guitar, and he asked me if I would like to get up and play. He was making a lot a wrong notes, sort of slowing them down, and nothing was coming out. I liked him as a person, though. I remember he let me touch his frizzy hair! But his playing was strange.'

Over on the West Coast, the band played support gigs and on alternate weeks stayed at Judy Wong's house in San Francisco. In between weekend gigs, Peter and Judy would go to see bands at the Carousel Ballroom, which later became the Fillmore West. It was there that they met acid tycoon Owsley, but the significance for self-effacing Peter of that first US visit was that, like it or not, his playing on the *A Hard Road* album had carved out a reputation for him up in rock music's hippest echelons. The Beatles' George

Harrison already admired his talent. Peter said at the time, 'I really enjoyed seeing Howlin' Wolf, Buddy Guy, Freddie King and white bluesman John Hammond. He came as a big surprise to me. I never liked him on record, but he was very good. We also heard Big Brother And The Holding Company and The Grateful Dead. Also, Janis Joplin with The Holding Company. She's incredible. I've never seen anything like that.' On the other hand, in terms of Fleetwood Mac establishing their name Stateside, the trip was a disaster. 'It wasn't even hard work. You can't work hard when there's no audience,' Peter now ruefully explains.

Another setback greeted Peter and the band on their return to England in early August: their latest single 'Need Your Love So Bad' had been in the shops some three weeks and was doing no more than bubbling under the Top 20. This soulful blues ballad was Peter Green's version of BB King's version of a 1950s more uptempo R&B hit, written and recorded by Little Willie John. At the start of 1969, Peter told the *NME* that his biggest career disappointment to date was that this single didn't make it in England. Evidently, he was getting very hungry for a hit.

Although still blues, Mike Vernon's production was the most commercial and accessible of all three Mac singles. Previously, Vernon had collaborated with Mickey 'Guitar' Baker (as in Mickey And Sylvia's 'Love Is Strange') and brought him in on this project. Vernon flew Baker over from Paris to write the score for the string arrangement, which, along with Peter's vocal phrasing and Christine Perfect's organ playing, turned the single into hooky stuff. But not quite hooky enough.

At the beginning of August, Mac's leader had turned his attention to helping his mate and biggest fan, Danny Kirwan (Peter's nickname for him was 'Young Eyes'), to audition dozens of potential recruits for a band to be fronted by Danny. The 18-year-old had decided to quit his job as an insurance clerk in Fenchurch Street and turn professional. However, Mick soon suggested that Danny join Fleetwood Mac. Although, looking back, Peter is rather guilt-ridden about going along with Mick's idea, at the time it had a definite and positive effect on Peter's playing and composing. 'I wouldn't have done "Albatross" without Danny' is his pithy testimonial, which speaks volumes.

Danny's debut with the band was at the Blue Horizon club in the Nag's Head pub at Battersea, London, on 14 August 1968. Andy Silvester went along to watch: 'Peter announced him by saying something like, "Now Danny Kirwan is going to do his first number of the night for us, and he's going to blow your minds!" Sitting in the crowd, I thought that an introduction like that just put too much on his shoulders. Poor kid.'

An ominous observation, as it turned out.

6 Albert Ross, Man Of The World

BBC's Radio 3 might have called it a musical *volte-face*, to Radio 2 it was probably more welcome easy listening, whilst Radio 1 gushed forth about a brand-new, happening sound. Just like Alec Issigonis's 'Mini Minor', launched some ten years earlier, the single's appeal couldn't be categorised – 'Albatross' was classless.

While the instrumental prompted BB King to eulogise about Peter's 'sensitive touch', a concert violinist wrote to the BBC enquiring who the composer was and where he might obtain sheet music for the piece. Meanwhile, professional blues purists like DJ Mike Raven shook their heads and walked away muttering 'sold out'. So, while 'Albatross' broke down musical barriers, it also brought out the snob in some.

'Peter Green's Fleetwood Mac,' commented Raven soon after the single's release on 22 November, 'are already too commercial and have lost their original guts.' In the late 1960s, Radio 1's *Mike Raven's R&B Show* in some ways epitomised the elitist 'if it's mainstream, it must be crap' attitude at which Peter in effect cocked a snook with 'Albatross'. In its heyday, the show was Auntie at her best: pukka, exclusive and yet just slightly patronising in its educational tone, something that Mick Jagger parodied brilliantly in an interview with Bob Dawbarn of *Melody Maker* in 1968. 'I must apologise for this next record, which is so old you can't really hear it, but it was recorded in a barn in 1933 and the music is first class,' Jagger laughed. 'That radio show is really in the BBC tradition

– or perhaps the Alexis Korner tradition – but it's a great programme, really worth listening to.' Even droll 1960s libertarian John Peel admitted he couldn't get into 'Albatross' at all, choosing instead to play the B-side, Danny Kirwan's 'Jigsaw Puzzle Blues' on his *Top Gear* show. At gigs, Peter nicknamed his instrumental 'Albert Ross'.

Just one week after Danny joined the band, Blue Horizon released Fleetwood Mac's second album, *Mr. Wonderful*, recorded in April. As summer drew to a close, 'Albatross' was nearing the end of its long incubation in Peter's head and would soon be put down on tape at CBS's New Bond Street studios. 'I got the idea for the name "Albatross",' Peter grins, 'from a poem I read at school called "The [Rime Of The] Ancient Mariner", and from that young girl's voice in the middle of Traffic's song "Hole In My Shoe" – "I climbed on the back of a giant albatross". That did trigger my mind, as did the Stevie Winwood thing. I wrote parts of it in an aeroplane, but the whole thing took years. I composed in the way musicians do, by feeling it out over time. Then, when Danny came along, we did the second-part harmony. Once we got Danny in, it was plain sailing.'

So, creatively, Peter needed Danny in the band. As Mike Vernon explains, 'Danny was outstanding. He had a guitar style that was totally unique. I seem to remember him playing this Watkins beginner's guitar and yet making these wild sounds that reminded me in a way of Lowell Fulson. I'd never heard anybody play like that and I was desperate to record him, but I didn't think his band [Boilerhouse] had what it took. When I found out that Peter had been talking to Danny about maybe joining the band, I was 100 per cent for it, and of course the results speak for themselves in that the musical direction of what Fleetwood Mac were about changed when Danny Kirwan joined and gradually became of secondary importance.'

Visually, the addition of Danny Kirwan in the line-up added a kidnapped-choirboy dimension to the group's ragged image. An

East End Jewish boy playing more Chicago than black Chicagoans is extraordinary; an elfin belting out macho Elmore James riffs is weird vaudeville; but a young lad looking like an early-teens innocent yet playing blues with the tone and authority of Lowell Fulson is surreal.

Danny spurred Peter on to some of his best playing, and this was partly because the leader now had someone to bounce ideas off and spark some creativity. 'There was never a lot of creative energy coming from the band,' reflects Peter. 'When Lindsay Buckingham and Stevie Nicks came into the group, there was creative energy. When Bob Welch and Bob Weston were in the group, there was the possibility of creative energy. But before that, there was only me and Danny. There wasn't enough creative energy coming from Fleetwood Mac, the two people. It seemed to me that Mick and John weren't so much into playing; they were more into making money. Danny and I tried to bring the band with us, and I suppose sometimes they did move a bit, but it was like budging along the bottom of the ocean.'

Not long after its release, Peter would enthuse about their second album, even though it lacked the energy and enthusiasm of the first and certainly didn't sell as many copies: 'I like our album *Mr. Wonderful*. It was where we were at the time.' This is indisputable in that four of the ten tracks featured with that same and by now well-worn Elmore James wah-dah-dah-wah-dah-dah riff. The remainder was Peter either in an acoustic Lightnin' Hopkins mood, playing with one-man-band Duster Bennett on harmonica, or doing a BB King boogie shuffle. The anguished 'Love That Burns' is most notably a recording where Peter breaks forever the mould of faithful, fanatical reproduction and puts his own stamp on the blues. His understated guitar is often hardly audible and seemingly phrased against the solid slow beat of the song. Completely original.

Not only did 'Albatross' open doors into the pop world for Fleetwood Mac; almost overnight it transformed Blue Horizon from a specialist independent label into something with a bit more clout. As Mike Vernon explains, 'Because it sold a million records and got to Number One, we realised there was money to be made in commercial records. When "Albatross" was recorded, nobody sat down with the specific intent of making a hit record. What happened was that Peter was a fan of Santo And Johnny's earlier hit "Sleepwalk", and he liked the quality of that Hawaiian-guitar sound. He felt he could adapt that and make something with a blue feel. It didn't have to be bluesy; it just had to have a blue feel. The rest of the band were really into it. The slide-guitar parts were done by Peter, the bass parts were double-tracked and Danny and Peter did the bits with the mallets.'

'Albatross' was recorded at CBS's New Bond Street Studios, originally Oriel Studios. The band spent two days recording and mixing just that track – an exceptionally long time to spend on a single in those days. On listening to the final mix, everyone in the band and the engineer, Mike Ross, agreed that it was a beautiful record.

Without a doubt, Peter was ambitious for a hit around that time. He obviously felt he had the talent and believed that 'Albatross' could be the one.

For almost a month after the record was released, CBS's initial reservations proved to be correct: absolutely nothing happened. The pluggers at CBS had been trying desperately hard for the *Top Of The Pops* television show to take it, but they refused, saying that they didn't think it would be a hit and couldn't find a slot for it, certainly not with the band performing the piece.

Then one week the producers discovered that they had a 45–50-second slot at the very end of one of the programmes when the credits went up and decided to fill the slot with 'Albatross'. The show went out on a Thursday. By Friday, CBS had orders in for 60,000 units and the record went smashing into the charts. The BBC also played it in a documentary programme, which obviously boosted sales still further. Released on 22 November, 'Albatross' entered the charts at Number 23 three weeks later on 14 December. The following week it rose to Number 19, then went to Number One over Christmas, at which point the band was holed up in snowbound Detroit, one-third of the way through their second US tour and, for a while, unaware of their new-found status as a pop group.

The astute Clifford Davis wasted no time in securing more 'poppy' bookings for his boys. Quite soon, Alan 'Pop Pickers' Freeman would be introducing Fleetwood Mac at Wembley Empire Pool (now Wembley Arena) on the same bill as acts like Barry Ryan and The Paper Dolls. But, of course, a pop group isn't truly a pop group until it has a fan club – or rather an appreciation society.

Jane Honeycombe, then a 16-year-old Londoner and British blues fan, plucked up the courage to approach Mick Fleetwood after a gig in the autumn shortly before the band set off for America: 'I told them about my idea for a fan club, and Mick said, "Oh, that sounds like a great idea!" and gave me his telephone number. Although I was just 16, I was cynical and didn't for one moment think that that would really be his number, but I was wrong. A couple of days later, I took out the piece of paper, swallowed hard and rang the number and was astonished to find myself talking to Mick Fleetwood, who at that point was sharing a place in Ealing with Andy Silvester. Mick still liked my idea and suggested that I go and see their publicist – a lady called Valerie Bond – and Cliff Davis.'

Clifford played Jane the new single, 'Albatross'. Her response was far from positive: 'I nearly walked out! That wasn't my band – they'd gone commercial!' Undeterred, Jane started the appreciation society, with Peter as her main link with the band. 'My first impressions of Peter? Well, you have to remember I was 16 and partly in love with him, so naturally he terrified me! Even then he was strange and very different from everybody else. Right from the start what was quite obvious was that Peter was the leader and the nucleus of the band and everything really revolved around him. Without Peter, the band was nothing and they were all to some extent in awe of him. This was particularly the case with Danny when he joined.

'But Peter wasn't ambitious in terms of stardom. When they returned from the States, I remember I went to one gig at the Empire Pool, Wembley, with Mick, and already there were some changes. Mick was dressed up as a baseball player with a helmet on and we travelled back in this huge limo. There were actually girls on the roof as we were leaving. Suddenly Fleetwood Mac were stars. We all laughed and thought it was very funny, but it didn't interest Peter at all.'

If Peter wasn't ambitious in the sense of bigger venues and more money, Clifford, their manager, obviously was. He was naturally very proud of the fact that, for much of that year, Fleetwood Mac were the highest paid band around: they often went out for £1,000 a night, which was a phenomenal amount of money but possible because they were better live than on record, whereas for most other groups in the charts the opposite was true. Clifford was very clever in that sense. Pop fans would go along to their gigs expecting more of 'Albatross' and instead would get rhythm and blues, rock 'n' roll and a great night out.

'But Peter's one weakness,' recalls Jane, 'was that he was gullible; he could be taken in by people he didn't know very well and yet be very dismissive of people who had his best interests at heart. I don't think the success of "Albatross" changed him fundamentally; I think it just brought more pressure and he had to learn to deal with lots of new people in new situations. Press interviews, for instance. Peter would often speak openly and then think his words had been twisted around. Mick was more articulate – he probably should have done all the interviews, but everybody wanted to speak to the leader. Then, of course, there was the pressure of the next single which couldn't be too commercial but still had to be a hit.

'If I had to summarise Peter's personality at that time and even now, he is a very critical person. He can be very cruel and he's self-opinionated – and that is said with the greatest amount of love. Although I never heard him criticise the band in a nasty way when there were other people around, he was the kind of person who was never really satisfied with himself or others.'

So the autumn of 1968 was at once the start of much bigger things for the band and also the beginning of Peter Green's fleeting rock superstardom. In only two years' and four hits' time, he would be out of the business, up in the backwoods of Maine with musician friends, happily jamming with warbling birds in the trees and, crucially, trying to restore the inner peace that had been lost amongst all the adulation, swollen egos and crushing workload.

But in 1968, the process that he was about to go through – the heavy industry of rock 'n' roll – was pretty much irreversible. Other creative free spirits with whom he was now rubbing shoulders, admiring and being admired by – Joplin, Hendrix – would die careless, solitary deaths in a few years. In that sense, Peter was lucky. Even so, looking back in the mid-1970s, he said, 'I tried to remember how it was before the hits, just to be playing for pleasure, and I couldn't bring back that feeling. It was terrible. Terrible.'

Paul Morrison, manager of the Orange Music shop, which had opened for business in London's New Compton Street a little earlier in 1968, noticed a change in Peter when the band returned from their second US tour. As well as selling highly desirable second-hand American guitars, Orange designed and manufactured their own range of amplification, which Fleetwood Mac were kitted out with in November and, despite massive air-freight bills, took to the States with them in December for the tour. In the UK, Paul – himself an accomplished classical guitarist who also played in London blues band Black Cat Bones – often went to Mac gigs as technical support and in time became good friends with Peter. 'When he returned from the second US tour,' Paul reflects, 'Peter was unhappy about something – the conversations I remember were ones standing at urinals at gigs! It wasn't clear to me why he was unhappy, and it's something I've never quite sorted out in my own mind, but he was beginning to feel detached from the whole Fleetwood Mac process. This may have been due to delusions of grandeur after "Albatross", or that he genuinely didn't feel part of things any more. Or it could have been part of health problems which were beginning to take hold around that time. I think a lot of that illness was reactive: he was put in a position that he could not cope with, namely being a very wealthy and successful young musician. But the thing you have to remember is that here was a young man in his 20s with the world at his feet and he's living at home with his mum and dad. Now, that's not exactly normal, and I think the reason is that he felt very vulnerable out in the big wide world. He was never able to cope with being a star. Part of him absolutely loved it and part of him was horrified by the whole idea. Once he'd made it, there were expectations of what he should be doing and how he should be living.

'Peter's parents were very proud of their son's achievements, but they also kept him down to earth. Yet perhaps with the very best intentions this may have made his confusion worse: to be told on the one hand, "You're just an ordinary Jewish boy. I'm a postman. This is real life and you stay here," and then on the other, "You're a superhuman being and extraordinarily special," which undoubtedly he was, then inevitably there is conflict. Once he was famous, I think he was constantly torn between these two states of mind.'

Nonetheless, Jane Honeycombe thinks Peter's relationship with his parents and his domestic set-up was always a good thing: 'What everybody forgets is that he was very young when he made it, 22. Some people are quite mature at that age, but I think he was, in the nicest possible way, pushed by his parents. They'd always been very supportive, but I think in part he was actually doing it for them. Once there was money coming in, it was a sensible thing to do to buy a house, and I think he realised it would be best to stay with them because it gave him stability and also meant he was protected. By then, everybody wanted to speak to him. His parents were able to shield him a bit.'

Paul Morrison smiles as he recalls one incident when Peter took great pleasure in the fact that he was famous by playing an elaborate game with a couple of girl fans: 'Peter was a great people-watcher and loved to observe how fans reacted to him. After a while he came to the conclusion that fame was really all in the mind: if he walked down the street behaving like an ordinary person, he didn't get recognised, but when he behaved like a star – posing, looking and feeling self-important – then people would notice him.

'One night we went to a club and chatted up a couple of girls. Peter behaved "normally" – not once did he mention who he was, but you could tell that they were unsure. We drove the girls back to their parents' home, they invited us in for coffee and the whole time Peter behaved like an ordinary guy. He kept up the act to the very end and the girls had to play along with it. Even though they might have known this was Peter Green, he managed to avoid the star situation for the whole evening and was just this guy Peter. We said goodnight to them, got in the car and drove off, and Peter laughed his head off.'

Without a doubt, stardom to Peter Green wasn't always simply a case of agonising introspection about his excessive wealth and the world's in-built social injustice; here was a young, good-looking guy who as a performer sometimes craved attention, like all performers do. 'I don't have this fan-fever thing,' he told a journalist around the time 'Man Of The World' had consolidated his pop-star status. 'Our followers are really very quiet.' He then admitted to the reporter that it gave him quite a kick to be recognised and stopped in the street, because it happened too rarely.

'Man Of The World' was recorded mostly in New York during a lull in gigging, on their second US tour. After the commercial success of 'Albatross', the pressure and responsibility of the follow-up smash was squarely on Peter's shoulders. The single turned out to be significant on several counts. Most importantly, it came out on the Immediate label, not Blue Horizon, to Peter's dismay and Mike Vernon's fury. Like the first hit, it was a sleeper which required some serious plugging before it rose to Number Two in the charts. Also, it was a classy, crafted pop ballad – all links with blues, even in the broadest sense of the word, appeared to have been severed.

A closer look at circumstances surrounding the split from Blue Horizon makes this the first crucial 'what if?' juncture in Peter's career. It is perhaps also a revealing insight into the music business in those pre-mega-corporation days which proves, if proof were needed, that big money is invariably accompanied by some conflict of interests.

Clifford Davis still remains convinced that 'The biggest coup I ever pulled off for Fleetwood Mac was getting them out of their Blue Horizon recording contract.' As an ambitious manager, he was doing his job by getting his 'hot' act out of an independent label and into an appropriate major record company. From Clifford's point of view, Fleetwood Mac, with one worldwide Number One to their credit, could hardly be regarded as beginners; they were a highly marketable asset. Mike Vernon would naturally disagree, while Peter now re-affirms that 'Blue Horizon was sensible for what the group was at that time – we were all beginners, apart from John McVie.' On the other hand, there was the songwriter, the artist. Peter had established a good professional and personal rapport with producer Mike Vernon, and once out of Blue Horizon he felt exposed and at something of a loss.

The band (minus Jeremy Spencer) would spend the middle part of 1969 recording their third album, *Then Play On*, with Peter ostensibly in the producer's chair, as well as being songwriter and star musician. He now reflects on his role as a producer: 'We should have had a producer on *Then Play On*. Then it might have sold better. We tried to produce it ourselves, thinking that might be more fun. We did have a lot of fun, but then it's all very well to say, "Yeah, let's produce our own records from now on; we don't need anyone," but we weren't completely aware of what the producer's job was.

We should have kept Mike Vernon. I didn't want to leave Blue Horizon but Clifford Davis was going for bigger money.'

Twenty-five years on, Mike Vernon still smarts at the memory of losing Fleetwood Mac, albeit from Blue Horizon's burgeoning roster, which by this time included Chicken Shack, Eddie Boyd, Champion Jack Dupree, Duster Bennett and Gordon Smith: 'Losing Fleetwood Mac was a battle, and I would like it to go on record that it was not a direct battle between Blue Horizon and the band but between Blue Horizon and the band's management, who created, I think, totally unnecessary barriers between the band and us. All right, Blue Horizon had grown up as a blues label, but it was never the idea that it should just stay a blues label. Nor for that matter did I think that Fleetwood Mac should stay a blues band. They wanted to develop, and to me "Albatross" and "Man Of The World" are examples of that. I spent time with them in New York on their second tour doing "Man Of The World" and then came back to London and finished it off with engineer Martin Birch at Kingsway Studios in Holborn. Martin ended up finishing the record without me because there was a certain feeling that maybe I was not into what they were doing, but that was not the case. What was happening was that I was being railroaded by the management, who had realised that the contract had run out and promptly thought, "We can get a bucket-load of money elsewhere."'

To Clifford Davis, the deal that Peter had struck with Mike Vernon prior to Clifford's arrival on the scene as the band's manager was simple: one year's recording contract, followed by two one-year options on Blue Horizon's side, to be taken up only if they still wanted the band: 'I just sat praying that Richard Vernon wouldn't notice the renewal date for the contract coming up. And he didn't! I notified Blue Horizon the following day that they had failed to take up the option and therefore Fleetwood Mac were free of any further contractual obligations to Mike and Richard Vernon.' To make the Vernon brothers' oversight even more painful, all this actually happened while 'Albatross' was high in the charts.

Mike continues, 'I can understand Clifford trying to get a bucketload of money, but he didn't actually come to us and say, "We've just had a massive offer, £250,000 from Immediate. Can you match or better their offer?" There is no question that CBS [Blue Horizon's distributors] would have matched or funded any deal to keep Fleetwood Mac, but we were never really approached; we were just told. Okay, we made an error, and we admitted it, but we said, "Let's renegotiate with CBS and make this band the international success we can make it."'

Mike recalls further how Clifford had promised that, even though it was outside the contract, 'Man Of The World' would still come out on Blue Horizon; Fleetwood Mac had made it with Blue Horizon and would honour that. But it came out on Immediate and the band never saw a penny of that quarter of a million pounds that Immediate had promised. Clifford ended up doing a deal with Warner Brothers. The Warner-Reprise deal was reportedly to have been good, but not as good as the £250,000 CBS would, according to Mike Vernon, willingly have come up with.

When told of Peter's views about the producer's role, Mike now wryly observes, 'It's the same old story – musicians only see their music from their own point of view. They see their performance, their song, their sound and their arrangement. But what does Joe Blow think about it? The producer is the guy between the man in the street and the band. When I heard their next album, *Then Play On*, I was disappointed. I really felt I could have made it sound more tangible and given it more of a groove. As it was, I think it sounded a little synthetic, and I know that we tried desperately hard with their other albums not to have that. Their first 'Dog And Dustbin' album has got so much feel to it and the second one was deliberately given an old sound. Funnily enough, a similar thing happened with John Mayall – his early records, the *Blues Breakers* and *A Hard Road* albums, had a strong feel, but gradually, as John started to take over control in the production of things like *Bare Wires*, he began to lose a bit of that. Thankfully, he's got it back now.'

From Clifford Davis's point of view, Mac's manager undoubtedly kept his cool during the split with Blue Horizon, especially when the brinkmanship with Immediate (at that point already a sinking ship which went under later that year) began to go against him. Clifford gave them the 'Man Of The World' tapes for two good reasons, both in Peter Green's and Fleetwood Mac's long-term interests: first, a couple of years earlier Peter had signed away his copyrights in a so-so publishing deal with Malcolm Forrester; second, it was crucial to get an 'Albatross' follow-up out without further delay.

Peter had been introduced to Forrester in his Mayall days, and the publisher was now connected with Immediate. Davis and Forrester are thought to have cut a deal where Clifford would get back Fleetwood Mac's songs and copyrights and Immediate would match CBS's offer for a three-year recording contract. As things turned out, he got the single in the shops and retrieved old copyrights, but that was about it. Even though no money actually came his way from the negotiation and Immediate stitched him up, Clifford then promptly put himself even more out of pocket, once again looking after Fleetwood Mac's and his own long-term interests.

'Man Of The World' was released on 4 April 1969. At first, sales were slow – the single needed a leg-up. Today's plethora of 24-hour satellite television channels and music shows often means that it's the media who have to court record companies by seeking exclusive 'firsts' in screening new videos, but in those pre-video, pre-satellite days of television the very opposite was true: there was *Top Of The Pops*, BBC2's *Disco 2*, Radio 1 and Radio Luxembourg, and that was it. So opportunities for nationwide on-air promotion were absurdly restricted and – to put it politely – some television- and radio-show producers and DJs exploited the situation to supplement their frugal BBC salaries. Ever since the Alan Freed case in the 1950s, payola (an American euphemism for this sort of bribery) was endemic to the music business: at the end of the 1960s and in the early 1970s, certain BBC DJs were caught in sex-for-airplay barter deals. Clifford Davis knew that 'Man Of The World' had to be a hit and acted accordingly: 'It was a big hit. I made sure of that. I spent a lot of money making sure it was played on the right programmes. And you can read into that whatever you like!'

Mike Vernon remembers 'considerable input' from Danny Kirwan in the making of 'Man Of The World' as gradually his presence was taking the band out of mainstream 12-bar blues and into blues rock and rock ballads. Peter and Danny's harmonised guitars seemed to keep Peter amused – for a while, at least. Today he's still amused by memories of Danny's eccentric, eclectic musical taste, taking in a wide range of influences from Django Reinhardt and Louis Armstrong to George Harrison and even Peter Green: 'We used to call Danny "Ragtime Cowboy Joe". He was into all that Roaring '20s band stuff, as well as country and western.'

While they were over in America on that second US tour, Fleetwood Mac continued to forge a new, rockier style. Even so, during that visit some out-and-out blues sessions took place, most notably Otis Spann's *The Biggest Thing Since Colossus*, an album that features 'Peter Green, Original Blues Man' approaching a peak. According to Mike Vernon, Otis – former pianist with The Muddy Waters Band, and the Clarksdale legend's half-brother – loved Peter's playing almost as much as he loved bourbon. That this was the case can perhaps be best heard on the piano/guitar/drums rave 'Walkin'', a simultaneously intoxicated and intoxicating piece of Chicago blues rock (Mike Vernon: 'Otis's head sometimes touched the ivories as often as did his fingers'). *Colossus*, Spann's penultimate album, was recorded in New York shortly after the *Blues Jam At Chess* sessions in January. A victim of cancer, Spann died in April the following year, 1970, aged just 40.

Mike Vernon still regards the Chess sessions as 'a very good piece of product', but looking back Peter and John McVie are not so sure. 'Those black guys,' Peter stresses, 'knew that you can't get the hang of it. They knew that whatever a white guy tries to do is not gonna be the blues of coloured people. It's a pose all along. In Chicago that time, I played too forcefully – too much and too loud – because my experience in life didn't match up to theirs. Perhaps white folks should've left those coloured tunes alone and stuck to singing hymns! At those Chess sessions, my voice sounds like I've been drinking ginger beer or am singing down the toilet!'

As far as John McVie was concerned, those Chess sessions dented his professional pride: 'From the moment we arrived in the studio, those guys made it quite clear that they didn't give a shit about who we were. We were just a bunch of white kids and they had a "whitey plays the blues" attitude. I also got the feeling right from the start that Willie Dixon didn't care for me!' So 4 January 1969 was a long day for John, in which it was his turn to have the blues about the blues.

Country-blues master John Hammond now thinks that Chicago in the 1960s was an exception and that skin colour has never held back determined blues talent: 'In Chicago, there were too many bluesmen and not enough work. Every working musician, regardless of skin colour, was looking over his shoulder in those days.'

Certainly today, as third- and fourth-generation black and white bluesmen tell it like it is, the question of skin colour is irrelevant: Robert Cray in some ways has been influenced by Eric Clapton, who in formative years looked to Freddie King, who influenced Albert Collins, who gave Cray the idea to start a band in the first place. In the early 21st century, it's taken for granted that the music is a melting-pot of styles, coming from blue souls wrapped in all shades of skin.

Danny Kirwan, though, still seems locked in a 1960s time-warp. When he talks about blues, his demeanour is suddenly transformed. In serious and heavy tones, he reflects, 'Peter Green and me, we stole the black man's music. What we did was wrong. The feel of blues music...' – mid-sentence Danny adopts a French accent, perhaps finding himself in Django mode – 'belong to ze black man. It's ze way he feel when he wake up, go to work and go out on a Saturday night. Now a white man can never know or feel zat feeling; he can only imagine it.' Several people who have seen Danny recently have formed a similar impression: here is a musician in self-destruct mode and seemingly driven by remorse at having once dug his heels in too deep on strange and sacred ground: black man's blues.

Of course it would be fatuous, fanciful and, in this context, rather sick to talk about dark, diabolic forces at work against Danny and, to a lesser extent, Peter as well. But it's also impossible not to hold some niggling doubts. Their massive blues-guitar-playing talent, in both cases so precocious it was unreal, certainly turned out to be Danny's making and breaking. Blues, at the intensity with which Peter and Danny explored and lived the music back then, thrives on danger. To spend a couple of hours in Danny's company at some seedy Soho pub now is to discover another aspect to this mighty, cathartic music. It's horribly sad but seemingly inevitable that the next headline about Danny Kirwan will be one announcing a destitute, alcohol-related and premature passing in a London hostel or side street.

Back in Chicago's Chess Studios in January 1969, though, the white boys did themselves proud. Perhaps the most poignant and historic moment came when Jeremy Spencer got up to belt out Elmore James's 'Madison Blues', accompanied by none other than James's original sax player from the 1950s, JT Brown. Peter's high points during the sessions include Chester Arthur 'Howlin' Wolf' Burnett's 'Sugar Mama' and the Perkins/Day classic 'Homework', which Peter would go on to produce for manager Clifford Davis as a solo single. Other local musicians on the Chess sessions included Buddy Guy (who for contractual reasons was transparently disguised as 'Guitar Buddy'), Willie Dixon, Otis Spann, Honeyboy Edwards, harp player Walter 'Shakey' Horton and Spann's drummer, SP Leary.

Blue Horizon waited almost a year before releasing the sessions as a double album, *Blues Jam At Chess, Volumes 1 And 2*, on 5 December 1969. The release irritated Peter: 'On some tracks there is only one of us playing, and as we didn't record enough for a double album there must be numbers by other people. So it can't be a Fleetwood Mac album. It is a bit annoying that Blue Horizon can't wait until *Then Play On* is out of the charts, and they are not going to be able to release anything near comparison to that.' Clifford Davis, ever the diplomat, was more forgiving: 'Of course we're not falling over backwards to promote this LP, but we're not ashamed of it. It should make quite a good collector's item.'

The fact that these and other business hassles cropped up with monotonous regularity during 1969 made Peter yearn for the life before the hits had begun to come. Then it was all about the joy of the music, no two nights being the same. Now gradually Fleetwood Mac was also becoming a money-machine. In July, shortly after the chart success of 'Man Of The World', Blue Horizon re-released a remixed version of 'Need Your Love So Bad' just a year after the original had come out. The strings were more prominent on the remixed version and Clifford Davis refused to have anything to do with it, while Peter, who never liked the idea of re-releases, thought that, if the record was going to make it, it would have made it last time.

Business matters also prompted the band to cancel its third US tour, scheduled to start in mid-July, as Fleetwood Mac found themselves in the middle of a litigious bunfight between the Columbia and Atlantic recording companies in America. Columbia had placed a restriction order on Atlantic which in effect prevented 'Man Of The World' and the imminent release *Then Play On* from reaching the shops in the States. For Peter, this was all very boring and a far cry from no-contract-necessary gentlemen's-agreement gigs at the Fishmongers Arms and the Toby Jug, Tolworth. He was already getting jaded, admitting at the time that he was not that keen to work: 'The others are in a big hurry, but I don't want the band to work too much. It's a complete waste of time.' Peter disliked the routine, the same thing every night. He believed they should have used the time to make albums: 'If there's a good album, everyone can hear it. If you play in one place, you can only be heard in one area of the country. I don't like big concerts and all that bit; I've always liked the small, packed club.'

Peter was becoming increasingly keen on doing free concerts around this time, mid-1969, but even here some downers lay in store. When Fleetwood Mac agreed to do the Camden Fringe Festival at the end of May, organised by Blackhill Enterprises and also featuring Rory Gallagher's Taste, Edgar Broughton and Duster Bennett, crowd violence brought proceedings to a halt. Before an estimated crowd of 25,000 gathered at Parliament Hill Fields, Fleetwood Mac went on stage around midnight only to be greeted by a squad of skinhead 'bovverboys' whose chanting and bottle-throwing forced the band back off again. Whilst Peter shrugged the incident off as yet another bit of showbiz blues, it made his father Joe's blood boil enough to write in to *Melody Maker*.

In a letter headed 'Sterner Measures For These Hoodlums', J Green of London W14 wrote, 'My son travels all over the country, playing to different audiences practically every night, and last Friday was one of his nights off. But instead of taking advantage and resting, he offered his services with the rest of his group to play a free open-air concert along with other artists. Everything would have gone off fine, when along came a small band of hoodlums – not, may I add, long-haired freaks, as is their usual description, but a gang of crew-cut young thugs who seemed to delight in spoiling a night out for the vast majority of people who were there to enjoy themselves.

'After many nasty incidents, the concert had to be abandoned, much to the disgust of the organisers, who went to a great deal of trouble to arrange it. It is time sterner measures were taken by the law and stiffer sentences imposed on these so-called citizens of the future.'

Charlie Watkins (of the Watkins Copicat and WEM Public Address Systems) was sound engineer that night at Camden: 'Before they went on, I'd had some aggravation backstage about the sound from a woman who was with the Fleetwood Mac party, and I was being all apologetic. Then I remember Peter Green just staring at me, or more like staring through me, and he didn't say a word. I felt very uneasy. Then he just walked straight past me – all bad vibes – and never said a single thing. I'd been told by people in the business about what a nice guy this Peter Green was, so when he was like that to me it came as a bit of a shock.'

During 1969, what was becoming quite clear was that Peter was beginning to despise actively the success that previously he had courted, almost with a vengeance. Spiritually, a void was looming. On his return from the second US tour in mid-February, he told both Jane Honeycombe and Paul Morrison that he had experimented further with LSD and mescaline. He told Jane that, contrary to what he had expected, drugs had made him far more, not less, introspective. He told Paul of one time on mescaline when afterwards he couldn't remember a single thing he'd said or done for over half a day. Such drug-induced trauma, together with the pressures and hassles of leading a band virtually single-handed onto full-tilt big time in the UK and America, were all starting to take their toll. Increasingly, he was living out the angst and ennui he had fantasised about when he wrote the lyrics to 'Man Of The World' about a year earlier. For Peter, growing up into a rock star meant living in a cossetted world of empty dreams.

Even the BB King Blues Band/Fleetwood Mac UK tour in April was in one sense a disappointment for him. Here he was, playing in some of Britain's finest concert halls with a living legend, Riley 'The Beale Street Blues Boy' King, who had probably inspired him most of all and who was a cousin of Bukka White, another of Peter's all-time favourites. At the opening night at the Royal Albert Hall, London, on 22 April, some 'Mac have sold out' purists gave the band a hard time during their set, only to see Joe Green rise from his seat in the front stalls, defy them and proudly stick up for his son, pronouncing him 'the best'. Later on in the evening, headliner BB King articulated similar sentiments as part of his act.

At one point, BB broke a string and put it down to nerves, explaining to the audience, 'Man, you'd be nervous if you could see who I can see right now.' He was referring to George Harrison and Eric Clapton sitting in a private box, enjoying the show. But then BB declared, 'But I've got to say that, I'm sorry, Peter Green is the best.' Then, a couple of nights later, live at the Regal, Cambridge, mentor and protégé exchanged musical ideas, figures and history backstage. Peter would play a rhythm, saying, 'This is something John Mayall brought back from America.' BB would take it up, hammer it for a while, play various other riffs and finally announce, 'Robert Nighthawk is the one who really made it. That's the cat. Earl Hooker did it, too.' Just a year earlier, Peter would have been knocked out by this kind of thing, but now the thrill was going. Instead, after the eight-concert tour ended, the band let it be known that they were dissatisfied with the half-hour slot given to them during each of their two sets per night and were therefore planning a concert-hall tour of their own.

Peter recalls one incident during the 1969 tour when, perhaps encouraged by the generous words of praise BB publicly had heaped on him at the Albert Hall, he tried to get closer to the man. 'One time on the tour coach,' he reflects, 'I got up and went over to sit next to him. Around then I was spending a lot of time thinking about religion and faith, and I kind of hoped he might have something to tell me, things that we might talk over. But I guess he wasn't comfortable doing that. One thing he did say was that, playing guitar, I had a sensitive touch.'

A couple of years later, Peter took part in BB's rather star-studded *In London* album, along with Alexis Korner, Ringo Starr, Steve Marriott, Klaus Voorman and many other names. BB now remembers noticing a big change in Peter's personality: 'In the studio he was quiet and I got the impression that he was very disillusioned with the whole music business. He played great on "Caledonia", but the way I remember him is sitting around. I was just pleased to share his company, and he seemed to get some comfort from mine.'

Conga player Nigel Watson, who collaborated on early-1970s singles like 'Beasts Of Burden', points out that Peter didn't really approve of BB King's musical direction at the time: 'In the early 1970s, Peter even became disillusioned with what BB King was playing: he called it showbiz and thought BB hadn't really taken the music any further.'

In fact, 'Showbiz Blues', with country slide inspired by Bukka White, was one of the tracks recorded during the spring and early summer months of 1969, in Kingsway Studios, Holborn, as the band finally finished off their third album. At first rudely entitled *Bread And Kunny*, until their new label, Reprise, stepped in as arbiters of non-dubious taste, *Then Play On* once again put the pressure on Peter to come up with something new. Danny's input – seven of the album's 14 tracks – drew from material he had written over the previous two years, whereas Peter's stuff had to be of the moment or, to use a cliché of the day, 'progressive'. It was really getting to Peter that the band were not always pulling their weight creatively, a criticism that John McVie is now quick to contest: 'Peter was the spearhead, the leader who we followed. I didn't write the songs, so all I could do was follow.'

According to Paul Morrison, when it came to recording his own new batch of songs for the album, Peter deliberately froze the rest of the band out: 'I remember when they were making *Then Play On*, Peter wouldn't let the band in the studio. He wanted to do all the parts himself, bass and drums as well as guitar. It was around the time he was heavily into classical music, and Vaughan Williams in particular. I had a classical guitar that he really liked and I was flattered because a lot of times he would let me in the studio, but not the band. I remember once going to John's flat. There was a guitar lying around, so I picked it up and started playing. John said, "That's nice. What is it?" and I told him: "It's on your new album!" He hadn't even heard it. So to Peter, at that point the band was becoming something very peripheral. I think he even felt he could play drums better than Micky Fleetwood and saw flaws in everything they did.'

Road manager Dennis Keen could see all of this – Peter's isolation – too but felt powerless to do anything so bold as gee the others up and give them the spur which, he says, was due: 'We were in Kingsway, all five of us [Jeremy didn't participate on *Then Play On*]. If Peter didn't get his guitar out, there wouldn't be a sound made. If Peter was late, they'd just spend the time sitting about, drinking coffee or whatever. Instead of Danny saying, "Oh, I've got a number; let's work it out and when Pete comes we'll see what he thinks," they'd do nothing. It was like that. Pete would have welcomed any input, but that was never the case around that time, although it was better a bit earlier around "Man Of The World". I could see Pete really enjoyed doing those two studio jams, "Searching For Madge" and "Fighting For Madge". He used to play back the tapes, take them home, listen again, come in the next day and engineer Martin Birch would play around with the mix. The rest of the band never contributed one iota to that. Peter did all the editing and cutting.'

Obviously, Paul Morrison and Dennis Keen have different interpretations of what was really going on during the making of that third album. While Paul saw Peter drawing away from the band, Dennis felt at the time that the leader was looking to them for creative energy but then always seemed to hit a brick wall. 'Part of the problem,' Dennis surmises, 'was communication. Peter was the leader, but he wasn't one to start flashing the sergeant's stripes. He did towards the end, you know, tell John what part to play, but only because he had to. I can only remember one rehearsal in the whole time Peter was with them, and that was at the Lyceum one afternoon, when they tried out a big new PA system. So it had to be during gigs that Peter tried to get them to "join" him in some way. Thinking about it now, perhaps he wasn't able to get this across.'

What can't have helped matters much was that the backdrop to all this – the mood of summer 1969 – was rather crazed anyway. While children were starving in Biafra, Neil Armstrong became the first man to pogo on the Moon's surface (at vast expense), and on the day of the Moon landing counter-culture psychiatrist RD Laing stood somewhere in north Africa and drunkenly ranted up at the astronaut for 'trespassing'. (Laing was the definitive 1960s shrink who declared that psychosis was an entirely reasonable reaction to the mad ways of the world, and for some time the world of psychiatry listened. In the mid-1970s, as it happens, Peter might have done a lot worse than have a few sessions with him, but no one thought of that then.) It was also during that summer that Brian Jones was murdered, one conspiracy theorist now alleges, as revellers partied on by the side of his swimming pool, too out of it to notice or to care that their host was being rubbed out before their eyes. Not only that but violence broke out in Ulster. For anyone with Peter's spirit – one that naturally tapped into a more collective consciousness – these were without a doubt crazy-making times.

Chris Welch recalls a fittingly weird scene at around this time involving Peter at his office in London's Fleet Street: 'I remember one time, it must have been 1969, he suddenly burst into the *Melody Maker* offices, unannounced. It wasn't very grand – one room on the third floor, full of desks and filing cabinets stuffed with cuttings and photographs. Peter burst in and said, "I want all my pictures back. I don't like any of the pictures of me that are appearing in newspapers." He went straight to the cabinet, which you're not supposed to do, opened a file and started throwing pictures around, trying to find photos of himself. I think the idea was to tear them up or throw them away. He didn't speak to me – that was the other strange thing – although we'd got on well that time before in the Red Lion. Eventually, the librarian persuaded him to put everything back, but something had obviously upset him a great deal.'

Evidently, Peter's mindset at this time really was that line of prototype rap he'd recently written: 'Don't ask me what I think of you. I might not give the answer that you want me to.'

7 Weird Scenes, Acid Queens, Jesus Freaks And Gurus

During the last part of their second US tour, in early 1969, Peter began a spiritual journey which was probably set in motion by LSD. 'When I took LSD,' he reflects, 'it was like breathing underwater. When you come down off it, you're back to the same thing again: you can't breathe underwater. Ever since then I've been trying to work out what it was, to see if that feeling, that ridiculous high, is attainable to us in any other way without taking the drug, to rediscover it without someone blowing your mind. And I can't work out what it was with acid that made you feel so free and so happy. But the thing about all the trips I took – about eight in all – was that the only time I ever had it was when it was given to me. I never bought it.'

What Peter couldn't have known was that by then the original Haight-Ashbury peace-and-love movement had changed into a tacky perversion of the original credo: already, many hippies' preoccupations were moving away from ideals and prophets to ideal profit. Increasingly, Peter was surrounded by guru hustlers and streetwise chameleons who changed hats lots of times each day according to whether it was enlightenment, highly lucrative drugs or both these things that they were peddling at that particular moment. Four or five years earlier Peter's honesty would have been in its element in San Francisco, but in the late 1960s they must have seen him coming. He was spiked the first few times and after that his own curiosity got the upper hand.

Stan Webb of Chicken Shack has trenchant views about spiking, the drug dealer's speculative and free introductory offer, based on some horrific personal experiences: 'When Peter first came across acid, he wasn't at all that way inclined. Later on, when he got into it, it became a challenge for him, like it did for Eric Clapton – Saint Eric as I call him – who somehow went there yet got back.

'Peter was a very strong character, but he got into taking those weird things. When I first knew him, before "Albatross", he'd have the occasional smoke and that was his lot. What happened to him might well have been exactly the same as with me, because I got spiked once on LSD, which gave me a nervous breakdown and just about screwed me up for three years: for ages after I would sit watching television and suddenly burst out crying. When it was done to me, I ended up on a tube train going to Kilburn Art College for a gig. Someone said hello to me and I tried to stab them. I didn't know what the hell I was doing. I ended up in this ambulance with the old blue light going and a nurse giving me glass after glass of orange juice, as well as three great spoonfuls of Marmite for the riboflavin in it, which calms you down. We had a Swiss road manager once who became deaf in one ear after he got spiked.'

Some still insist that Peter was first spiked with acid in San Francisco in 1968 and then a couple of years later, more insidiously in a hippy hang-out just outside Munich. Munich has since been seen as the most convenient explanation of how such a clean-living and focused musician, whose extreme simplicity was also his genius, could then appear to disintegrate into an acid casualty fazed by life's complexities.

In 1968, when Fleetwood Mac, the four-piece nothing-but-the-blues combo, flew out to the United States for their first tour, each of them tried LSD for the first time, although Peter was least keen.

He and Jeremy stayed with Judy Wong, now a no-nonsense music-biz trouper who's seen it all. Back then, though, she was a demure and rather shy oriental woman who, in her own words, 'hadn't heard the F-word or the C-word, never mind used them'. With Peter and especially Jeremy *in situ*, all that was going to change.

'Peter sometimes swore, but Jeremy was literally two people,' Judy reflects. 'I didn't expect some lunatic Englishman to open my windows at four in the morning and shout obscenities for the sole purpose of waking up the neighbours.' Jeremy said in a 1974 interview with Steve Clarke of the *NME* that Peter did not drop acid on this first US tour, yet many know otherwise and some even suspect that Jeremy may have had a hand in first 'turning on' the uninterested guitarist.

Jeremy can only have been a part of it because, to all intents and purposes, Peter's fate was sealed the moment he arrived. He was already a cult celebrity over there and, as such, a highly desirable prospect for the drugs underworld. His reputation as Eric Clapton's successor in The Bluesbreakers had gone ahead of him, and this meant that, when he started hanging out with Judy at music haunts in San Francisco's bohemian sleaze quarter of Haight-Ashbury, there were some heavy names on the scene eager to shake hands. The Grateful Dead's Jerry Garcia was one of them. The Dead were looked after by the electronics genius who had conceived of (and paid for) their huge public-address system, which they would use at musical 'freak-outs' where the audience was tripped out on acid. The acid was, reputedly, supplied by the same electronics genius, one Owsley, Tycoon of Trips. It made for great business.

Augustus Owsley Stanley III was the grandson of a Kentucky senator and twice a dropout. Here was a bohemian scientist with a calculating business brain quick to realise the market potential of the 1960s peace and so-called 'underground' movement. He may not have made money out of Peter Green directly, but Owsley's cachet allegedly came from rubbing shoulders with famous rock stars. It was his purest-of-all acid that reportedly fuelled The Beatles as they dreamt up the psychedelic vistas of their *Sergeant Pepper's...* concept album.

Profit margins to be found in LSD manufacture when Owsley set up his Baer Research Company in the mid-1960s were as mind-blowing as the stuff itself: $20,000 worth of basic chemicals would gross maybe $2-3 million on the streets. Although in 1966 he was ahead of the game, by 1968, when Fleetwood Mac were in town, the police were after him. As soon as he heard Peter was around, Owsley was very, very interested in meeting him, as Judy Wong remembers: 'Peter and I went to dinner with him somewhere on Broadway. He was a very intelligent person who impressed Peter by being knowledgeable on a wide range of subjects. Owsley only ate meat – no potatoes or vegetables. The three of us would hang around together, and although I knew that he passed around acid, I think he was just genuinely interested in getting to know Peter.

'One time we went over to Owsley's house in Berkeley, which is just across the Bay from San Francisco. His house was just off the campus of the University of California, completely out of the way, which suited him just fine. When we got there, Peter and I were amazed to discover that the whole place was decorated with owls – not stuffed owls, but owl salt and pepper shakers, owl figurines, owls everywhere! And his fridge contained only one thing: meat. We're not talking chops; we're talking legs and huge joints. To this day, I've never seen anything like that, and of course to Peter it was a weird bit of *déjà vu* going straight back to his butchering days.'

Owsley always stressed that he wasn't an acid missionary like Dr Timothy 'turn on, tune in, drop out' Leary. He assured Judy that he would supply only if that was what was wanted, and she was quite comfortable about the whole situation. However, one night, backstage at the Fillmore West – then called the Carousel Ballroom – Owsley offered Judy what she thought was Coca-Cola. 'Then, in a mad-scientist, ghoulish voice,' Judy recalls, 'Owsley inquired, "And I wonder how Mr Green and Mr Fleetwood and the others are doing?!" I dashed off into the hall, where the boys were listening to the band. When I found them, I remember Mick saving he felt strange but all right.'

Later on, when they got back home to Judy's place, Jeremy experienced problems coming down off it and, he has since said, was scared witless, thinking about death and his own mortality for the first time in his life. Mick and John enjoyed the experience sufficiently to trip again soon afterwards, on the mountain near Sausalito. And Peter? Well, at that point he could take or leave it – only instead, he was given it.

After that first tour, none of the band continued with the acid experimentation back in England, but when they went back to America in December for a three-month stretch, Owsley eventually hooked up with them in New Orleans. 'In New Orleans,' Mick Fleetwood remembers, 'when we were playing with The Grateful Dead, we had taken some acid and we knew that the whole audience had been spiked from the water fountains at the Warehouse club. After the show, one kid went home and announced to his parents that he was Jesus. Mom and Dad got scared and complained to the police, who went straight after Owsley.'

Mick's ex-wife Jenny Boyd remembers this rather heavy night and also recalls a somewhat paranoid Peter, perhaps freaked at having being spiked to the point where he couldn't even play guitar: 'That was the thing I couldn't really understand about [Peter] and drugs. That time in New Orleans, at the Warehouse gig where we all got spiked, I remember being back in our hotel room with Mick. Peter was with us and we were all still on Owsley's acid. I remember looking at Peter and thinking that this wasn't natural to him because he had his own energy and didn't need anything. There was one incident with Peter at that concert: they were all so high they couldn't play their instruments and were having a mass panic. Danny rushed up to me and said, "Jenny, I don't know what to do! I can't play anything!" At one point, Peter couldn't play anything either, and only Mick was able to perform a bit, but to me he looked like a skeleton on stage...complete madness! Afterwards, we were all still out of it and I remember walking towards Peter and suddenly he said, "Oh no! Stay away from me! I don't want to get caught in your world!"'

While Mick cannot condone Owsley's questionable legacy, he still has fond memories of the man: 'He was the wicked pixie, and I always told him that. I still keep in touch with him. He makes exotic jewellery and lives in a tent on the Gold Coast, near Cairns in Oz. He lives in the right vortex at the right time – when the end of the world comes he'll be on the right axis and won't get sprung off the Earth. He was responsible for turning half the planet on and a lot of heartache has come out of it. But on the other hand, he has turned a lot of people's lives around to the positive by a once-in-a-lifetime experience. The fact remains that he made millions out of acid. This chap was on the front page of *Time* magazine.'

Owsley and his wife (a chemistry student) met at the California college in Berkeley dropped out and went into the acid business. They had a production plant in Berkeley, then in Los Angeles, and first produced the stuff when it was still legal. For years he stayed out of jail because he had so much money, but then it ran out and the FBI clamped down. They caught him the night he spiked Peter and Mac in New Orleans, as Mick remembers with mixed emotions: 'It was purely by coincidence that we escaped the police that time. Pete couldn't play because he was too high. I was so high that I literally drove us back to our hotel with my feet – I was sitting on the back seat of a Mercury station wagon absolutely out of it on acid and turning the steering wheel with my feet while somebody else worked the pedals from the front passenger seat. We tried to follow Owsley and The Dead's car along the cobbled streets but got lost. Thank God! They got busted down on Bourbon Street. The police were really wanting to bust Owsley, and he'd only managed to elude them because he had the finances. He was on some vague probationary thing. But that time they got him and put him away for five years.'

When the band returned from that second US tour, people close to Peter started to notice a change in his attitude and demeanour. Ex-girlfriend Sandra Elsdon-Vigon feels that it was drugs that eventually undermined their deep friendship, a process which started around then. Sandra, now a psychotherapist living in Los Angeles, was very anti-drugs. She still recalls her anger at people like Owsley and Jeremy who led Peter in that direction: 'I remember Owsley coming to visit one day at Peter's house in New Malden when he was over with The Grateful Dead. He brought with him a huge vial of acid that he left with Peter. It was something that we would really argue about.'

By all accounts, Owsley truly believed he was doing Peter a favour. Carlos Santana, whom Sandra remembers as a very sweet man, at that time was into everything, and Peter kind of got drawn in. 'There was an outdoor festival at Shepton Mallett with Fleetwood Mac and Led Zeppelin. Peter and I had a big fight because Carlos was plying him with cocaine and acid and whatever else. It was awful for me because I could see that Peter was someone who just shouldn't touch anything like that. But to Peter it was all very exciting; he really admired Carlos and his band and all the San Francisco lot. He just got swept up in it.'

Peter had met Carlos on Mac's first US tour, a couple of years before Santana made a monster hit out of Peter's 'Black Magic Woman', recording a version that fused Latin and African rhythms.

Fan-club secretary Jane Honeycombe only got to know Peter a little before that second tour, but like Sandra she noticed a difference when the band returned in February 1969: 'Shortly after they returned, John held a small party at his place and Mick was there with Jenny, Danny was on his own and I ostensibly was with Peter. The conversations were all to do with drugs – we were all smoking. Suddenly I didn't feel terribly well and went to the loo. Mick and Peter came to the door after a while to see if I was all right, and to my surprise Peter sort of told me off for smoking dope. Rather foolishly I told him later that I'd really like to try acid. Peter got very angry. He said, "If anybody ever gives you any of that stuff, I'll kill them."'

This instance of 'do as I say, not as I do' was typical of the 'old' Peter Green at his most forceful and opinionated. But it wasn't to last: trip by trip, line by line and toke by toke, the drugs – by his own admission – 'turned me into a softy'.

8 Closing My Eyes To Hear
The People Laugh

In that same summer of 1969, Peter was searching intensely for an answer and was quite desperate for relief and respite from all the new-found traumas and stresses of showbiz. Drugs provided at least some temporary escape from business hassles and the trappings of fame. Yet the musical ideas kept coming through thick and fast, often to disappear before he had time to capture them on tape. Here was a musician in the mainstream of life who, whilst drawing from a seemingly bottomless well of creativity, was also teetering close to the edge and at some considerable risk of falling in.

Experiments with drugs had left Peter more disillusioned than traumatised or agitated, and whereas he had expected it all to liberate him and make him more carefree, it had actually made him more introverted. The constant question was 'Is there more? There has to be more to life than this.' This was when the religious thing started.

Peter engaged in long conversations about faith with Jane Honeycombe, who had been brought up a strict Roman Catholic. 'When I first knew him, that wasn't at all the kind of conversation he was into,' she recalls. 'I think that gradually developed into his worries about money. Peter, always looking into things and typically taking them to their extreme, would want to do or become the things that he believed. This apparently frightened Mick and John because Peter was, they believed, the kind of person who, if he felt strongly about something, needed everybody to agree with him.'

Also around this time, Jenny Boyd – younger sister of Pattie Harrison/Clapton, inspiration of Donovan's 1960's hit 'Jennifer Juniper', future wife (twice over) of Mick Fleetwood and now a writer and psychologist – shared a London taxi with Peter that summer. 'Just after Mick and I had got together again in 1969,' Jenny recalls, 'Peter rang me up. I hadn't seen him in years and the very fact he called me was quite unusual because at that time there was this unwritten rule that you don't talk to your friends' girlfriends because…they're your friends' girlfriends! Anyway, he called me and said, "Do you mind if we meet?" It so happened that I had to go up to Oxford Street for an appointment, so I said, "Let's share a cab." So we met up and once in a taxi he said, "I know you've been to India and you've been on this search for years – Mick's always told me about it. What is it you've found?" It was like he'd just discovered this great spiritual awareness, and he knew that I'd been on that path for quite a few years. And so, in the cab ride from Kensington Church Street to Oxford Street, he wanted me to give him the answer, to tell him what it's all about. But he did it in such a beautiful, open way. Of course, I felt totally inadequate, because something like that obviously needed so much longer to talk through.

'All I could do was reassure him that yes, he was right, it is there. He was always very curious, always asking himself questions. Now, while that's an admirable quality, it is such powerful stuff that it can drive you crazy. You have to make a real conscious attempt to keep your feet on the ground. Otherwise you can get taken away.'

Sometimes Jenny would accompany Mick on tour, and towards the end of 1969 she began to notice changes taking place in Peter's personality: 'It worried me when I saw him on the road with the band because I wondered how much of his ego was also starting to play a part. The thing is that, with the other thing – the spiritual part – ego doesn't play any role at all. Yet he was almost starting to believe that he was some kind of messiah. If you believe that everything has a light and a dark side, then that taking over was the dark side of it. With someone as intense as Peter, it's as bright as it is dark – the brighter the light, the darker the dark.'

Peter then radically changed his appearance – donning religious robes, growing long hair and a beard – as if to advertise his radical new attitudes and beliefs. Girlfriend Sandra soon grew concerned: 'That summer, Peter was really excited by all the possibilities that were presenting themselves. This correlated with a spiritually exciting period. We were both for quite some time very spiritually connected and searching. I was into Eastern philosophy and belonged to the Buddhist Society, so we'd go to Watkins bookstore and get all these esoteric books. We went to a Tibetan Buddhist retreat in Scotland. Then I made the robes – one white and one red velvet. For Peter, they were nothing to do with any Christian faith. I think psychologically it was definitely a move into psychosis, or perhaps a precursor of it – he was getting stuck into identification with God! Because of all the adoration people were giving him, he was finding it very hard to differentiate between that exalted state and mere mortality – albeit with a God-given talent – and at that point he was acutely aware that he had a gift which then became a power. As I see it, he wasn't strong enough then to contain that power, and it soon led to lofty identifications.'

'Now, when I talk to God, I know he understands; He said, "Stick by me and I'll be your guiding hand. But don't ask me what I think of you; I might not give the answer that you want me to."' With such self-aggrandisement, this, the second verse of 'Oh Well', is in sharp contrast to verse one's 'I can't sing, I ain't pretty' sentiments. Elevation follows self-deprecation, all set to music which, on the A-side, is aggression tastefully running riot, whilst the classical stuff on part two runs the gamut from repose to melodrama.

Peter Green's *magnum opus* was perceived as exactly that at the time by everybody but his own group, and so its release served to set him apart from the band for good. Perplexed Jesus freak or no, the single's sheer creativity must have been daunting for those around him. Mick and John even bet him that it wouldn't chart. 'Mick and I,' John now wryly concedes, 'each bet Peter £5 that the single wouldn't chart. We just didn't have Peter's vision about the parts-one-and-two idea.' They disagreed so much that at one point the leader was seriously contemplating releasing it as a solo effort. But Peter won the bet and collected almost immediately as the single went to Number Two.

After that, the situation within Fleetwood Mac became more and more fraught. The leader privately told manager Clifford Davis that he wanted to leave, but he was persuaded to stay on for the sake of the others. If evidence of dissension were needed, there's a video recording of 'Oh Well' played live that captures the band's very obvious lack of *esprit de corps* around this period. In it, Mick screws up the rat-a-ta-tat cowbell bit and, right on camera, a biblical-looking Peter then laughs goadingly at his hapless drummer's efforts. Meanwhile, Danny is characteristically oblivious to all around him and instead is bending notes to insane effect whilst Jeremy, playing maracas, looks bored and out of a job. It's almost as though the wacky leader is berating his play-it-safe colleagues for ever having entertained doubts about his abilities and offbeat beliefs.

Peter now explains away that phase as an identification with Jesus, but he's quick to emphasise that the way he saw and felt the transformation in himself was not as some 'drug-induced delusion of grandeur', which is how others saw it. Identifying with Jesus, he says, was more a gesture of humility. Mich Reynolds, then married to manager Clifford Davis, remembers an instance of this shortly after Peter left Fleetwood Mac: 'Star-struck young girls were still coming around to his house in New Malden. Sometimes he would come out and chat to them. After one such occasion, an over-protective father got to hear about this, went round and just hit Peter in the face when he answered the door. He told me about this and I asked him what his reaction was. "I just smiled at him, turned the other cheek and stood there in the doorway."' At this point, the assailant apparently sloped off, looking very confused.

'There was a time,' Peter admits, 'when I did start reading about Jesus and thinking along the lines of "He has returned and I am Him". Then I started reading the Bible and coming up against riddles: Why did He have red hair, supposedly, and I didn't? Then I'd remember that I did have auburn hair as a child. These thoughts, though, were before the acid; once I took LSD, that got rid of all that, all that vanity.'

'Closing My Eyes' from the *Then Play On* album was written when Peter was in this frame of mind and captures the intensity of his spiritual awakening – the feeling of being compelled to search but not knowing what it is he is searching for. It also describes the inevitable deflation that followed when Peter tried to externalise such a deeply personal experience and explain it to friends like Jenny Boyd. Inevitably, he found himself lost for words. 'This song,' Peter said at the time, 'was written around the time I had such a great faith in Jesus that I felt I was walking and talking with God. I wanted to tell people about it, but they turned it round and tried to shatter my dreams. This was written after they had broken my faith.'

The fact is that nobody in his circle of friends at the time remembers anything remotely like this spirit-breaking malevolence being directed at Peter, so the 'they' who broke his faith more probably came from within and, as such, were an early sign of a deep depression that was looming as, tour by tour, hit by hit, nervous exhaustion began to set in.

As Jenny Boyd sees it, the acid experience disturbed (although for a while it did boost) his already massive energy levels, his sensitivity and his need to search. 'That taxi ride,' she points out, 'was Peter in his curiosity stage. He was almost continually breaking down inner walls within himself. Like the classical music he explored with 'Oh Well'. As a rock guitarist from London's East End, for him to even attempt something as beautiful as that says a lot. He was just breaking down these walls of restriction and realising that there was a big, big world out there – and a big world inside, too. Music became his god and, especially after the acid, he found a lot of spirituality there. I remember after that New Orleans trip we all started having far more philosophical discussions about the band's performance, and we started to see it as a spiritual thing: the group were giving their unity to the audience. It may sound obscure and very 1960s now, but I was likening it to the fishes and loaves, nowadays the fishes and loaves being like the music. The audience has an energy from its togetherness, so there's an exchange.'

In a way, Peter still echoes Jenny's thinking today: 'I don't quite understand performance. I think a lot of it is luck and a lot of it is happiness – you have to be happy with yourself and pleased with your efforts. It's a magical thing.' Obviously, this kind of performance magic is volatile in the extreme, and the downside is that the musician or performer easily can become a victim.

Zoot Money, Peter's musical companion from purple-heart all-nighters at the Flamingo, emphasises how the dangers inherent in the performer/audience situation night after night were ones which may not always have been good for Peter's mental health: 'You have to understand the dilemma of the structured set-up in the late 1960s, in the aftermath of the Vietnam War and all that stuff. Put simply, freedom was rife amongst young people and so, perhaps forgetting Bob Dylan's advice, they did need to follow leaders and somehow contain or control that freedom. Young people looked to somebody. But fame, from the performer's point of view, is a bit like being caught up in a tide: you start off with good intentions and good feelings and you want to spread them through playing music. That becomes a spiritual thing, or whatever it is when it makes contact with other people who then enjoy it. Anyway, it becomes ritualistic, involving many, many people.

'At that point, it takes on a power of its own which is then no longer something entirely controllable by you, and so you have to find ways of making it work for you. You can either let that power subside naturally or smash hotel televisions and set fire to things! But for any musician, the most difficult task is to keep that power working over time; once someone like Peter gets so much fame in a short space of time, then you have a lot of mental balls to juggle at once. Initially it's simple enough to control a crowd of 200 or even 2,000 people, but things get far more difficult and stressful when you get up to 20,000 or 60,000. Nonetheless, the process is the same: it starts off with you and then extends along the stage and makes contact with a lot of people out there who have brought their own energy as well.

'Merely making that work in a good way, night after night, is impossible. As audiences get bigger, so does the risk of technical hitches that can turn you off. So suddenly, from every night being a good night and spiritually uplifting, you're now lucky if it's one in ten. That's the best average I've ever had, and that's really lucky! So just holding onto that positive spirituality that strengthened you in the first place and drew you in becomes a major problem. At the tail end of the 1960s and the start of the 1970s, that was where Peter and many other musicians found themselves, so those people – myself included – naturally started looking to mystical books and the Tarot in the hope of finding something that might help. And then there were drugs. You hoped all these things might lead you to a spiritual revelation in some form.'

Without a doubt, Peter's 'Closing My Eyes' was inspired by some form of revelation: feeling a higher presence around him day after day. What this perhaps served to do was send him on a quest, a quest in which his spirituality was almost completely linked to his music, and as Jenny Boyd says, his god was his music. Zoot Money lightheartedly alludes to this serious matter, remembering the unique mood of the 1960s, when it seemed as though certainly everybody under the age of 30 – from astronauts to potholers – was on some kind of inner as well as outer search: 'The thing about my generation during the 1960s is that we had to go out and artificially create the traumas for ourselves. We didn't have to fight a world war in the trenches, which was the kind of trauma where many who did that get an incredible, blinding revelation. My generation did get something like that when they had taken too much acid, when even in familiar surroundings you are in fact subjected to the same kind of mental stress or trauma. It is a totally mental thing – if you're blind in the middle of a battlefield and you don't actually see the carnage all around you, then of course you'll be at peace with yourself. That's a wicked analogy. What I mean is that, in a way, you do become lighter in death and within the sea of trouble when you actually give yourself over to a higher spirit.'

So for Peter in 1969, with music as his higher spirit, creatively he was soaring. 'Peter at his happiest,' Jenny Boyd points out, 'was an inspired person who placed complete faith in his inspirations, wherever they took him. There was "Albatross", the classical music, then the improvising and jamming, and then, in a similar way, there was his idea about Fleetwood Mac being like a band of gypsies enjoying themselves by roaming the world and giving their money away to ease suffering. That idea he regarded as an inspiration that came to him, and he believed in it just as he did the music for "Albatross". But sadly, what I then saw in Peter was that same energy and flow of creativity turn inwards and turn into something much darker when the rest of the band, Mick especially, didn't agree with him. Peter and Mick up until that point were very close – they loved each other – and I don't think either really ever got over what happened. Neither of them understood why.'

So in the context of that defiantly idealistic era, the 1960s, Peter's desire to help feed the world should not, in theory, have been construed as insane, but it was, and he was locked away because of it. In effect, his was a low-key Live Aid but without the egos, knighthoods and instantaneous global music-business career launches.

In March 1970, just a couple of months before he left Fleetwood Mac, Peter's charity-band ideas were reported in the music press. In an article entitled 'Giving Away The Green Stuff', the 14 March edition of *Melody Maker* reported, 'Peter Green surprised the pop world this week by announcing intentions to "give away" a large proportion of his income as a guitarist with Fleetwood Mac. A spokesman for the group said on Monday, "All the group agrees with Peter's aims and they will probably give several charity performances. Peter plans to give up his own money as well, although we don't know exactly what he intends to do with it."'

This deft bit of music-business PR did its best to mask the reality of the situation, which was of course that, with the infamous Munich showdown only a couple of weeks away, the band in effect was rearranging deckchairs on the *Titanic*. Peter was intent on one thing, and the rest of the band would soon be forced to declare their hand and trash his philanthropy.

In another interview, this time with Nick Logan of the *NME*, the group leader explained his thinking further: 'I'm not going into poverty with people on the other side of the world who are starving, although I did think of doing that. It would have made me feel better. This way, the more money I earn, the more I can give away.' During the interview he was anxious that Nick Logan did not regard his second-hand £700 Jaguar XK150 (£700 would be nearer £7,000 today) as an extravagance: 'I would love to go yachting. I love cars. I would love to buy an AC Cobra, but the thing is that, before I do that, I would like to know that everybody is getting their bowlful of rice every day.'

However, Sandra Elsdon-Vigon now has a very different view of Peter's motives, seeing the charity notion as not really about charity or being altruistic. She now believes that Peter thought that if he got rid of those things – all that 'unclean' money – then he would somehow also get rid of some of the power and get back to where he was before: a gifted guitarist who didn't find himself identifying with God. Ironically, this move to regain his freedom backfired on him: news spread like wildfire, and after he declared in the music press that he wanted to give his money away he was inundated by begging letters – 'My grandmother's dying...', 'My mother needs an operation...' Of course, Peter soon realised that he couldn't answer all their pleas, and that scared him too.

So to describe Peter at that point as anxious about the question of money is an understatement; it had become a painful obsession and a neurosis. This is confirmed by Paul Morrison, his friend from the Orange Music shop, who remembers well a car journey with Peter at around this time: 'We were driving along and he was describing to me in great detail the inner turmoil he felt about whether to buy a particular car. He really wanted an AC Cobra, which was the fastest car around then, but he couldn't bring himself to spend the money – I think they cost about £5,000 at the time – so instead he bought the old Jag XK150 for £700. For him, this was a really unhappy compromise. The pop star wanted the fast car but the ordinary Jewish boy wouldn't let him. He was never able to resolve that conflict, and I think it was that that brought on the illness.'

In the few months before the split in May 1970, for the first time ever Jenny sensed negativity coming from Peter and a loss of interest in the band after it was decided that Fleetwood Mac were not going to do the charity thing. It was a major disappointment for him and was also the turning point. When Peter went to Mick and Jenny's wedding in June 1970, shortly after he'd left the band, Jenny noticed a cynicism she'd never seen before. Mick had asked Peter to be best man, but Peter just didn't turn up in time for the wedding ceremony. 'Mick was incredibly hurt,' recalls Jenny. 'Peter and Sandra eventually arrived hours later, but I think it was a kind of 'Fuck you!' He didn't believe in marriage as an institution and felt we were giving in and becoming the conventional middle-class mortgage-and-kids thing while he was a free spirit. The fact that he did that to Mick I think shows just how much Peter felt he had been let down.'

But Peter's relationship with the band remained one of love and hate right to the end, as revealed in an interview given shortly before leaving for the European tour in March: 'I'd say that, like the last time we came back from America, the band is closer than it has ever been, and Danny and I are now working and playing together, which we haven't done before.' He then went on to disclose that he and Danny were planning an album based around their two guitars and that he was going to record a solo album for release at Christmas: 'We've got about 20 new numbers as well and we should really he recording now, but we've got so much touring to do.'

It's quite possible that, more than anything else, it was the pressure of touring that caused Peter to leave Fleetwood Mac. After the three-month American tour at the end of 1969 and beginning of 1970, there were already plans to return to America in the autumn: 1970 was going to be the year that they'd conquer America. Whereas previously they were main support for headlining acts like Jethro Tull and The Joe Cocker Grease Band, it was decided that next time around there would be no more supports; their leader's talent would get them headlining every time. Dennis Keen, Mac's road manager then, recalls the group's bullish attitude: 'They'd been playing second or third on the bill up until that point, but promoters were beginning to notice how they were packing out places like the Whiskey A Go Go in Los Angeles as the sole act. So in autumn 1970 we were going to break out and be as big as Jethro Tull.' There was just one snag: when could they record the new album if the year was already completely taken up with tours?

Peter's mother, Anne Green, now remembers just how gruelling her son found those tours: 'When Pete came back from America towards the end of his time with Fleetwood Mac, he would go upstairs to his bedroom and virtually sleep for a whole week. He would come down for the occasional meal or cup of tea, but most of the time he just wanted to sleep.'

Still drained by the recent American tour, anxious about the band not spending enough time in the studio, receiving begging letters daily in the post and with the engineer overworked and overpaid, as he saw it, Peter was on the brink of nervous exhaustion. The train gathered speed through Europe on a gig itinerary that took in Paris, Basle, Amsterdam, Rotterdam, Londerzeel, Copenhagen, Odense, Gothenburg, Stockholm, Hanover, Berlin, Hamburg and Düsseldorf. Then, during the last weekend in March, Fleetwood Mac had an afternoon gig in Munich. Backstage, a classy, bohemian German rock chick had Peter marked out. Swathed in a mink mini-coat, she was raunchy, irresistible, into acid and full of anti-capitalist attitude. Peter's resistance was particularly low.

9 Trauma City
The Munich Trip

John McVie described Munich and its aftermath as 'Trauma City'. Although at the time it was just another gig on one more gruelling tour schedule, many say something happened there that has moulded the rest of Peter Green's life, something malevolently in-keeping with the political climate that targeted rock music on the world stage and particularly in West Germany at that time. Another conspiracy theory, no less.

Anarchism and alienated youth often seem to court each other, but in 1970 Europe's live-music circuit became youth's unlikely target. Well, not really that unlikely, when you consider how the face of rock in the early 1970s was changing. Forget all that rubbish about free concerts and happenings in the 1960s; rock by its very nature was starting to grow up into the big capital-intensive business it is today. Do you want to hear loud, quality music and see a good show? Well, that costs money: bigger PAs, road crews, lighting rigs, juggernauts and so on.

In just a couple of years, ticket prices soared to cover costs and create, it must be said, realistic profit margins for an industry set on long-term growth. The Germans particularly resented this and proceeded to riot outside pop concerts, demanding to get in for free. The Rolling Stones' autumn 1970 European tour was littered with nasty incidents – forged tickets, arson and violence – and it all came from streetfighting men and women who refused to pay. As a result, Fleetwood Mac's manager pulled his band out of a planned European tour at the end of the year that Peter left. But in Munich that March weekend, all these things were still in ferment. Looking back, John McVie describes that anarchic mindset: '"I'm not bothered what the action does; it's the action itself that is important." That's what we were up against. Those people who lured Peter away and spiked him, they were sure they were doing right.'

Fleetwood Mac were in Munich for three days, and on day one played an afternoon gig. Road manager Dennis Keen takes up the story: 'We were in the dressing room after the gig and a group of people came in – this always happened over there, as we were more popular in Europe than anywhere else. Amongst them was this gorgeous, really gorgeous girl. Pete was a sucker for nice chicks, and she just asked him if he wanted to come to a party. Pete said yes, but the rest of the group weren't in the mood, so only Pete and me went. Eventually, we got to this big house with a huge grand drive. When we went inside there was a party of about 20 people sat around, we were offered a glass of wine, and the next thing I knew all hell broke loose in my head – we'd been drugged. Nobody had offered us any tablets; they just went and spiked us.

'I was wandering round this house, talking to people in English and, surprise surprise, not getting any response. I didn't have a clue where I was or what was going on. I was 25 and a strong man in mind and body, and was I high! Nowadays I'd have freaked.

'I only have one memory of Pete in the whole 24 hours that we were there. I was going round the house trying to talk to these people and I went downstairs to the basement. They had a studio there and I could hear all this sound coming out, so I opened the door and there's Pete playing this guitar with all these other guys. But the sound they were making was awful, this kind of freaky electronic droning noise. It wasn't music as I knew it.

'After what must have been about eight or ten hours, I was wearing off, and I couldn't have liked what was going on because I was thinking about ringing the hotel in Munich. I always used to carry a book of matches with the name and telephone number of the hotel on it which I would show to taxi drivers in order to get back. I didn't ring Clifford Davis until the morning but then asked him to come down and get us out of there. By then it was all going a bit weird. I don't know what it was that wasn't right, but I just knew we had to get out. So Clifford, Mick and Dinky, our road manager, drove down and they got us out.

'For all I know, during the time that I was out of it they may have been drumming something into Peter. They might have been saying, "You've got all this money. You should be giving it all away." But it wasn't like it was with Spencer a year later, who everyone could see had been totally brainwashed and, in my opinion, brainwashed for the better. Jeremy looked a lot worse before he went and then looked alive afterwards; you could see he'd found what he'd been looking for. In Peter's case, he started to go down after Munich. As the tour bus travelled on from Munich the next day, he told the band of his decision to leave.'

Twenty-five years on, Peter's own memories of what happened in Munich differ somewhat from those of Dennis Keen: 'We were met at the airport by this girl and boy, both of them wearing fur coats. I found myself walking with them instead of our group – it was nice for me to walk with them. They came back to the hotel with us and there they told us that they had this commune in a big old house. To my knowledge, only Dennis and myself out of the English lot went there.

'While I was at the house, I remember playing lead guitar – there was a kit of drums and an electric piano. Some of it got recorded and I kept the tape – it was different and good, one of my favourites, this LSD tape, which many years later I gave to my wife in Los Angeles.

'I was put to bed by this girl. I don't know where Dennis was at the time. I was just lying there on my own, on just a mattress, and thinking I was made up of crystals. Some people might be frightened to sleep if they felt like that, but I was so tired I just went straight off to sleep so that I'd be ready for the next gig and I could play well. On the next gig we played, I felt marvellous – fresh and not grubby.'

During an interview with Mark Ellen of *Mojo* in early 1994, Peter recalled, 'They had a mansion, a great big place it was. I went back with one of the road managers. He gave me some LSD, I ate it, and as I'd got my guitar we played with some music for a while. Then I just sat around thinking and thought about everything. I was thinking so fast, I couldn't believe how fast I was thinking! And I ran out of thoughts. I must have been thinking solid for about an hour, just sitting down on my mattress.'

Curiously, Spencer has implied that he also went to the Munich house party. In a 1974 *NME* interview, he told Steve Clarke, 'I don't know why Pete left the group, exactly. It looked like it was coming up. He met some of these people in Germany – I didn't in fact have anything to do with it – but we took some acid and played some music. It was pretty weird. I didn't like what he was playing. He was just jamming. But there was no point in trying to stop him leaving.'

There's also little point in trying somehow to extrapolate the truth about what really took place in Munich that time. Bearing in mind that it happened so long ago, and that during those 24 hours in question the key players in the drama were both on acid, in these circumstances lofty notions of truth fly out the window. Perhaps Munich's real significance in the 1990s is all the mythology that has been attached to it ever since. It is possible that the German hippies were part of some extreme cult, or that they were political activists. It is possible that attempts at brainwashing – sadly so fashionable in those days – did take place whilst Peter was downstairs in that basement studio, but no one can ever know for sure.

Similarly, no one can ever prove that Munich was the trauma that set off some or all of Peter's subsequent health problems and erratic behaviour. Given this eternal uncertainty, it is perhaps better to stick to what few known facts there are, even though these might demystify the legend somewhat and replace it with something more mundane yet credible. Legend by definition cannot be mundane, but life – even on the road – often is.

Given Peter's sensitivity, not to mention his fazed and confused state of mind at around that time, he was courting disaster to drop acid just when he did. Perhaps he was simply desperate to bring things to a head with the band. It was Dr Timothy Leary who preached the importance of 'the set and the setting' to would-be space cadets by emphasising how they should drop acid only at the right time and place and in the right company, conditions hardly applicable to Peter on that day. Peter knew a split from Mac was looming and, what's more, he knew that they knew that he knew – that was his mindset. As for the setting, there may well have been some heavy mind games lurking behind the Munich commune's camaraderie, but exactly what these might have been is not known.

What is known is that he enjoyed the music that was going down. At the end of the day in question, Peter did not freak out; he went to sleep exhausted, feeling as if he was made up of crystals. So if it was bad, impure acid that he was handed out there, it wasn't bad enough to permanently wipe out millions of brain cells in Dennis Keen's cranium. He's as sparky and sharp today as he was back then.

The facts that are available suggest that Peter and Dennis spent just one night at the commune. It was not the three-day acid binge which is now part of rock legend: in purely practical terms, the band's tight tour schedule rules out that possibility – after Munich, during that last weekend in March, they had three more gigs in Germany before the tour drew to a close in Helsinki on Friday 3 April.

Munich's real legacy for Peter Green was that it consolidated ideas that he was already forming about an eccentric change in musical direction. The music coming up out of the basement that sounded so awful to Dennis was a glimpse of the guitarist's new vision, more Stravinsky than Vaughan Williams (Peter studied both these modern composers and had, in John McVie's view, woven Williams's *The Lark Ascending* into 'Oh Well, Part Two'). His new music may have been dark, unstructured and scary. It was certainly uncommercial.

The band's reaction was understandable: this was the leader whose inspiration in the shape of 'Albatross' 18 months earlier had dragged them out of the blues clubs (just in time, as the late-1960s boom began to implode) and on to *Top Of The Pops* and the concert halls. And he was now seriously suggesting that they give away part of their earnings and play music that was commercially unsound.

Conga player Nigel Watson collaborated with Peter in the early 1970s on tracks like 'Heavy Heart' and 'Beasts Of Burden', both defiantly uncommercial singles. He now recalls how even two years later, in 1972, Peter was keen to play him the Munich 'LSD tape': 'We were a bit spaced out and sat listening to music at my place in Woldingham. I remember Peter played the single 'Green Manalishi' at 33rpm by accident. The power coming out of those opening chords was mindblowing! Then he put on a tape he'd recorded in Munich while he was on acid. I found the playing weird, even scary at times, but it was still there, freeform in one sense but spot on in another. He was obviously really pleased with it.'

This does suggest that not everything going on at the Munich mansion amounted to a sinister assault on Peter's psyche. Even so, anarchy was very cool in Germany at that point, and because Peter was so exhausted, his hosts were in a good position to coax him out of the tacky capitalism of big-time rock 'n' roll for good. After all, as John McVie says, they knew their actions were right.

10 Manalishi

The Green Manalishi defies analysis, really. In fact, the word derives from *greenbacks*, American slang for dollars. A song about money as the devil incarnate marks in a way the start of Peter Green's slow retreat from a crazy world to a place and time of his own.

Between 1970 and 1977, attempts to go back and regain the simple inner peace that he had taken for granted as a butcher gradually became more desperate. More than anything else, it was the trauma of fame that had hived him off from everything and everybody, and in 'Green Manalishi' – like Bowie's 'Space Oddity' a couple of years later – he sketches out rock-star alienation. Whereas Bowie would describe it as 'floating in a mowstapeculiar way', Peter Green, when he wrote 'Manalishi' in 1969, was still resisting, trying to hang on and 'trying to keep from following you'.

The song augured feelings that eventually overwhelmed Peter, and writing and recording it, he now says, sapped all his strength: 'It took me at least two years to recover from that song. When I listened to it afterwards, there was so much power there. It exhausted me.' Yet the experience remains one of his happiest musical memories from the Fleetwood Mac days, as he explained to Mark Ellen of *Mojo*: 'Making "Green Manalishi" was one of the best memories. Mixing it down in the studio and listening back to it, I thought it would make Number One – lots of drums, bass guitars, all kinds of things, double-up on bass guitars, six-string basses, tracking on it. Danny Kirwan and me playing those shrieking guitars together.'

The track was recorded at Warner-Reprise's studios in Hollywood on their third US tour and then mixed back in London about a month before Peter left the band on 28 May 1970.

All kinds of inspiration made Peter's songwriting prolific throughout 1969: listening to Vaughan Williams and Stravinsky, learning the cello, perfecting his use of the wah-wah pedal – and then there was the acid and mescaline. 'Green Manalishi' was the product of a mescaline-induced dream Peter had had in which he was seemingly dead. It was not, he now stresses, a wake-up-screaming nightmare; it was far more insidious than that, like a new reality, full stop. Death's siren, in his case, was a green dog barking at him from over the other side, and the fact that it was green to Peter meant money – greenbacks: 'This little dog jumped up and barked at me while I was lying in bed dreaming. It scared me because I knew the dog had been dead a long time. It was a stray and I was looking after it. But I was dead and had to fight to get back into my body, which I eventually did. When I woke up, the room was really black and I found myself writing the song. Next day I went to Richmond Park and did the lyrics – the words were coming through thick and fast. Then I went back home and worked out parts for all the instruments on my Ferrograph tape recorder.'

'Green Manalishi (With The Two-Prong Crown)' was released on 15 May, some six months after Peter had written it and just two weeks before he left Fleetwood Mac. When the group went to promote the single on *Top Of The Pops*, they had a bust-up with the BBC, who wouldn't let them use the eerie vocal effects. Peter refused to do the song live on television without them and so the single was promoted with stills of the band instead. It got to Number Ten in the chart, whereas his three previous hits had notched up either the runner-up or the Number One slot.

The eight or so weeks between Peter announcing his intention to quit in Munich and playing his final gig with the band on 28 May were extremely busy and a sign of the times. With help from his older brother, Len, he organised a charity gig at London's

Lyceum in aid of the Jewish Welfare Board. Fleetwood Mac were supported by 'friends' – two groups, Idle Race and Masterpiece. This concert was a blueprint for live rock music as Peter Green thought it should be: loosely arranged jam sessions between slicker 'official' sets by each of the three acts. A variety show.

Peter put in three appearances during that spring Sunday evening. The first was with electric fiddler Nick Pickett in the quartet Masterpiece, then with Fleetwood Mac for a long set, after which he assembled an impromptu band comprising himself, Mick Fleetwood, Danny Kirwan, Pickett and Jethro Tull's bassist and drummer, Glen Cornick and Clive Bunker. Green was on stage for a total of four hours.

What was intended to be his last London gig was at the Roundhouse Pop Proms on Friday 24 April. At 12:15am, as the crowd yelled for more, Peter stayed on stage after the rest of the band had gone off, quite ready to play more. A week or so later, up in the Northeast at the Redcar Jazz Club, they played a three-hour set which included a taste of Peter's new interest in African drumming. At one point during a Danny Kirwan song, 'Coming Your Way', some three-man drum rhythms were laid down: Peter played an African talking drum, Danny used a single stick and cowbell and Mick pounded away on his full kit – real showtime, and ironic that, just three weeks before their leader's departure, Fleetwood Mac were getting their act together in a more dramatic, brash American style. They'd always played superstars, but now they looked as though they played like superstars as well.

A touch of B-movie melodrama brought to an end what was scheduled to be Peter Green's last gig with Mac at Bath City Football ground on Saturday 23 May. With the all-day festival running way behind schedule, the band came on stage at 10:45pm, and at midnight, when they were only halfway through their set, the organisers turned off the floodlights and power supply to the stage. Mick Fleetwood provided a lengthy and defiant drum solo as a farewell to his leader whilst the crowd lit bonfires around the ground.

The band were not able to play another single electric note that night. It could have been such a legendary ending to Peter's time with Mac; instead, all was darkness and muted confusion.

The following Thursday, back in London, the group had arranged an extra concert at London's Lyceum along with The Grateful Dead. As it turned out, the Musicians' Union barred The Dead's appearance, so Mac did this final, final gig on their own. There were reports after the show of Peter backstage, blitzed by Owsley's acid and trying to set the amps on fire.

Peter's last television appearance with Fleetwood Mac was broadcast on the 30 May broadcast of BBC2's *Disco 2*, which had been recorded eight days earlier. Less than a year later, in America, he would fill in for Spencer, who had left the music business to join the Children of God. What happened to Peter and his former colleagues in the intervening time serves to illustrate how one year can be an eternity in rock music.

11 Free Form

On 20 June 1970, Mick Fleetwood was quoted in the *NME* as saying, 'I think if we could have done a month ago what we are doing now, Peter might never have left, I really do.' The months following were not going to be easy and, as John McVie just about remembers, 'much hash' was brought in to help the four musicians reframe their hapless plight. Then, in the late autumn, Mac (now with Christine McVie on board) bought Benifold, a house near Haslemere, where they lived and recorded: a rock band with a country seat.

Peter now explains how, originally, that had been his idea, too, but the suggestion, he says, fell on deaf ears at the time: 'We were due to get some royalties from Warner Brothers and my idea was to live in a commune, a house somewhere in England where we could all live, do our practising and make our records, but any overflow of money we had we could give away to help the starving in countries like Biafra. When I spoke to them about this in a hotel somewhere, John McVie and Spencer agreed with me at first, but Mick Fleetwood didn't. Danny wasn't around at that time – he might have been in another room – and Clifford Davis didn't know what to say. Mick said that he would rather give up the group than give away his money. So I said I was going to break up the group and reform it with people who wanted to do this idea. Mick still wouldn't do it, so I told them I was only bluffing. And instead I left for my freedom.'

Freedom for Peter, in those first few weeks after leaving the band, amounted to being busier than ever, which is ironic given that he was the most exhausted of them all in the original Fleetwood Mac's final months. But the big difference now was that this new life was free from business pressures and responsibilities.

When the charity-band notion was being thrashed out through long nights in grand European hotel rooms thick with dope fumes and misunderstandings, Mick Fleetwood was under the distinct impression that Peter's designs were far more radical than 'overflow' or 1960s 'getting it together in the country' band-commune scenario. 'When this whole charity thing started,' Mick explains, 'it was a case of "We can't make any money; we've got to give it all away and play for nothing." I didn't want to give my money away, and I suppose Peter didn't like that. John was supportive of Peter's position, and I remember asking John at a gig why we couldn't use the money to finance an orphanage or something like that. I mean, this was all such naive commentary which was so typical of the time we were living in. The bottom line, according to Peter, was that we would be like monks in a monastery – able to survive, feed and clothe ourselves – and everything else would go to the cause. Well, I just didn't want to do that. I remember thinking, "I've got a girlfriend. I've got a flat to pay for. What do I have to do, give it all up?" That was the thing that freaked me out.

'Looking back now, what we were actually seeing were the beginnings of him changing – a major metamorphosis – but at the time we didn't see it like that; we just saw him pulling away from us, and somewhere in there we were lost. We were hurt and we were devastated when he left. Were there bad vibes? Specifically, no, but...we were like lost sheep.' Mick still shudders at the memory.

Over the next year or so, Peter would work on his music more intensely than at any point before or since. It didn't seem like work because financial considerations never came into it. After four years as a pro, the reluctant entertainer, bound and gagged by contracts, had broken free and was able to be an artist. The metamorphosis went on apace.

'When you play for money, it crowds in on you; when you're not playing for money, you're free to walk off any time you like, and the audience can see you're not playing for money. If I hadn't gone professional,' Peter still maintains, 'I might have played more Shadows, even The Beatles. I changed back to lead from playing bass because I thought that by doing that I could go professional during the blues boom. I had to go that way to accomplish something I wanted to do.'

Manager Clifford Davis sympathised with Peter's changing attitudes at the time: 'He's always had a big thing about going on stage knowing that the audience has paid £1 to see him [roughly £10 today] and feeling that sometimes he's had to put on a big act to give them the best he could for their money. I think he often felt that he was letting them down.'

Peter's departure from the mainstream music business, then, reflected his disillusionment with business, not music. Playing music remained his lifeblood, a fact illustrated by his schedule in the wake of his decision to leave. In between farewell gigs during his last weeks with the band, he played all the instruments on and produced a single called 'Come Down And Follow Me', recorded by his manager Clifford Davis. Then he spent the first week in June helping Memphis 'Every Day I Have The Blues' Slim out with his *Blue Memphis* album in London.

Among others at the sessions were John Paul Jones, Chris Spedding, Duster Bennett and Conrad Isadore. The *Blue Memphis* project echoed Muddy Waters' *Electric Mud* psychedelic blues album, recorded a year earlier, in that it melded traditional blues with modern effects: Slim's piano with Peter's wah-wah guitar. Peter felt it was an honour to be playing alongside Memphis Slim, whose one-time guitarist Matt Murphy was a guiding influence for him back in his Putney days.

Blue Memphis was too modern for some. In fact, much of Peter's work over the next couple of years would be met with a similar response by music critics.

Whilst guesting on *Blue Memphis*, Peter was also tentatively organising his own solo project *End Of The Game* (see Chapter 12). With only one week until the sessions were due to start, the musicians he had in mind were American keyboardist and session man Nick Buck, Zoot Money, Alex Dmochowski and John Morshead (both ex-Aynsley Dunbar Retaliation) on bass and guitar and Godfrey Maclean on drums.

On Sunday 14 June, Peter made his live post-Mac debut at the Salisbury Hotel, Barnet, for free, although his bold idea of putting on good music and charging only five shillings admission no matter who was playing, whether it was Ten Years After or inspired local three-chord tricksters, lost the promoters a lot of money – approximately £120 on the day.

Peter did the gig, one of seven acts on the bill, as a duo with American keyboardist Nick Buck. It was all improvisation. The *NME*'s Nick Logan, who was in the audience, later wrote, 'Playing from the heart, and quite brilliantly at times, he was well received by an attuned audience, although it remains to be seen how long this formless format, carrying with it the threat of self-indulgence, can be sustained.' At least another two years, as it turned out.

Other, similar low-profile and impromptu pub gigs followed, and even one big, high-profile event when, two weeks later, Peter went to the Bath Festival of Blues and Progressive Music to rejoin his old boss John Mayall on stage in a one-off line-up that included Aynsley Dunbar on drums and Ric Grech on bass.

It seemed as though everyone now wanted the chance to play with freewheeling Peter Green. After the midnight Mayall gig at Bath, he stayed at the festival site, ready to jam on Sunday. 'Electric-Afro' percussionists Noir borrowed ten £10 to buy petrol to get them from London to Bath in a hurry that day because they'd heard that Peter was looking for them. Sadly, when the four-piece black group arrived and were setting up their gear, rain stopped play, but the following weekend Peter said he'd join them on stage at the Afro-Rock Carnival at London's Roundhouse. However, just one month or so into his new way of life Peter, the altruistic hippy found himself once more surrounded by somewhat less altruistic hippies hoping to rip off a teeny-weeny bit of the man's reputation for their own good.

Peter had first spotted Noir (a name carefully chosen for its Black Power connotations) when they stole the show at an Eric Clapton concert at London's Lyceum, no less. That led to the Bath Festival hook-up and then all manner of Peter Green/Noir rumours. Noir's place in rock 'n' roll history has to be that of a band who spoke of 'light groups', such as Led Zeppelin. By 'light', they meant heavy on guitar but light on percussion. According to this definition, the heavy percussion bands of the time were Chicago and Peter's favourites, Santana.

Noir – three Jamaicans and a Ghanaian – were black Londoners with attitude. Prototype rappers, they were hoping to spend time in the Congo playing with local drummers (rather like Mick Fleetwood would some ten years later with his The Visitor project) and they wrote songs attacking 'the system'. The system, they maintained, was a music business which allowed only one black group to get through every ten years or so. Noir were determined to be The Next Black Big Thing, and they could well have been that until their manager tried to do it on the back of Peter Green.

The day after the Roundhouse gig, when Peter was reported to have joined Noir for a jam, their manager promptly told music weekly *Disc* that Noir was to be his permanent backing group, that they were currently rehearsing together and that their debut gig would be that Wednesday at London's Marquee. It was textbook Tin Pan Alley hustler stuff – tell the press something's already happened and who knows? It might just come to be.

Peter wasn't having any of it. 'I'm not playing the Marquee date,' he told *Disc* from his New Malden home. 'I've not spoken to their manager. I've only met two of Noir. There is a possibility that I may play with them some day, but nothing has been fixed.' Peter gave hot-and-happening Noir the freeze.

At around the same time, two other characters met with more success in exploiting Peter's trusting nature. Both were musicians with name bands on the British blues scene, which by 1970 was well on the way out. Times being hard, they fastened onto the idea of starting up a small factory making African-style talking drums. The partners knew of Peter's interest in African drumming and persuaded him to stump up the capital. Not a single drum was ever produced by the company, and the backer never saw a penny of his investment again. 'Some friends wanted to do this musical experiment, and they asked me if I had any money they could borrow,' he sighs. 'All I had in my bank account was £600, so I lent them that. They never gave it back to me.' This was but the first of many such incidents. During the course of the 1970s and 1980s, a succession of till-dippers – friends, drinking partners, even lovers – came and then disappeared when the money ran out.

This aside, June was an exhilarating month for the ex-leader and pretty much as he had intended life after Fleetwood Mac to be. He absorbed and expended prodigious amounts of creative energy on an extremely varied musical diet. Having spent the last three years motivating the same four musicians (with, he now says, varying degrees of success), in just one month he must have exchanged musical ideas with a couple of dozen fresh faces.

12 No Way Out

June 1970 was the month that Peter had to complete his debut solo album, *End Of The Game*. Zoot Money remembers a phone call one night: 'It was Peter saying, "Do you fancy coming down to the studio tonight? I have to complete an album for Warner-Reprise." I answered with a very definite yes. At that point he had a deal, but I don't think he actually wanted to do any more records and had to be pilloried. I'd known Peter since the all-night jams at the Flamingo, and when he called I felt very much the same way, musically – that it should be a free expression of ideas. So I arrived at the studio at ten in the evening and just played for three or four hours. There was no structure, just an exchange of ideas, and when we finished I put on my coat and said, "See you on vinyl," and left.'

While Zoot got the impression that the album was something Peter was forced to do, guitarist John Morshead (not long out of The Aynsley Dunbar Retaliation and also taking part in the sessions) remembers that he cut a rather isolated figure in the studio: 'He was in a corner by himself, very much in his own world. There was hardly any talking, just jamming. Some of it was really good and other bits were not. When I heard the actual album, I remember thinking that some of the good stuff had been left off.'

Bassist Alex Dmochowski, another Dunbar exile, made an altogether darker contribution to those sessions, according to conga player Nigel Watson, who would collaborate with Peter on some of his early-1970s projects like the singles 'Heavy Heart' and 'Beasts

Of Burden'. 'That album was a battle, made under some heavy pressure from Alex,' he says. 'They were all totally stoned, all of the time. It was like a competition with Peter and Alex each trying to play what they were tripping. Peter had been on medication, but Alex had got him off it and they did other drugs. All the time around then he was looking for musicians who could join him to create a new feel. The feel in *End Of The Game* was very introspective: Peter was trying to find out what was making him scream, musically.'

The pushy musicians around Peter can't have helped his state of mind. Alex had high hopes at around that time of persuading Peter to form a supergroup with him called Horsepower, but after much vacillating Peter knocked the idea on the head after someone blabbed to the music press and the rumour became front-page news.

From the moment Peter left Fleetwood Mac, everyone wanted a piece of him, while all he wanted was a bit of peace. Sick and very tired of the big time, he was content to play low-profile gigs with Nick Buck (formerly of Hot Tuna) whereas, when many who Peter had regarded as friends saw him, they saw dollar signs on the horizon. This made him cynical, suspicious and eventually paranoid. Sadly, the transformation from a sparky, trusting and pure person to a disillusioned shell of his former self happened in no time at all. The change is brought into focus by the optimism clearly heard in his voice during one of his last BBC shows with Mac, as he told DJ Brian Matthews excitedly about his plans for the future: 'The main reason [I'm leaving Mac] – there are many little reasons – is that I feel it's time for a change and there are a lot of things that I want to do. I'm not sure if I'll form another band – if I found a perfect situation, I might do that – but if anyone's planning any free festivals, non-profit-making, or if anybody's got any ideas for charity work, I'd be interested to know more about them.'

Until this point in the interview, Brian Matthews sounds just a touch patronising, yet his tone is definitely perplexed as he asks, 'You don't want to really earn a living from music?', to which

Peter, polite as ever, replies, 'That is necessary so I can keep alive and have instruments and amplifiers. So I'll earn money from records, which is the main thing, to make lots of LPs. I've got lots of ideas for that, and the first thing I'm going to do as soon as I've finished with Fleetwood Mac is make my own LP.' Peter then introduces his song 'Sandy Mary' as one of the numbers he would possibly include on that debut album. He didn't, but Cliff Bennett did subsequently release it as a single.

As Zoot Money sees it, '*End Of The Game* was a sonic kind of last statement that music should always be that way. That way to Peter was after drugs, much religious searching and some revelation. The positive side of what happened to Peter then – and I think he was a great example – is John McLaughlin. John had some kind of revelation as to what he should be doing with music, instead of adopting and assimilating other people's styles. He's gone along a path which embodies the way he lives, his beliefs and also the way he plays.'

The title of the album was a pun inspired by Alex Dmochowski which refers more to the hapless plight of near-extinct species of animals or jungle mammals than to the world-weary ennui of a guitar hero. In Peter's eyes, the open-ended project failed. 'There wasn't enough there,' he admits. 'When I was editing it, I found out that there wasn't enough to make up a record; it was only freeform. The jungle idea wasn't mine – I'd already written about that with "Before The Beginning". My idea of a jungle is the Indian jungle, where the elephants quietly work. In the African jungle, they run around screaming.'

Although the term *avant garde* is often used by critics to talk up what they feel is incomprehensible rubbish, *End Of The Game* really was ahead of its time. Today bits of the album could be edited down to make a good acid-house dance single, while other bits would now be called ambient or new age. But in 1970, the best that *Melody Maker* could say was that it was 'certainly the most disturbing album release this year'.

Following a summer spent gigging with Nick Buck, Peter agreed to visit the keyboardist in New Orleans in the autumn, after he had checked out a Free College he'd been told about in Vermont and hooked up with some musician friends in Boston. Andrew Kastner, now a guitarist with LA soul-funk band Jack Mack And The Heart Attack, then had a local band called The Act. He had first met Peter when Peter was with Fleetwood Mac playing at the Boston Tea Party. Kastner remembers jamming with him, following him all over the place and how, one morning after a night's playing, he found Peter outside on the steps of the house happily jamming with the birds as they sang their dawn chorus: 'That knocked me out, to see this awesome guitar player trading licks with the birds!'

What was less invigorating for Andrew, however, was to see how the whole rock-star experience had left Peter so deeply disillusioned about the music business: 'We had one conversation where he told me that if he had known what working in this line would be like he wouldn't have done it. Either he was talking about the business side or being in a band, I don't know, but it was during the time they were making *Live In Boston*. My dream then was to do what he was doing, and I found what he said pretty heavy because I was a young, naive person. Even so, having thought about what he said, I decided to give it a try anyway!'

Around the time of his stay with Andrew Kastner and friends, Peter also spent some time at the Godard Free College in Vermont. The term 'free' is a little ironic, as Stan Webb wryly points out, 'because it was full of extremely rich kids – doctors' sons and daughters'. Chicken Shack on tour in the States at that time bumped into Peter there: 'We landed on this strip of tarmac which they called an airport and there was this reception party standing around a big table with champagne on it waiting for us. When we got to the college, the first person we see, lo and behold, is Peter – and what's more, he's dressed in a kaftan. I thought, "What's happened to him?" because at one point he was so much like me, you know? A laugh with the lads and screw anything in a skirt. But now he's wearing a kaftan, holding court out on the lawn and being all philosophical, with young students hanging on his every word and looking up in admiration.'

Chicken Shack bassist Andy Silvester also remembers a philosophical Peter at Vermont: 'The morning after our gig, some students were sitting out on the grass, playing some talking drums or something like that, and Peter joined in with them on another drum. I can remember him giving me this long talk about the planets, the moon and "Why are we here?", and all I could tell him was that the best thing to do is enjoy life while it lasts. Funnily enough, at the time he agreed with me about that. Before this, it was me who went to him with questions. I always found him very helpful and able to give me good advice. He was always so positive and powerful. But what seemed to be happening was that, while he was very coherent, he was becoming negative.'

Peter enjoyed his stay at Godard. 'You could do whatever you liked there,' he says. 'You could spend your time doing whatever you liked. Some people were making candles while others were just wandering around. I was one of those who were just wandering around. They had a music room where I used to play my guitar nearly every day. They had a stage and touring groups came and played – Rod Stewart, Savoy Brown, The Faces and Duster Bennett – and the kids who were there could play their instruments with the groups for a while.'

When he left the college, he flew down to New Orleans to stay with Nick Buck, and it was during what should have been a pleasant social visit that something sinister happened to Peter, totally by chance and totally in keeping with the cultist early 1970s, when brainwashing was regarded as kind of hip. At that particular stage, Peter needed it like a hole in the head. It's something that he will still bring up out of the blue in conversation, using phrases like 'the night someone stole my soul'. 'I was with Nick in New Orleans,' he recalls, sounding bewildered, 'and we went round to this guy's flat. He was rolling weed and we were happily smoking. Eventually

Nick decided to go, and I should have left with him, but the guy said I should stay. I did – I don't know why. I was captured by this bloke. He said he was a warlock – a male witch – and although I was tired, I still couldn't get away from him. He just kept on asking me questions. I couldn't find an answer to any of them. He was staring right at me, asking me more questions, and I stayed until we saw the sunrise. I don't think I ever saw Nick Buck again.'

Nine years later, in an interview with Steve Clarke of the *NME* at around the time Peter's comeback album *In The Skies* came out on PVK, Peter brought up this same incident. As he remembered it then, the warlock – who previously had been a professional guitarist – wasn't asking the questions; he was giving all the answers, and the gist of his message was that Peter should give up the selfish life of being a musician to concentrate on mending fences with his long-neglected friends.

Back in England in the late autumn, Peter seemed unaffected by the New Orleans brainwasher. One of the first things he did was to get in touch with Andy Silvester, with his mind set on forming a new band. Andy recalls, 'After Pete had left, the rest of Fleetwood Mac moved into their communal country house, Benifold. Pete invited me and Dave Bidwell [The Muskrats' and Chicken Shack's original drummer, sadly deceased] down for a jam, apparently with a view to forming a band. It was really embarrassing for me and Dave because Mick and Jenny Fleetwood and John and Christine were there at the time. We went into this music room to play together. It didn't lead anywhere, and I think it was then that he realised he couldn't really improve on the rhythm section he'd already had with Mick and John. I don't know what he was trying to achieve, really. It was like he was trying for something that didn't exist, or perhaps that did exist but was above everyone else's heads. After a while he gave up and turned it into a joke – he put on one of his favourite jokey voices, which was like an old cowboy, saying, "Heh, heh, dis whirl ain't big 'nuff fer you an' me, boy, heh, heh!" And so he went on in that voice until it got on your nerves a bit.'

Peter also remembers this awkward social situation he masterminded – not for its awkwardness, mind you, but as one big laugh with Dave Bidwell: 'Dave and me just couldn't stop laughing. Don't know what it was, but we just kept looking at each other and laughing.' Sour grapes and pique must have figured to some extent in Peter's strange sortie to Mac's house, of all places, although the event must have left him in rather a depressing quandary: one by one, the perfect scenarios he had conjured up in his imagination, to parry the blow when Mac wouldn't go along with his charity-band notions, were turning into pipe dreams. So what next?

Well, he returned a favour to drummer Godfrey Maclean, who played on the *End Of The Game* sessions by helping out on a couple of tracks on Godfrey's soul-jazz album *Juju*. As 1970 drew to a close, he teamed up with Alex Dmochowski, jazz sax session man Ray Warleigh, former Graham Bond Initiation, Brian Auger and Warm Dust drummer Keith Bailey for a few London pub gigs. This band didn't work out as Peter had hoped, and in 1971 he was reported to be looking for musicians to play on a second solo album, scheduled for March, which would feature vocal tracks like 'Sandy Mary'.

The hand of fate, however, was soon to intervene. Out of the blue, Peter got a phone call from Clifford Davis, who was on tour in Los Angeles with the Kiln House line-up of Fleetwood Mac. Mid-tour, Spencer had debunked to join the Children of God and Clifford was calling to ask whether Peter would come over and save his old band from financial ruin by playing for the last six weeks of contracted gigs. Peter agreed, but on two conditions: first, that conga player Nigel Watson would accompany him and second that there would be no 'Fleetwood Mac's greatest hits' nonsense on stage – they would jam from start to finish. Although this thought horrified the band, they acquiesced; as they say, when you're up to your neck in alligators, it's easy to forget about getting stuck in the swamp.

Nigel Watson remembers the scene in mid-February after Peter got the SOS: 'We took a flight from Heathrow at two in the afternoon and got to Los Angeles 14 hours later. Clifford [at that point also Nigel's brother-in-law] met us and drove us straight to the Swing Stadium at San Bernardino for the gig. They rehearsed in the dressing room for half an hour, then went out and did the gig. Afterwards we all got absolutely pissed. Peter could have played all the old Fleetwood Mac numbers, but he just didn't want to do that. His attitude was "If they want Peter Green, they'll do the music I now want to do." Once they got into the tour, Peter began to take the leading role for the whole gig, which annoyed Danny Kirwan, who felt overshadowed.'

Nigel remembers one occasion in the dressing room, after a gig where Mac were headliners on a bill including Van Morrison, when Danny threw a bottle of beer over Peter because he was so jealous. Peter just laughed it off. 'It wasn't that Peter was out to put Danny down on stage,' he says. 'He just played around him, trying to egg him on. But Danny didn't have the fire, or the skills of improvisation, and so he got very frustrated.'

Danny, by then 21 years old, was already pretty lost in a drink-and-drugs wasteland. Jenny Boyd noticed a big change in him after Peter left, when a lot of pressure fell squarely on his always rather paranoiacally hunched shoulders: 'At first, Danny was like a son: he used to come and have supper with Mick and me a lot in our flat at Benifold. He was like a little Peter Pan. Once Peter had left and they were all rehearsing at Kiln House, it was pretty stressful because they didn't know if they could make it as Fleetwood Mac on their own. Danny suddenly started having these total outbursts and tantrums that had no grounding to them at all – a side of him would just kick in and be totally inappropriate to the situation. I think drugs and alcohol got Danny totally nuts in the end. He was just too sensitive a soul.'

Peter's six weeks as a ringer came to a climax at the Fillmore East in New York when he took the place by storm with a four-hour improvised version of 'Black Magic Woman'. Until then, he'd kept a low profile on stage, occasionally indulging in a bit of irreverence (like calling the audience 'Yankee bastards'). That night at the Fillmore, he was more upfront and promoter Bill Graham almost had a riot when he tried to end the gig at midnight. The guitarist finally ran out of ideas, or rather the stamina to play them, at 4am. Although John McVie now remembers that kind of jamming as 'invigorating', at the time he confessed, 'We were scared stiff. We'd go on stage every night, look at the audience and didn't have a clue what we were going to play.'

Mick Fleetwood has since spoken of the band being 'bored out of our minds' playing the music that Peter wanted to play, so there was never really any question that the tour was just a stop-gap. 'After the US tour,' Nigel Watson continues, 'when Spencer disappeared, Mac all went home and we stayed on for a month to visit San Francisco, Nevada and Denver, Colorado. In San Francisco, we stayed at Mike Shreeves's [Santana's drummer] house in Mill Valley, and one day we got chatting to a half-Indian guy called Hank from Nevada who made moccasins for a living. He invited us up to stay at his cabin in the woods past Sacramento, where he taught us a lot about survival out in the wild. It was this visit to Nevada that inspired the song "Beasts Of Burden" [recorded and released in mid-1972]. Peter had always loved animals and, especially after his experiences in the music business, had reached the conclusion that he much preferred them to humans. At least animals sniff you out before making friends. People smile in your face and tear your bollocks off with the other hand. That's how Peter saw it.'

On his return from America, Peter spent time applying for jobs at London Zoo and Chessington, but was turned down because of his lack of qualifications. Then, during 1971, he stayed with two friends, Adrian and Lynn Boot, at their house near Surbiton. Adrian, now a photographer, was then a chemistry student at Surrey University. He, Peter and others were not averse to the occasional highly controlled experiment with lysergic acid diethylamide: 'I met Peter through a circle of friends, and for some time I didn't know who he was. He was looking for somewhere to stay, so we let him stay at our maisonette in Lovelace Lane. He was with us for nearly a year – he taught me to drive in the time. I was a student and did odd jobs during the holidays. One summer I worked as a gardener at Mortlake cemetery, which was how I got Peter the job there. He didn't play very much then but was still very interested in listening to music, although his taste in music then was totally uncommercial: African music, Etta James, Donny Hathaway.'

It was no surprise that Peter admired Donny Hathaway, a young black American whose material melded Beethoven and gospel. In Hathaway he saw qualities he felt were lacking in himself. A highly trained musician and accomplished pianist who, although he came from the classical school, became a session musician at Chess Studios, Donny's musical vision in summer 1971 was to take the musical colours he'd glimpsed in Ravel, Debussy and Bach and make use of them in both an acid-rock and country-and-western format. Attitude like this blew Peter's mind.

'It was clear,' Adrian reflects, 'that he was disillusioned about so many things. The fact that he couldn't get a job as a zoo-keeper depressed him, but then being in a position where he couldn't do things was all part of the game. He really enjoyed working at the cemetery because the people we were with were very eccentric people often with long and complex stories to tell. I remember a couple of Second World War casualties there. One had been a doctor before he joined up, went away to fight and had lost touch with his family for a couple of years. When he arrived back after time in a prison camp, he went to where he used to live in the East End of London and all he found was bomb crater where his home used to be. He went to the pub on the corner to discover that his whole family had been wiped out and no one had bothered to tell him. He cracked up and had been working at Mortlake ever since. Peter really identified with this guy, a professional who could, if he wanted to, do other things but found sanctuary in pushing a lawnmower round a cemetery.

'Working there was fun. We weren't hassled because there were no taskmasters, and you soon got used to the grief surrounding you. It was very easy to insulate yourself from all that, so one didn't feel morbid at all – it could just as well have been a park. I left at the end of the summer to return to my studies but Peter stayed on and was still working there when I returned mid-term. He obviously enjoyed it: it certainly had an immensely therapeutic effect. I'm saying that now, with the benefit of hindsight, because at the time I wouldn't have thought any therapy was necessary – there didn't seem to be anything unusual about the guy other than the fact he used to be a pop star. Okay, many people had been dropping acid, and some of them had been affected quite severely and gone completely off the rails, but they were few and far between. Then there was a band of people who I guess were temporarily fazed by it all, but I wouldn't even put Peter in that category. It's quite plain to me that, both musically and politically, he was just too radical for his time: he wanted to use his money constructively; he wanted to get involved with running a zoo; he was interested in all sorts of causes in Africa and Third World development. It was a Live Aid syndrome but ahead of its time, and as thinking like that wasn't at all fashionable then, everybody thought he was a lunatic.'

Adrian recalls their experiments with drugs as always being under very controlled conditions: 'We were all science students and terribly cautious as to what we took. I think what Peter wasn't able to get when he needed it most was somebody he could respect and talk to. At that point he didn't like any formal religion – he was spiritual but not really religious. Also, I never regarded his decision to quit the music business as at all odd. Having worked in the business, I could see it was really only about money. So I thought it was far more important for him to do what made him happy.'

It was while Peter was staying with the Boots in Surbiton that he got the call to replace Jeremy temporarily. Before going out to

America, he'd been in the De Lane Lea Studios, Holborn, along with Nigel, Snowy White and others, for a week of jamming from which his first solo single was taken, a sombre instrumental called 'Heavy Heart' b/w 'No Way Out'. It was released in June, and the critics had a field day rubbishing this seven-inch paradox, a cavalierly uncommercial single.

Peter himself recalls vividly the night before he joined Adrian as a gardener at Mortlake: 'With things like acid and mescaline, it's so easy to go on a trip, and it should be easy enough to come back afterwards, but after one trip I took on some stuff called Sunshine I had such a ridiculously good time all night long. When the morning came, I came down off it a bit hard. I'd decided the night before that I was always going to feel this good. I would get a motorbike and go round visiting friends and roll joints and smoke ganja weed and grass. I bought the motorbike, but I didn't really go round and see anybody much. That made me realise that it was going to be harder than I thought staying on the trip.'

Madge Jones – the Madge of 'Searching' and 'Fighting For' on the *Then Play On* album – was staying with a girlfriend in London at this time. One afternoon Peter, knocked on the door, paying them a social call. 'We were both really surprised,' Madge recalls, 'to see him after all this time. He was wearing a biker's jacket and looking far more macho than I remembered him in the early blues-band days. He had really changed as a person as well. He sat down, started to roll a joint and began talking about politics, world problems and things like that. Very soon I could see that the things he was saying really rubbed my friend up the wrong way. I couldn't believe how he'd changed from a shy, polite person into this arrogant, opinionated sort of guy. In the end, my friend virtually had to ask him to leave.'

Bob Brunning, who didn't know Peter as a drug-taker, also received a visit from him during his biker stage: 'After Peter and I had done the Dave Kelly solo album, I was really disturbed by what I saw. I rang him to tell him the album was out and invited him round to our house. He came in saying, "I don't want to hear the record. Let's go down the pub instead." I just couldn't believe it. He'd come across on his motorbike, all macho, but it just didn't sit right. We went down the pub and talked, but he clearly didn't want to talk about music. He said he'd given away all his guitars, didn't want to play music and didn't want to talk about it. Peter was always a very sensitive guy, and you could see that it was all going wrong.'

The Dave Kelly sessions that Bob Brunning is referring to took place only a year earlier, and Dave himself remembers a very affable Peter at the Philips studios in Marble Arch: 'It was just after he'd done his *End Of The Game* album, which I always thought was absolutely brilliant. I remember he arrived at the studio in his white Jaguar XK150 with his girlfriend Sandra, who proceeded to get on with her needlework as we played – a real hippy scene! Peter asked me what I wanted him to do and I explained. He was very helpful, very constructive in the studio and a charming man. We recorded two tracks, one of which we didn't in fact use in the end, because of...let's call them "external pressures". Philips must still have that one in their vaults.'

In June 1971, just before the summer and autumn he spent working at Mortlake, Peter recorded one track for the all-star BB King *Live In London* sessions, 'Caledonia'. BB now remembers 'a disillusioned and very quiet Peter in the studio who didn't say much at all, but I got the feeling that he just seemed to find it a comfort sitting near to me for a while'. Following that, Peter found time to record 'Beasts Of Burden' b/w 'Uganda Woman' with Nigel Watson, although it would be almost a year before the record was released as a single. 'Beasts Of Burden' is obviously written by a very angry young man: angry at the contradictions and hypocrisies of the developed Western world and drawn to the simplicity and harshness of primitive life on other continents. The first verse reads, 'Creatures dying, vultures flying, songbirds singing, hyenas laughing, ageing horses who gave all they had to give, beasts of burden who worked for the right to live.' 'Uganda Woman' is a musical reference to the basic beauty found in an image of a black woman walking along, carrying a pot of water on her head.

Peter encouraged Nigel to join him in his pursuit of primitivism: 'We once spent a few days sleeping rough in the New Forest. I'd come back early from the Fleetwood Mac Bare Tree autumn 1972 US tour. Danny had been fired by then and I was blown out by all the weird scenes going on in the group. Peter and I spent three days in the woods, living off our wits. We killed a rabbit for something to eat, gutted it, ate it and were promptly sick. We communicated to each other by whistling and tried to be as one with nature. We swam in the river and had tick-checks. It was all a bit of a game, really, because when we got really hungry we nipped off to the nearest shop!'

Soon afterwards, Nigel hospitalised himself, having developed the muscle trembles symptomatic of Parkinson's disease. Eventually, this was proven to be psychosomatic, something which he regards as the after-effects of life on the road: 'I spent three months in hospital, blown and trying to recover from my music-business experiences. For me, as for several others, Fleetwood Mac was too much, too quickly. One minute I was laying down carpets for a job, and next thing I know I'm in Los Angeles playing in front of thousands in a football stadium. A bit mindblowing, really.'

For Peter, 1972 saw a continuation of his gradual retreat from the music business and the insidious approach of depression and nervous exhaustion – a condition which would be exacerbated over the following two years by Draconian medical treatment. At one point, in the summer of that year, he looked set to replace the late Les Harvey as guitarist in Maggie Bell's Stone The Crows (Harvey had been electrocuted on stage in Swansea the previous year). In the May 1994 edition of *Mojo* magazine, Maggie described what happened: 'We picked him up at the station. He had a rucksack and his hair cut really short. He looked very healthy. We were supposed to do the Lincoln Festival in May and we spent six weeks rehearsing at keyboard player Ronnie Leahy's house. Peter played so well right through rehearsals, and then two days before the festival we got a phone call to say he couldn't make it.'

Peter's departure from the business for what turned out to be six years came in January 1973, when, uncredited, he helped Fleetwood Mac on one track of the *Penguin* album. The song in question was a Bob Welch composition, 'Night Watch' (Californian Welch had replaced Spencer in spring 1971). Welch made an interesting observation about Peter at around the time of that session. 'Bob called me a chicken-killer,' Peter points out, obviously amused. 'I guess what he meant by that was that I never played with musicians who were as good as me. I always played with chickens that I could kill!'

13 Lady's Man
A Jewish Hippy's Love Story

Peter's all-or-nothing intensity, a quality believers would describe as typically Scorpionic, fired several of his love affairs in every sense. In The Peter B's, the earnest 19-year-old popped the question to Beryl Marsden at a stage in the relationship when she was quite happy just kissing on the back seat driving to and from gigs. Once he was a rock star, too many temptations and distractions presented themselves on the road for his long-standing relationship with Sandra Elsdon-Vigon to survive. As his health vacillated in the early 1970s, he needed an angel. Luckily, he met one in 1971.

A nice Jewish girl whose middle-class parents had emigrated from Iraq to live in a suburb of London, she was there when hospitalisation – and its debilitating medication – put the man everyone once knew as Peter Green in limbo. She was there when Peter returned from his first blitz of ECT (electro-convulsive therapy), which left him in a state of distraction; he would mutter the start of a sentence, pause, and then perhaps finish it 45 minutes later. Yet, having gone through all this with him, she called the whole thing off two days before their wedding, late in September 1975, and walked out, with Peter's tacit agreement. For the first time in their four-year on-off relationship, the instinct for self-survival got the better of her. The lady in question would prefer not to be named, so let's call her just that: Lady.

Back in the late 1960s, one Saturday in summer she was walking through Hyde Park to the sounds of Pink Floyd billowing in the distance as they performed a free concert. It was a fateful moment: 'When I saw what was going on, I thought it was fantastic, and the following Monday I rang *The Daily Telegraph* information office to find out who'd organised it. I was told Blackhill Enterprises. I went along to see them and offered my services for free for the first six months. One of the first events I organised for them – Andrew King and Peter Jenner – was Stones In The Park. We'd put Blind Faith on the month before and Mick Jagger came backstage to suss it all out. A few days later, his agent phoned and gave us about three or four weeks to organise it, which was plenty.'

Lady helped to organise the free festival at Parliament Hill, where Peter and Fleetwood Mac had tried to play, before crowd violence brought proceedings to a halt: 'I didn't even stay for their performance, because at that point we were a bit anti-bluesy at Blackhill. My band was Edgar Broughton, and although I'd listened to a lot of blues at college we were more into underground. The Third Ear Band were on that bill: it was pouring with rain until they came on, and then suddenly it stopped, so of course as spaced-out hippies we all took that as a sign from God, and all that rubbish!'

Not one to be in awe of famous rock stars, Lady's first meeting with Peter at Blackhill's offices in 1971 was just an everyday kind of thing: 'He was living at Lynn and Adrian [Boot]'s and he came along to the office perhaps to see Lynn. I think we needed a lightbulb replacing in the loo and we weren't brave enough to go up there, so I asked him to do it for us. I knew who he was, but while he was fitting the light I yelled up, "We'll have some tea while you're up there!" Perhaps he wasn't used to being treated like that, without any reverence at all. I was going out with somebody else at the time and wasn't the least bit interested in Peter, but then I wasn't going out with anybody else and suddenly I was!'

The first time Lady and Peter went out together was on a trip to Bournemouth with Lynn and Adrian. They travelled in Adrian's Mini-Moke beach buggy. It was raining and they got soaked. Peter invited Lady to stay with them at his parents' house. Peter took

Lady for a walk along the seafront and proposed to her. 'At that point, I'd known him for about six hours, so it was incredibly strange, but I thought he was really quite cute. Up until that point he knew I was Iraqi but he didn't know I was Jewish – he proposed to me when I told him I was Jewish. I think it meant quite a lot to him.

'My first impression of him that time at the office was that he was quite strange and faraway, and at that point I rather liked people who were strange and off the wall. But in conversation he was obviously all there, and it's something that I've always thought about him, that he is incredibly intelligent but never had the education to express it.'

Peter's family was totally alien to anything Lady had ever known. She was from an Iraqi Sephardic (Middle East/Spanish/ Portuguese) Jewish family, which she describes as the lower of the two types of Judaism: 'Because I was brought up in northwest London in a predominantly Jewish area, I rebelled against it and very rarely admitted I was Jewish. I didn't like the typical northwest London Jewishness and wanted to be as far away from that as possible. But I'd gone to a direct grant school and had a very nice family who gave me everything, financially and emotionally. So I found it very strange that a boy should be subsidising his parents – not necessarily wrong, but completely alien. He told me that his father had given up work the moment that Peter had made his first large sum of money – he went off sick with a bad back or something!'

Although intense, Peter was witty with a dry sense of humour which appealed to Lady, and she was soon drawn to him: 'At the time I think he took to me because I was quite a sort of down person, quite boring, mundane and ordinary. Although I'd worked in the music business, we never spoke about that or about his experiences. What he wanted from me was my ordinariness.'

The only time Lady can remember Peter's past catching up with him was during a visit to Hale, Cornwall. The couple were having a drink in a pub when someone came up to Peter and said, 'You're

Peter Green, aren't you?' Peter grabbed him by the lapels and said, 'What of it?' Then Peter and Lady left.

So Peter had at last found a supportive 'Jewish non-princess', as she describes herself. Between 1971 and 1975, theirs would be a stormy relationship with several final partings followed by as many impassioned reconciliations. Very early in the relationship, she twigged that the Green household was zany in the extreme: 'Compared to my parents, it was like a mad family. His father looked like Alf Garnett, sounded like Alf Garnett and said the same sort of things as Alf Garnett. At midday he'd come down in his pyjamas and dressing-gown, take the cover off the green parrot's cage and start dancing around the lounge with the parrot, which squawked in a way that terrified me. Meanwhile, their dog, a Border collie, would get in on the act by humping Joe's leg as he waltzed round the room. I honestly used to think it was all quite insane.'

Peter and Lady bought a house together in Ham, although they didn't stay together long after that. For most of their relationship, they would rent places or stay at Peter's house with other members of his family.

Within weeks of them coming together, Lady witnessed the selfless philanthropy that eventually got him locked up: 'He wrote out a cheque to War On Want for £80,000. I couldn't believe it. Perhaps he was testing me to see if I was after him for his money. Before he sent the cheque, he asked me to ring round all the charities, asking them how much they spent on administration and what percentage actually went to the needy. So when I first knew him, he didn't have any money left. Occasionally, when the pair of us were really broke, we'd actually go and do something. Sometimes a letter would arrive with a royalty cheque for £1,000 and we'd breathe a huge sigh of relief because we could eat properly!'

Manager Clifford Davis obtained films from people like War On Want so that Peter could see how his money would be used. 'Clifford showed me some films,' Peter reflects, 'showing where a lot of the money was spent on teaching people in starving countries new methods of agriculture so that they could grow their own crops. But I didn't think that was the best thing for me to give my money to; I thought I should give them food supplies.' The size of the sum was apparently decided when Peter went to WOW's offices. He would point to an area on the globe and ask how much it would cost to put things right there.

Peter's trip to Israel to work on a kibbutz also came quite early on in his relationship with Lady. 'How it came about was so typical of him,' she remembers. 'He literally woke up one morning and told me he had to go to Israel to be with his people. After I'd recovered from the shock, I understood completely, so off he went. After a few weeks, a postcard arrived from him with two lovebirds on it, which the dog almost chewed up on the mat, and on it he'd written that I was the only "real person" he'd ever met, but that he had to stay on and be with his race. He ended the note saying he was thinking of joining the PLO. When he got back, I discovered why: he'd gone to work on a kibbutz and they hadn't let him drive the tractor! He also said he'd really enjoyed sitting on the edge of the desert, watching the nomadic Arabs, and felt more akin to them. He actually ended up really hating the Israelis.' What Peter enjoyed most about his time on the kibbutz was the work routine, starting work at first light and finishing at dusk.

During this time, 1972/3, when Peter's illness really started to take hold, Lynn and Adrian Boot were spending a year in Jamaica. When they returned, in 1974, Lynn especially was astounded by the deterioration in his condition: 'He had put on so much weight because of the medication and just walked around like a zombie all the time. Whatever they did to him it was appalling.'

Mich Reynolds also spent time with him during this period: 'It wasn't a nervous breakdown; it was a slow decline. I spent many evenings with him, and sometimes he wouldn't talk at all, just observe people or observe me talking to people. He'd sit in silence, hair all over the place, and a lot of the time I thought he was taking the piss out of people. It was difficult to know when he was doing it for effect and when he couldn't actually help it. For example, I took him out shopping one day because his mother said he needed some new clothes – he'd put on weight by then. I took him to Wimbledon and we went into a café to get something to eat. When we came out, he started to imitate an ape as we were crossing the road: he stood in the middle of the road just laughing at everybody looking at him. It was obvious he was doing it for effect, but then later, when I lived at Longmeade, he couldn't always control his thoughts and actions. He once swore that he saw a spaceship at the bottom of the garden coming towards him before disappearing. Much, much later, he said he kept seeing things crawling up the walls.'

Peter and Lady never tried to make out to each other that everything was all right and that it would all miraculously somehow come right in the end. They tried to confront his illness whenever possible, but in time this became very distressing for Lady to have to deal with: 'There was something wrong with him – we both knew that. There would be long loaded silences and a change of mood from the start of a sentence to the end of it, not all the time but at pretty regular intervals. One moment he'd be talking and loving me with every word that he spoke, but before he got to the end of the sentence he hated me. And I had no idea why. I hadn't physically moved or thought of anything or done anything to be loved or hated. But to get all those emotions within a period of 15 seconds was really hard.

'Another time, we'd had this great reunion where everything was wonderful and we'd gone out for a meal. Peter decided to have a really hot curry, so hot that the waiters were advising him against it. He seemed to change after he had this curry. We went back to the house and were looking at some books about Red Indians – Peter was very interested in Red Indians and how they lived so close to nature. We were sharing a chair and both looking at this book when he suddenly got up and said, "I hate your sort of person," went up to the bedroom and moved the wardrobe in front of the door in case I tried to get in. This was in one of the houses he shared with his parents. I put up with all of this because I really, really loved him, and we both hoped that it wouldn't be like that forever.'

But comic relief also sometimes sprang out of Peter's erratic mood swings: 'We rented a cottage in Cornwall for a few months and spent one hilarious Christmas there. That Christmas Eve he went out and left me on my own. Then, at two or three in the morning, he came back and said, "I've got your Christmas present." I got all excited. Then he brought in this cauliflower he'd nicked from the fields nearby!

'The day before, we'd gone into Penzance to buy a turkey. I'd never cooked a Christmas dinner before but I struggled on as best I could. I got up really early in the morning to cook it – you know, with all the trimmings. I put it all on the table and proudly announced, "Christmas lunch is ready, Peter!" He just looked at me and said, "I think we should be vegetarian." So I picked the turkey up, opened the front door and threw it out into the garden.'

When Peter was first hospitalised at West Park, Epsom, in 1974, daily phone calls to his partner were just about his only brush with sanity: 'I was staying at a friend's house while they were away. I'd just moved in and Peter was going to come over that night. He didn't turn up and I had no idea what was wrong. The next day was my birthday. Peter phoned me and said he was in a mental hospital in Epsom. After that, he phoned me every evening. I wanted to go and see him, but he categorically would not let me. I later found out that he'd been committed by a Dr Tintner, who his mother had worked for.'

Peter recalls the events that led to him being hospitalised: 'They tricked me into agreeing to go to a nice place where Jewish boys and girls would be and then took me to the hospital in Epsom, the madhouse. Dr Tintner was in my house and, I don't remember the exact words he said, but it was something like, "I've got this place I'd like to take you to tomorrow. I'll pick you up." I said, "What sort of place?" and he said, "Oh, you know, young boys and girls there." Anyway, I went down with him and next thing I knew I was stuck there and eventually they gave me ECT. They gave me injections and tranquillisers. I could hardly walk or keep my eyes open. I felt terrible there.'

Even so, his indefatigable and dry sense of humour didn't fail him, as Nigel Watson recalls: 'When I went to see him at West Park, the first thing he said when he saw me was, "Christ, you ain't in here as well, are you?" Then, still thinking I was also a patient, he said we could have fun and he started singing that pop song "Knock Three Times (On The Ceiling If You Want Me)". You could see he was well out of it on the medication they were pumping into him, like in a trance.'

'I don't think he had shock treatment initially,' Lady continues, 'because Peter told me that at West Park they laced the puddings and syrup with a drug to keep everybody quiet. I'd be talking to him on the phone and suddenly he'd go quiet then say somebody had come up and stared right into his face. It really scared him. I knew that if he was really scared by this then he shouldn't be in there: it's a place for those who are too far gone to feel fear. I just knew that there was no way that Peter was insane. Around then, we went through quite a lot of break-ups: he'd go away or go abroad, then come back. My brother had just bought a chemist's shop and I went in to help. Peter must have been an out-patient by then because he was having ECT at St Thomas's in London, which was, like, a couple of hundred yards away from the shop. Very often he'd come to the shop after he'd had the treatment and I couldn't believe it: he just stood there, like, for hours, with his arms slightly in front and in a trance, telling me how very frightened of it he was.'

Lady and Peter continued their relationship while all this was going on, but slowly she realised, ironically, that she was fighting a losing battle with the doctors. He was responding – if that's the right word – to the treatment by becoming more and more docile.

The loaded silences between the couple grew longer and more intense and things felt more and more strained.

Increasingly fazed by events, the couple nonetheless decided to throw in their lot together and buy a house in Ham, near Richmond, a place where they might be able to get on with their own lives. Even better news was the fact that they'd decided to get married in September 1975: 'I remember the day we had decided we were going to get married. We went downstairs and Peter said, "Mum, I've got something to tell you. We've decided we're going to get married." Because she had at least pretended that she liked me, I thought she would have given a nice response. I'll never forget what she said: "Dad and I will have to cut down on the phone and the other bills, then." The implication was obviously that I was out to cop the readies and Peter would stop the payments to them once we were married. I was so hurt. When Peter's parents met mine, though, she must have seen that my family were not exactly strapped for cash.'

A date was set – 6 September 1975 – and plans for the wedding went ahead with the rabbi of the bride's synagogue, who at one point took her to one side and advised her against taking the big step. Of course, outwardly this only strengthened her resolve, or so she thought: 'Then, two days before the wedding, we were sitting in our lounge, watching the yachts sailing past on the Thames. Suddenly there was a loaded silence for nothing that I was aware of having done, and looking out of the window again I saw a stupid gold aura thing that came out of the river and into our lounge window. Written on it was, "Go home to your parents." I wasn't in the least bit astounded when I saw this: it was a message from God. I very quietly went upstairs, packed a few things, came down and told Peter I was leaving him. I asked him if he'd mind driving me back to my parents' house and he very calmly said, "Not at all." He didn't try to fight it and we didn't argue. He must have seen it, too. My father was so calm about it and accepted everything, but my mother went hysterical, probably at the thought of the wedding having to he called off with two days to go.'

To this day, Peter remains the Iraqi lady's great love, even if the relationship was virtually doomed from the start. Watching her go about her work at Blackhill's offices, Peter had handed her a note. It read, 'The depression you try to escape from/Is your lonely soul's broken heart/Realising its mistake, and crying/You are torn between the tragic truth of a lost soul/And the falseness you have been led to believe is your way of life/I choose the first to be my *self*/If you look hard and deep you will see it in all man/If you don't see it – you will see madness.'

14   What Am I Doing Here?

When the so-called shotgun incident story broke, the national press made a meal of it. Fleet Street couldn't have wished for an easier target at whom they could direct that day's fickle finger of scorn: 'Pop Star: Free Me From My Cash' read the headline on an inside page of *The Daily Express* on 27 January 1977. The article, which was as accurate as it was understated, used a formula of journalese that would repeat itself when even nastier men of the press began to stalk Peter in the late 1980s. The *Express* piece read, 'Peter Greenbaum, who was lead guitarist with Fleetwood Mac, has been arrested following a row over £30,000 that he did not want… He was so desperate to stop the payments that he had to be arrested at the office of accountant Clifford Adams in Paddington last month… Green admitted having a pump-action .22 rifle without a firearms certificate at the accountant's address. He denied threatening to damage Mr Adams' office and no evidence was offered… The guitarist's father said at his home in Canvey Island, "The magistrate made the right decision. Peter definitely needs help. He must have given away tens of thousands. He would help the whole world if he could. He lives in an Alice-in-Wonderland world of his own."'

This piece in the *Express* prompted more press reaction, which was a pity because it contained some crucial inaccuracies. There was no confrontation at the office of the accountant, whose correct name was David Simmons (Clifford Adams being a pseudonym for Clifford Davis, Peter's manager). It is also debatable whether the crux of the story – the £30,000 that Peter was supposedly desperate to return – is a fair representation of what actually was going on at the time.

John Junor – subsequently knighted for his brand of hard-hitting and responsible journalism – took the story in *The Daily Express* at face value and went on to add injury to insult in his *Sunday Express* column that weekend. Aptly entitled 'Careless Talk', Junor wrote, 'The Fleetwood Mac pop group was never exactly a household name, and it has been nearly six years since Peter Greenbaum stopped being the group's lead guitarist. Yet a court is told that even today Greenbaum is receiving £30,000 a year in royalties for past recordings. Greenbaum seems to be an eccentric. He didn't want any money from his past. He tried to have it stopped. He had a row with his accountant and brandished a gun, which was why he appeared in court. The court's decision was that he should be admitted for treatment to a mental hospital. But when the economy of our country is so balanced that a minor pop guitarist can earn £30,000 a year for recordings he did six years ago, isn't it the rest of us who should be in a nuthouse?'

However, the damage had been done. The tale was now a news story and, in the normal run of things, would eventually mature into legend. Chris Salewicz of the *NME* wrote a more informative and considered piece a week later (5 February 1977): 'Appearing under his real name of Peter Greenbaum, former Fleetwood Mac guitarist Peter Green (30) was last Wednesday at Marylebone Court, committed for treatment at a mental hospital. This followed an incident last month when Green was arrested following a row with accountant Clifford Adams at his Westbourne Park address over Green's demands that royalty payments from his hit records be stopped. Amounts involved are in the region of £30,000 a year. Green admitted having a pump-action rifle without a firearms certificate, but denied threatening to damage windows at Adams' West End offices. In his defence, David Bray told the court that, since his client left the group in 1971, "It appears there have been some difficulties, and his attitude is that he wishes to make his own way through life rather than make use of any royalties from his past records." Making the hospital order, Sir Ivor Rigby told Green, "I hope you understand that I am really only interested in trying to help you."

'Since Green decided to quit in 1970, this was not the first time that he spent time in a hospital. The stories that have filtered out in the media about Green's existence since he left Mac have been appropriately colourful: Green going to work as a gravedigger, Green playing in a pub band in Southend, Green flying out to Los Angeles with only a one-way ticket, getting sent back, buying another ticket (return this time) in London and going back again. The reality, as might be expected, is less romantic. As old associates of Green's who have still remained in touch with him tell it, a picture of him emerges that is considerably different from the legend. Apart from the odd days when he'd return to stay at the home near Southend, which he bought his former-postman father, his life has been one of dossing around London, sleeping on music-business acquaintances' floors.

'Always penniless, he apparently considers his royalty money to be "unclean"; he is apparently well into passing off demands that he should pay large phone bills and asking friends to buy larger houses so that he may live there as part of his "hippy" philosophy. Of late, in addition to having declared that the coalman's life was the one for him, Green has become even more obsessed with his "Jewishness" than he was in the years immediately after leaving the band. It was then that he changed his name back to Greenbaum and visited Israel. Lately, as well as being more insistent than ever that his money should go to Jewish charities, Green has apparently been engaged on something of a desperate search for the perfect Jewish wife. He has also been particularly anxious to maintain links with other Jewish musicians. For a while he stayed with Marc Bolan. Bolan, presumably in an attempt to help Peter get himself back

together, gave him a guitar. Green left it in the boot of Peter Bardens'
car. At the time he was arrested at his accountant's, a warrant was
also out for his arrest on various petty motoring offences. Only the
other week he was so impecunious that a journalist from *Sounds*
lent him £10. "People," comments one person with whom he's
being staying recently, "say that Peter's just suffering from San
Franciscoitis – that he just did too much dope – but that's not true.
He doesn't smoke or do dope at all.'"

What actually happened, say Peter and his brother Len, was
rather different to the headline news. Peter now has detailed
recollections of events leading up to the incident, and of the
telephone conversation between himself and his manager, Clifford
Davis, that somehow ended up being reported as a confrontation
with Peter in person at Clifford's offices 'brandishing a gun': 'I'd
just come back from a holiday in Canada,' Peter points out, 'staying
with a girl I knew out there. Before I came back to England, I had
some money left over – about $80 – and I didn't know what to
spend it on. Anyway, when I was going to collect my plane ticket
I passed this really good gun shop and went in. I told the guy that
I had $80 to spend and he said, "You can't have a handgun because
you need a licence for that, but what I have got is a pump-action
.22 fairground rifle." So I bought that and a couple of boxes of
cartridges and I was on my way. It broke down into two pieces
and I carried it in a cardboard box. So when I got back to England
I just strolled through Customs and didn't declare it.' Peter left the
gun at his parents' house in Canvey Island.

'Then,' Peter continues, 'when I was talking to Clifford Davis
on the phone, I wondered if he had any money for me because I
didn't have any after the holiday. He told me he didn't, but that
David Simmons had it. David Simmons was an accountant's boy
– you know, made coffee and things like that – and eventually he
did all right and became my accountant. I remember I made the
phone call from Our Price records. On the telephone to Clifford,
I forget how it came out, but I said, "I'll shoot you." And when

Clifford told me David Simmons had my money, I said, "Well, I'll shoot his windows down, too," because he had a place on a posh street in London. Clifford might have thought it was the gun I already had, which was a rather rare single-barrel 12-bore shotgun. I never used it because there was nowhere to shoot unless you belonged to a gun club, which I didn't. But when I made the call, I didn't have either gun in my possession; my mother and father were looking after them at Canvey Island. So it was an idle threat. But when Clifford asked if I was threatening him, I don't remember exactly what I said – it might have been yes…it probably was.

'The next thing I know I was round a girl called Betty's house and the police knocked on the door. They said they had a warrant for my arrest for using threatening behaviour towards Mr Davis and Mr Simmons and asked me to go with them. First of all I spent a night in Marylebone police station and then next day they took me to a jail somewhere – it could have been Wandsworth, but I'm not sure because they moved me about a bit.'

In Peter's opinion, though, it was an idle threat: the gun was 50 miles away, still in that cardboard box. In fact, he never took it out of that box. He had however smuggled the gun in and had in this respect broken the law.

While he was in prison, Peter was held under observation. He subsequently failed a psychiatric test and was sent back to a hospital in Epsom. 'I'd been there already,' he recalls. 'The thing is, you're not *held* there by anything – you're *stuck* there. After the injections you haven't got the strength to walk to the toilet, never mind go home. So I stayed at the hospital until I was able to actually walk away.'

Mich Reynolds, Clifford Davis's ex-wife, who now runs the Fleetwood Mobile Studio (still a successful enterprise some 20 years after it began operating), has remained a good friend of the Green family. In the early 1970s, she tried to help Peter through his bleakest times. Mich remembers a call out of the blue at the start of 1977: 'His mother phoned me to say Peter was due to appear in court and had nobody to represent him. I went to Marylebone Road and sat in the gallery. When they called his case, Peter came up looking for all the world like a tramp. They started to read the charge and I could see he honestly didn't have a clue where he was. He looked round, saw me and said, "Mich! What are you doing here? You shouldn't be here with all this: this is crazy, insane. Go home!" I wanted to see him afterwards, but they wouldn't let me. I went to see him at Brixton – I used to take stuff and took an acoustic guitar in for him.'

Mich has few doubts as to why Peter was charged in the first place. She maintains that the court case was blown up out of all proportion, probably due to Clifford and David, who knew that if Peter kept giving his money away then they too would lose money, so they took seriously something Peter said in jest. 'I had many conversations with Peter during that time,' recalls Mich, 'and it still upsets me that people considered him insane just because he wanted to give his money away. Peter knew he had a God-given gift, and he told me on several occasions how he thought the best thing he could do with that gift was help people who were less fortunate than himself.'

It is tempting to view this incident in terms of the idealistic artist on the one hand and the profit-orientated big-band manager on the other. It's an old cliché: nobility versus base instincts, and money as the root of all evil. Yet something says it can't have been quite as simple as that.

That Peter went through hellish turmoil as he tried to break away from the business of rock stardom is beyond doubt, but it should also be remembered that at one point, right at the start of his career, he and manager Davis were coming from exactly the same place: East Enders out to prove that barrow boys can make it in the big wide world, just like anyone else. And although their paths diverged, Peter today still acknowledges Clifford's role in building up his career.

Seeing Peter's charity notion from Clifford's more sceptical point of view is to understand that Clifford had made a big investment in Fleetwood Mac and Peter Green, both financially and emotionally. Of course, he was in it for the money – that's why groups appoint managers in the first place. But for Clifford's talent, it's conceivable that the original Fleetwood Mac could have been one-hit wonders. He was astute enough to realise that 'Man Of The World' had to be a hit, whatever the short-term personal cost to himself.

It's not the case that Davis stalked Peter throughout his career – for instance, when Peter left Mac, Clifford assumed that it would also mark the end of their partnership. He told *Disc* at the time, 'He won't stay with me for management because we've always had a verbal agreement that any time he wanted to leave, he could. Peter hates responsibility and I think I've been his shield in the past. The only way he can feel free is if I'm not around any more. He doesn't want people to depend on him.'

Yet Peter elected to stay with Clifford, who, from what Peter now says, did at first try to understand his ideas about giving money away, if not agree with them.

'The main reason they put me into hospital,' reflects Peter, 'was for giving my money away. They wanted me to realise that I was on drugs when I tried to persuade the rest of the boys to give away our overflow of money to Biafra. I was on a drug at the time, mescaline. I took it at first to see if I was strong enough to resist all these things, but I wasn't. I was taking it, and yet in the distance I could see someone – the strong person – who thought he could get through it.'

Clifford seems to have tried to understand the urgency of Peter's compassion, at one point approaching the charity War On Want to obtain some films for Peter about Third World development. So Peter's 'idle threat' could well have been the final straw for Clifford, a financially motivated man who was watching someone he knew well apparently squander his money for reasons that were not always entirely clear to anybody – Peter included, it must be said. What's more, his family also figure in the equation.

In the nicest possible sense, they had grown to depend upon their talented son to help them out financially when times were hard. Peter himself was happy to do this and had bought Albatross, the house in Coombe Gardens, New Malden, for them. It was a close-knit family, and it continues to be so to this day: without a second thought, Len and especially his wife, Gloria, are quite selfless in the way they now look after Peter. But as Len Green is the first to point out, when his youngest brother became famous, he also became the family purse: 'I remember one time – I think he'd just come back from touring the continent with Fleetwood Mac – Pete phoned me up from his accountant David Simmons's office. He said, "I've just had a cheque arrive here for £7,500. How much do you want?" He was used to carrying a wad of notes around with him all the time – about £1,000 or £1,500. Anything more than that he thought he didn't need.'

Len had struggled all his life to make ends meet, and by this time, having been out of work quite a few years, he owed water rates, house rates and several months' mortgage payments, so Peter's question was like an answer to all his prayers. 'Send me five grand and it'll get me out of trouble,' Len replied. The following morning the postman delivered a cheque – no accompanying note – for £5,000.

The significance of the so-called shotgun incident is perhaps threefold. First, it shows that, by 1976, an understandable conflict of interests had arisen regarding Peter's estate, and because he was still subject to erratic mood swings, no one was willing to take his altruism at face value, except the grateful charities on the receiving end of his donations. Second, the national press ridiculed and made a scapegoat of someone in no position to answer back and all for the sake of a good, though essentially inaccurate, story. (In today's climate, where showbiz personalities are quick to sue the press for hints of slander, Peter might well have been awarded substantial damages for what was unquestionably some sloppy and misleading reporting.) Third, and perhaps most disturbing of all, is the thought that a highly sensitive individual with a recent history of mental problems should be put through the trauma of police cells, court appearances and imprisonment in this way without any effective representation to shield him. The image of one of the country's most naturally talented musicians answering questions in court, clueless as to why he's there in the first place, reflects rather sadly on the nature of community care in Britain.

15 Los Angeles Smog In The Skies

The outcome of the court case was that magistrate Sir Ivor Rigby sectioned Peter for further treatment in hospital. The venue this time was Horton Hospital, next to Long Park in Epsom. Horton's eight-foot-high concrete perimeter wall obscures hospital annexes in which the ground-floor windows have been bricked up, presumably to keep inmates in and not trespassers out. Phil McDonnell, former roadie for Fleetwood Mac, was appalled when he heard about Peter being there and took immediate action to have him moved to the Priory. This was the £500-a-week private clinic at which, on a previous stay, he'd bumped into Lionel Bart, the brilliant writer of hit musicals during the 1960s, who was there, alas, trying to dry out.

Peter responded well to treatment at the Priory, and during this period of recovery his brother Michael made a career move which would pave the way for Peter's return to the music scene some two years later, in 1979. 'I joined PVK,' Michael explains, 'through meeting a guy called Peter Vernon-Kell. He had a record company and asked if I would be interested in joining as a plugger. He explained how he'd got together with this financial wizard called Peter Cormack who'd never even heard of Peter [Green] – his background was in plastics – but he had this knack of making companies profitable.'

Peter Vernon-Kell was a businessman, producer and musician, roughly in that order. In the early 1960s he'd flitted in and out of the London music scene (playing guitar with a band that eventually became The Who) and his early failures made him determined to succeed second time around. 'I decided that I would only return to the music business when I had the money and capital to make a real go of it,' he explains.

Before PVK Records got a cash injection from Peter Cormack, they'd had a taste of success with Freddie Starr. In mid-1977 the company put out feelers with Michael to get Peter onto his roster. 'I told Peter VK that I'd already thought of asking Peter,' Michael adds, 'but he seemed happy in his retirement now that he'd got over the court case and other things. Still, I had a word with him and to my surprise he seemed quite interested.'

Peter VK decided on a gentle approach in order to get Peter playing once more: 'I used to have these sessions in my studio with friends and Peter started coming along but not playing. Nobody shoved a guitar into his hands, and I think he found it unusual that we didn't appear to care if he should come or go. Eventually he asked to play bass, although I think he was more interested in my collection of cars, especially an E-type Jag that I had at the time and which he subsequently pranged. His mood was very in and out. I had a brother who suffered from epilepsy and Peter had the same kind of drugged-up look about him. Every now and then there was a flash of who he really was, when he would laugh or smile. He literally hadn't played a note in five years, but then picked up this battered old Fender Jaguar and went straight into working out an intricate instrumental called "Proud Pinto" – it was hard to believe. Apart from his fingers getting sore quite quickly, it was as if no time had elapsed whatsoever.'

Peter VK soon discovered that the best thing to do was surround Peter with good musicians and then just let him doodle, even though this could be a frustrating experience: 'He would often come up with an unbelievably good riff or phrase when the machine was switched off, and when I asked him to repeat what he'd played when the tape was rolling we nearly always drew a blank.'

So as 1977 unfolded, it was a promising time for Michael and all three Peters: the guitarist was off the medication, he'd begun to lose weight and he was becoming more positive, and it looked like a good album was starting to take shape. At around this time, Peter broached the subject of him and Peter VK going out to Los Angeles. Ever since meeting Californian Jane Samuels at bass player Steve Thompson's (formerly with John Mayall) house soon after leaving Fleetwood Mac, the two wrote to each other, something that fired the jealousy of Peter's girlfriend at the time: 'These letters would arrive from this girl who played the fiddle and I'd get furious – they were quite obviously love letters.' The notepad passion grew when Jane returned to Los Angeles, and in one letter that Peter wrote to her whilst recuperating at the Priory earlier in the year, he had proposed marriage.

Jane was at Los Angeles Airport to meet the two Peters when they arrived and they went to stay at her small house in the hills. She immediately took them out onto the veranda and insisted on playing her violin. Peter VK remembers her playing: 'She was terrible! But obviously for Peter love was deaf. He even wanted her to play on the album, which is what she was very obviously angling for. I told him if he wanted a violinist I would get him one, but that she was no violinist.'

Peter's family had met Jane when she went over to stay with them. 'She was a quiet girl,' Peter's mother recalls, 'but very fond of money, I felt.' Jane also brought out twinges of xenophobia in brother Len: 'One afternoon, Gloria made us all a really nice tea – cakes, sandwiches, scones and jam – and Jane kept on asking me for the jelly. I said, "Sorry, we've got everything else but we ain't made any jelly." Of course, she meant the jam!'

Amongst Peter's friends, the general consensus about the woman he now wanted to marry was less lighthearted and cosy: Peter VK didn't take to her born-again evangelism, which Judy Wong now remembers as possibly having something to do with 'Jews For Jesus' Messianic Christianity (Jane being Jewish). 'She converted

Peter,' Peter V-K points out, 'while we were staying at her house, and Peter tried to persuade me to do the same. I wasn't having any of it. At first he seemed inspired by his new faith – Jane wrote the words to that song "Seven Stars" [from *In The Skies*] during a Bible-reading session they both had. But in the long run I think it confused Peter and did him some real harm.'

Their wedding took place at Mick and Jenny Fleetwood's Bel Air house on 4 January 1978. On the previous night, back in England, brother Michael had had a panic attack about Peter tying the knot and stopped himself from ringing Peter to tell him it was wrong only for fear of further confusing him. Jenny couldn't really understand Peter's decision: 'We didn't know why he was doing it, but we sort of went along with him and supported him as friends.'

Jane became pregnant, but by the time their daughter, Rosebud, was born in the late summer, the marriage was floundering. Mick Fleetwood remembers how Peter shared some troubles with his bosom pal: 'I thought from the beginning that Jane was a little strange, a little austere and heavy. She was a born-again Christian, and of course there's nothing wrong with that, but suddenly Peter was surrounded by it. However, she was pretty, which Peter loved.

'But later, he told me how he was starting to feel that she was on the dark side of things: he felt that she was attacking him from within. It was very heavy. I remember when Fleetwood Mac were rehearsing the *Tusk* album he came along a couple of times [Peter's guitar is featured at the end of 'Brown Eyes' on *Tusk*]. He made it quite clear to me that he now saw this woman as a threat and that basically he felt that she had made a covenant with the Devil. Now, that may well have been Peter's paranoia, and I have to say that it would be unfair to blame her for what happened to him afterwards, but she was like one of those people who get caught up in cults, and that was worrying.'

What also can't have helped much was a fair amount of substance abuse throughout this time. Happily off the prescribed medication he so loathed, Peter was by all accounts tooting endless

ortrait from *Reaching The Cold 100* photo session, 2002. MONTY STRIKES

Peter and Danny Da Costa Bethnal Green,
summer 1971. DANNY DA COSTA

Nigel Watson & Peter. Bournemouth,
summer 1971. DANNY DA COSTA

Bournemouth, summer 1971.
DANNY DA COSTA

Peter and Maria Zantkuijl. Adrian Boot's
Surbiton flat. Early August 1971. MARIA ZANTKUIJL

1981 PVK era. Photo used for *Whatcha gonna do?* Album cover.

Rosebud Samuels-Greenbaum mid-1980s.

White Sky at The Venue. Ronnie Telemaque, Peter & Gregg Brown. Mid-January 1982.

Kolors 1984/85 Jeff Whittaker, Alfred Bannerman, Peter, Greg Terry-Short, Willie Bath & Emmanuel Rentzos.

The caring touch – eldest brother Len and Gloria Green 1994.

Peter's return to the stage. Buxton Opera House.
5th May 1996.

Splinter Group 1997: Peter, Nigel Watson, Cozy Powell, Neil Murray and Spike Edney.

Splinter Group 2001: Pete Stroud, Roger Cotton, Peter, Nigel Watson and Larry Tolfree. EAGLE ROC

Peter Green And Friends: Andrew Flude, Martin Winning, Mike Dodd, Matt Radford (obscured, on upright bass) and Peter. Sheffield O2 Academy, 8 May 2010. STEVE BLACK

anvey Island Yacht Club. July 2008. MARTIN CELMINS

eds-Liverpool Canal, Bingley, West Yorkshire. September 2009. MARTIN CELMINS

Peter reunited with his 1995 Gibson Howard Roberts Fusion III. August 2019. MARTIN CELMINS

Mersea Island August 2019. "I look like a saint..." was his comment about this photo. MARTIN CELMIN

lines as 'well-wishers' fell over each other to see him right. Meanwhile, any of the beneficial time-release effects of the stabilising medication he'd stopped taking almost a year earlier were wearing off. In this frame of mind, any decision-making that went on mostly did not take place in – to quote John McVie – the full light of day.

When both Peters first arrived in Los Angeles, there was no doubt that the guitarist was 'falling back into music again', as he himself put it at the time: Messrs Fleetwood and McVie had by then formed their own management company, Seedy Management, run by Judy Wong, and Peter, they all agreed, was to be their blue-chip client. Getting him a major deal with Warner Bros would be no problem – after all, *Rumours* was making the company a fortune at that point, which meant Mick had corporate *schlick*, as they say in Burbank-speak.

Mick went with Peter to buy him a replacement guitar – exactly the same kind of 1959 sunburst Les Paul that he had played in Fleetwood Mac, bought from a collector for £5,000. Peter was overjoyed to have it, yet shortly afterwards he gave it away to a stranger he met in the hotel lift who said he liked music. Peter VK freaked, not unreasonably, when he found out. Mercifully, the beautiful 1959 Gibson was soon traced to the local pawnbroker's, where its extremely temporary new owner – a hustler and space cadet – had promptly taken it to get $200 more with which to score that day.

As for securing a record deal for Peter, Mick had a meeting with Mo Ostin, head of Warner Brothers: 'The first thing Mo asked me was, "Is he together?", and in my view he was together so I said, "This guy is fine. I'm with him all the time. He's not going to jig out on you."' Mick got Peter a very good deal, going on for $1 million for three albums to be made in his own time. Then the day came for signing. 'I said, "Pete this it. If you wanna start making music, you gotta get the money and sign on the bottom line." Then right there and then in the office he suddenly turned and said, "I can't do this. It's the work of the Devil. This is not what music should be." Jane came down later that day and tried to persuade him to do it, without any success. So I went in to see Mo Ostin, apologised and said, "You can have your $400,000 back."'

Peter VK describes that bizarre business meeting as like 'a scene out of *Dallas*', but he could see that Peter knew his signature would lead to pressure from the record-company executives and that that was the very opposite of what he wanted. Peter wanted instead to go back to England and go into the studio, which eventually was precisely what he did do.

When Peter's brother Michael went to pick him up at a hotel near Heathrow, he wasn't at all prepared for the shock that was in store: 'When I first saw my brother, I had to go downstairs and have a drink, because it just wasn't the same person. His voice sounded very weird, muffled, and the first thing he managed to say to me was, "I look like Barry White." It broke my heart. I don't know what had happened to him over in the States but he'd just gone backwards: he had absolutely let himself go.'

Soon after that, in the spring of 1979, Peter VK released *In The Skies*, which charted at Number 32 in Britain but went on to sell a massive 800,000 copies in Germany, where it was welcomed as the return of a triumphant hero. The reality was somewhat less amazing: Peter's health was extremely fragile, too fragile to run the media gauntlet of press interviews to promote the album. Rock writer Steve Clarke did meet him in the Montcalm Hotel, London, for what was a very disjointed interview, subsequently published in *NME* along with a rather disturbing photograph of the guitarist that was taken against his will as he smiled uncomfortably on odd occasions during the talk.

In The Skies featured Snowy White, who, according to Peter VK, was badgered by Peter throughout the sessions to play all of the lead guitar. In deference, Snowy (formerly with Pink Floyd, Thin Lizzy and Linda Lewis) did his best not to, although he does solo on the title track and later secretly confessed to Michael Green,

'I'm not even fit to play rhythm guitar with him.' So reluctantly Peter was sometimes pushed to the front.

Peter Bardens joined him once more on keyboards, Kuma Harada (sessionman with Mick Taylor and Poly Styrene) on bass and Reg Isadore (of The Robin Trower Band) or Godfrey Maclean on drums. The album alternates blues, rock ballads, funk and classical guitar. 'Fool No More' is heartache blues played at a slower tempo than on the original version, recorded during sessions for the 'Dog And Dustbin' debut LP and eventually released in 1971 on *The Original Fleetwood Mac* out-takes album. Peter's playing in the late 1970s is less explosive, with few anguished outbursts and flurries of notes, but such restraint serves only to heighten the emotion. The track is a showcase for Peter Green's canon – namely that less, in fact, is more.

At around the time that most of the album was recorded, in autumn 1977, Peter Bardens was persuaded to put on a few London pub venues with Peter and Snowy by Gregg Brown (later in the White Sky band): 'I thought Peter sang very well on *In The Skies*, and it was a promising album. My friend Gregg Brown, who'd always been a great fan, built a band around Pete about then. I played with them on maybe two or three gigs and then resigned because it was just such a shambles. You'd have to gaffer tape a guitar onto Peter to get him to play; he was in no condition to go out and perform. Also, Pete wasn't really playing lead guitar – he'd leave it all to Snowy, like he did in the studio, and that was a bit of a shame because audiences would come along only to hear him.'

In Germany, the album stayed in the Top Ten for months during 1979 without any promotion. The pressure was soon back on to produce a follow-up.

Before *In The Skies* came out, Peter had suggested to Michael that they should form a publishing company. This he duly did, called it Tashman Music, and landed a three-album deal with Chappell. Peter put the deal Michael's way partly to boost his brother's finances. However, 18 months later, his generosity in a sense backfired by putting Peter under pressure to deliver at a time when his tank was running on empty. It was left to Michael somehow to sort it: 'We had a meeting – Peter, Peter VK, Peter's lawyer and myself – and Peter VK said to Peter, "We're going in the studio next week," and Peter said, "There's no point. I've got no songs. Mickey's got some so we'll have to use his." That's how *Little Dreamer* came about, with me burning a lot of midnight oil. Some of the tracks were written the night before we went in the studio – "Loser Two Times", "Walkin' The Road" – and then when we got into the studio I'd be worrying about whether Peter would be able to perform them. In the end he was all right, which was some achievement, considering his health at the time.'

The album's title track, 'Little Dreamer', is Peter in his element, improvising: '"Little Dreamer" was an instrumental he made up on the spot. He didn't really want to do one but I managed to talk him into it. He'd mentioned a couple of days earlier that he had a tune in his head so I suggested he went into the studio and played what was in his head.'

Guitarist Ronnie Johnson joined Peter on this and the following two albums, *Whatcha Gonna Do?* and *White Sky*. In an interview with *Mojo* magazine, Ronnie gave some insight into Peter's wacky ways in the studio and also his continual experimentation with the colours of sound: 'The sessions were interesting and a lot of fun. Peter arrived at the studio for the early sessions with these incredibly long fingernails, and the producer was frantically trying to cut them so Peter could play. Another time we were really going well and suddenly Peter stops and looks across at John [Edwards, now bass player with Status Quo] and says, "No, no, no. You're taking me to Brighton and I want to go to Shepherd's Bush." We just collapsed laughing. That may sound a bit bizarre, but in terms of the music there was an element of truth in what he said. Peter grew in confidence as time went on, and the last sessions I did for him were for an album called *White Sky* [May 1981]. He bought himself a Marshall amp with a Leslie hooked up to it and was trying out different sounds. On the days when he was all right, he was very together and playing extremely well.'

This pattern of good and bad days, introverted days and eccentric days, was and still is Peter's normality. As Peter was still prone to impulsive gestures of generosity, Peter VK and Peter's lawyer thought it wise to invest his money in property lest he give it all away on a whim, and in the couple of months that the conveyancing was going through for a small property in Richmond Peter stayed in Beckenham, Kent, with a guitarist called Kris Gray whom he'd recently befriended. At this point, *Little Dreamer* was out and *Whatcha Gonna Do?*, Peter VK's last production for Peter, was in the can. What's more, Peter had done sessions with early 1960s blues daddy Brian Knight for his new album, *Dark Horse*.

This period, as Kris remembers it, was one of rest and recuperation for Peter as he had time to try to make sense of the rather frenetic pace of life that had begun just two years earlier when he had met Peter VK and then moved to Los Angeles. 'I had a band called Hard Road,' explains Kris, 'named after the Mayall album, and I'd sent Peter and his brother a demo we'd done of "The Same Way". After a few telephone conversations, he asked me to pop by his brother's house, where he was staying. When he opened the door, he said, "Hello, are you Jewish? You look Jewish to me." I told him I wasn't but he still thought there was some Jewish blood somewhere going back. Anyway, after we'd gone out for a pint a few times I said that if he wanted a change he could come and stay in our spare room until it was time for him to move into his place at Richmond. It was obvious that he was a bit exhausted because when he moved in he spent a lot of time during the day in bed. He spent most of his time in pyjamas. He'd get up and I'd cook him something, which he'd eat, then sit around for a while and then go back to bed. When he was up he'd chain-smoke and listened to *Little Dreamer* or Thin Lizzy's album *Chinatown*, featuring Snowy White, again and again. Funnily enough, it didn't get on my nerves because he was kind of tranquil, not all agitated and restless.'

During his stay with Kris, Peter did talk about recent events. He told Kris about one incident with Jane in Los Angeles when he was dreaming that he was attacking her and had only realised that he *was* attacking her when he felt the police put a gun to his head. He described a lot of that period, from the mid-1970s onwards, as a dream, and how since that time he'd had trouble putting together what was real and what was fantasy. He very much felt that the ECT was the root of all his problems, making his condition worse and not better. One good thing had come out of Peter and Jane's marriage, though – his daughter, Rosebud – and Kris remembers how Peter phoned Los Angeles every week (always paying for the calls), to find out how his daughter was.

Peter's house purchase soon went through and he moved out of Kris's place. Kris visited Peter soon after: 'I couldn't believe how small and claustrophobic it was, like a telephone box with a bed in it. I went round a few times and the same guys were always there [some of them later formed Kolors]. They seemed to have taken over. There was a lot of smoking going on, and from time to time someone would tinkle with a guitar. I just didn't like the vibes – it was very oppressive, so I stopped going.' A loss of rapport between Kris and Peter followed, naturally.

Sadly, Peter's divorce went through in the early 1980s. To this day he remains somewhat baffled by the fact that the lawyer who represented him throughout the settlement, to his knowledge, was a friend and associate of his ex-wife's Los Angeleno lawyer. The first Peter knew of Margaret Bennett, he says, was at a rehearsal studio when she arrived and announced that she was his new lawyer.

16 Greenbacks: The Root Of All Evil

Peter Vernon-Kell bowed out of the business in 1981 after producing *Whatcha Gonna Do?*, thus ending a four-year collaboration with Peter which was extraordinarily fruitful, especially in view of Peter's erratic health. He admired the guitarist's prodigious talent with a pithiness that echoes his style of playing: 'His gift was simple: he had a natural ability to always find the note he wanted, the note he could hear in his head.'

One of Peter VK's greatest managerial skills in handling Peter's affairs was that he appeared not to be his manager. When the time came to make decisions, he made the guitarist feel that he was in the driver's seat, which in effect he often was, anyway. Then between 1980 and 1984 Jamaican percussionist Jeff Whittaker gradually took over Peter VK's role, although it must be said that there was little love lost between the two. Jeff feels that Peter VK used him for his many musical contacts on the scene during the late 1970s and early 1980s in black London, while Peter VK reviles the succession of bands that played with Peter during that time – variously called White Sky, Kolors and Katmandu – who in his opinion were all milking the guitarist's legend for what it was worth.

Peter VK was in the audience when one such line-up played in north London: 'I was disgusted. There was a blues legend fronting this cabaret band. I listened to about three numbers, by which time I'd had enough. If I could have physically got to the front, I would have got up on stage and chinned the one who kept reminding the audience that "Hey, man, this is Peter Green!"'

With the benefit of hindsight – which so often tends to be 20/20 – Jeff in a way now concurs with Peter VK that, during the four and a half years that Peter and he collaborated, live performances and gigging were not a good idea for Peter at that stage in his career: 'What I discovered quite soon with Peter was that, although he wanted to work, he didn't want to work just because he had to; he wanted to work when he felt like it. We should have been in the studio, making records, but with the exception of drummer Godfrey Maclean, Peter and I were playing with second-rate musicians.'

Whittaker, initially a dancer, had played in the early 1970s London musical *Catch My Soul* and was percussionist on Crosby, Stills And Nash's hit 'Love The One You're With'. He first bumped into Peter in the early 1970s during the *Gass* sessions. Jeff was working on a project in Germany while *Whatcha Gonna Do?* was being made and returned after Peter VK had departed. Peter, he says, at this point was once again disgruntled with the way the record company and accountants were interfering with the process of making music.

When Jeff got back from Germany, he learned a bit more about the guitarist's business affairs: apparently, after the divorce settlement and some steep fees from private clinics, Peter wasn't as comfortably off as he might have wished at the start of the 1980s. So, in a sense, for the first time since his early days as a pro he now *had* to work.

With the *White Sky* album finished by June 1981, the two musicians decided to go for a holiday to Barbados and plan their next move, forming a band. At this point, Peter's eccentricities left Jeff in something of a quandary: 'He wanted musicians around him who were financially independent and didn't put pressure on him to provide them with a wage. But as high-calibre musicians wouldn't tolerate Peter's ways, the only musicians who would work with him were those who were struggling and eager to break through and make a name for themselves. So the players on the *White Sky* album were not the same as those who did the four gigs that everybody got upset about; they were Gregg Brown, myself, Peter, Carlos Morela, Reg Isadore and, when Carlos wasn't around, Reg's brother.'

Although many people close to Peter were saddened by what they saw at the *White Sky* Red Lion/Greyhound performances, not everyone regarded the music as the pitiful fiasco that mythology has made it. In *The Guardian*'s arts pages of 18 January 1982, journalist Mick Brown reviewed White Sky's gig at London's The Venue: 'After 12 years, Peter Green seems committed to the idea of a comeback. He wrote some of the most memorable rock of the late 1960s. His current group, White Sky, is actually a black five-piece playing streamlined funk and rock which is a logical progression of the blues that was his main idiom. Inevitably, perhaps, none of the newer songs carried quite the impact of those old ones, but there was enough craftsmanship, glimpses of the old skills, to make one optimistic for Green's renaissance. All he needs is more belief in himself.' What with the ECT and medication, more self-belief was a very tall order.

After the famous four gigs, some promoters showed sufficient further interest to warrant putting a tour together, and so rehearsals began at the £100-a-day Orbis Studios. Already, though, Peter could smell a rat – or, with his sensitivity, probably a plague of them. 'We were rehearsing there,' Jeff explains, 'and Peter heard the tour organiser and some of the band arguing about money. Then, when Peter's lawyer came down, everybody rushed towards her thinking she was going to give them generous advance wages for the tour. Peter saw this, looked at me and said, "Let's go. I don't want this." This totally freaked Gregg Brown, who regarded White Sky as his band. He could see it all falling apart. So I had to tell him and others there and then that, after some three days of rehearsals, Peter didn't want to go on with the band any more.'

The band had already cost Peter money. Before the four gigs, they had rehearsed for about a month, Peter's company paying each musician £150 a week. Peter didn't like that, and he wasn't happy about White Sky's live set either, which included some of his old hits which he sang because of Greg, an old friend. By that point, what he really wanted to play was the material from *In The Skies*, which was more jazz funk.

Peter's lifestyle was very much that of a blues musician – that is, one of stylish squalor in a small terraced house, set in an incongruously bourgeois zone of beautiful Richmond. Incongruous because, according to some, it was as though the streetlife of the entire town used the *bijou* property as a crash-pad. Peter and his eldest brother, Len, both recall female visitors who persistently overstayed their welcome. One of them, Marie, Peter had met during one of his spells in hospital. 'Marie used to sleep on the couch when she stayed there,' Len explains. 'She came round whenever her social security money ran out and she needed drink. When we first met Marie, she was a really nice plump girl. Then she became an alcoholic, dried out, went back on the booze again and her weight went down to five stone.'

Another unwelcome hanger-on was a girl called Janine. 'She just wouldn't get out of my house,' recalls Peter. 'She once brought a cheap Spanish guitar with her, which I also didn't really want in the house. So after I'd asked her to leave many times, I lost my temper and smashed the guitar on her head. It was so cheap it just broke into three pieces. Perhaps I would have handled these things better if I hadn't been smoking weed, but drugs turn you into a softy and you let things go on too long.'

So it was in that kind of atmosphere that the Kolors project began to take off, rehearsing in Peter's front room. Kolors comprised Stephan Rene, Godfrey Maclean, Larry Steele and Peter. Next door to Peter lived a guy called Zilch, who was in partnership with Knocker. They were like brokers, connected with record companies, and were good hustlers within the industry. Jeff arranged to meet Zilch, who, although he had a Rolls-Royce, was obviously broke.

'When I told him about our line-up, he said, "Wow! With names like this, we could make money!" So he took down all our names and went straight to Phonogram Records in Germany – where Peter was still a big name – to get us a deal. When he came back, he had a £60,000 advance for us, which we thought was great, but of course we'll never know how much of that he kept for himself. While Zilch was negotiating with Peter's lawyer, he gave us the opportunity and equipment to go into a studio and start work on the album.'

Kolors went into the studio every day for over two months, Zilch paying for everything, but for some reason it just didn't come together. One of the band had a heroin habit and had turned to Buddhism for his salvation, which meant he thought he wasn't supposed to earn any money. In order to get any money, Jeff had to form a company, Zilch paid him and he distributed £6,000 to each member of the band. Peter wanted it that way.

Not only did the original Kolors sessions not go well but, after a couple of months in the studio, the band had little or nothing to show for it, although the Zilch company gave the impression that they were not really interested in seeing an album.

At the same time, Jeff had an ongoing project in colleges and kindergartens in Cologne, Germany, and had some contractual obligations coming up. He had a brainwave: 'I had to organise a finale concert of Afro-Caribbean music, due to take place in Cologne, so I thought the best thing to do was to get Peter down there to use him as an introduction. It also meant that we could get Kolors started.'

Kolors' debut live performance took place on Midsummer's Day, 1982, on the famous Dom Plaza in front of Cologne Cathedral. 'I was quite well known,' Jeff says, 'on the local arts scene in Cologne because I'd been working on that Kultur Stabil project for five years. I was due to do my last gig that day and I told the radio guys to expect a surprise, that I'd brought Peter Green with me and he was going to get up and play. Within five minutes, I saw at least 1,000 people gather in the square because of the radio announcement, and as I went up to the microphone to start the gig I got all emotional and had to back off for a bit. Peter saw this and started dying with laughter.'

But things turned very ugly with the Zilch company when they returned to England, as Jeff's wife, Dee Whittaker, recalls: 'The records from the Phonogram deal didn't happen and Jeff arranged to meet Zilch's business partner, Knocker, in a pub in Richmond. Jeff wanted the masters of the original Kolors sessions back from Zilch because they weren't producing an album out of it. So Jeff went to the pub as arranged, and the next thing I knew at about half past 11 that night I got a telephone call from a man who said he had seen two men outside a pub in Richmond holding Jeff, and another guy beating him up. He reckoned they broke his jaw and his wrists because they didn't want him to play, and put him in hospital for three days. Knocker was annoyed that the band had got so many thousand pounds each – which was in fact Peter's idea – and then nothing had come out of it, even though that wasn't the band's fault. On reflection, if we'd have been sensible at the time then the members of the band wouldn't have actually got any of that money – it would have stayed in the bank and been used to carry things over and whatever else. But the whole thing with Peter was to share it out fairly, because of his attitude to money.' Dee, now a headteacher, eventually became Kolors' tour manager during school holidays.

For the following 18 months, the band toured intensively in Europe and Scandinavia. A television recording taken from the German *Rockpalast* programme shows a gig in Hamburg. Wearing flamboyant red headgear, Peter looks like a nomad just in from a trip through the desert, and as he plays an off-beat reggae version of 'Black Magic Woman' he appears to be happily sharing a really good joke with himself. His playing is simple and sparse. 'By that time,' Peter points out, 'I'd stopped bending strings and liked playing the guitar straight.'

Life on the road during those tours was stressful for all concerned. Peter's health was, as ever, erratic, and Jeff felt it was his responsibility somehow to curb Peter's appetite for nocturnal *frissons* of one kind or another: 'After gigs in Europe, when the rest of the band went to sleep, Peter would go and walk the streets. Usually he'd bump into girls, and once they knew he had money in his pockets, they'd just put him into a room, lock him up and I'd have no idea where he was. So I soon learned that it was best to go with him everywhere – which meant I didn't get a lot of sleep for a year or two.' Uncannily, this is borne out by the fact that, in his 40s, Jeff actually does look younger than in shots taken of the band over ten years ago.

In 1983, Kolors toured Europe and Scandinavia once again and made the first of two trips to Israel. Shortly before Christmas, on 28 November, they played a high-profile London venue, the Dominion Theatre. Peter's performance here was rather inconsistent; most of the newer post-Mac material was good and funky, but some of the old numbers – most notably 'Love That Burns' – were so low-energy as to be comatose. Then, a few minutes later, and probably when his powers of concentration luckily had returned for a while, he stunned the audience with 'Black Magic Woman', played as strongly as ever before. What all this added up to was a very unusual concert in which the mood of the crowd never stayed the same for more than a few minutes.

After the Dominion, Jeff and Peter decided it was time to go back to the drawing board to find really good musicians and start again. A mutual acquaintance had met Ray Dorset (of Mungo Jerry) at a party. Ray had enthused about how much he liked Peter Green and so Jeff suggested that they went down to Ray's studio. Ray was running a video/commercials production company: 'When we got down there and were having a jam, one of Ray's clients from a Swiss company was there. He heard us playing and just said, "I'll buy anything they do." After that, he put his money where his mouth was – with £120,000. That's how Katmandu started up – as a studio band with Ray Dorset, Vincent Crane [of Atomic Rooster, now deceased], Peter and myself.'

Recorded between December 1983 and January 1984, this album is an inspired combination of classic and original blues. The groove and mood has an urgency that is absent – perhaps deliberately so – from Peter's other post-Mac releases. The album remains his favourite of these, especially the track 'Who's That Knocking?'. But while making it gave Peter a boost, the business side of things increasingly left him cold. It seemed as though each new project, each fresh line-up of musicians, brought with it legal and financial complexities which Peter was more than happy to leave for his astute lawyer to sort out. It was as though his solo career was bringing him full circle, back to that same disdain he felt in the Fleetwood Mac days, when the money-making always spoilt the music. Although Peter really enjoyed the Katmandu project, dividing the spoils marred the experience, according to Jeff: 'Peter realised very soon that Ray Dorset is a businessman, and after we had done the album, which Peter thought was great, he wouldn't have him working with us. Too grabby.'

Peter now feels that he was 'over-encouraged' by Jeff during their four-year collaboration – but then again, he must have enjoyed it from time to time because he's not a guy who has ever remotely contemplated compromise or eating humble pie for a living. Jeff, perhaps more so than everybody else, is matter-of-fact about the extent to which Peter's health deteriorated during the time they worked together. As he sees it, the problems were there from the start in 1980 – mood swings, day-long silences and a fear of being alone – and the percussionist tried to make appropriate adjustments, particularly when they were on the road. Most probably, being an active travelling musician was better therapy than the institutions that held him in limbo for stretches during the 1970s. Nevertheless, towards the end of 1984 events conspired to make him want to give up being a professional musician, and this time for good.

Two specific instances between 1982 and 1984 may well have

led to this decision, although equally likely is the possibility that by then Peter was actually beyond caring. The first is the tackiest record release in his entire discography, the *Kolors* album, and the second was the cloak-and-dagger ending to his second visit to Israel in the summer of 1984.

The first track on *Kolors*, which shows a picture of Peter Green on the cover, is entitled 'What Am I Doing Here?'. Things wouldn't have been so bad were this opener an incredibly witty pun or conceit on behalf of the record company. The irony is that, for the most part, Peter in effect just isn't there; bad mixing often put his guitar to the back of beyond. The thinking behind this compilation of rejects and out-takes is shameless. That it was ever released is a great shame.

In the summer of 1984, Kolors went to Israel after an extensive European tour. A three-day world music festival was planned in Tel Aviv featuring names like Al di Meola and Billy Cobham. Sadly, for the organisers and all concerned, the money ran out on the first day and Kolors played only one of the three gigs they'd been contracted to play. For the next two weeks, Peter and the band were holed up in the Carlton Hotel, Tel Aviv, in amongst some choice heavies and with slim prospects of getting out. As Jeff and Dee remember, 'Peter spent the time working his way through the menu in the restaurant of the Carlton and swapping anecdotes with Billy Cobham. Meanwhile, armed bodyguards were to be seen everywhere as deals went on behind closed doors. The Carlton wasn't good enough for Al di Meola, so they had to move him to the Hilton, where he proceeded to get very lonely and ended up slumming it with us in the Carlton! In the meantime the Israeli promoter of the festival, who went bust, was holed up on the three top floors of the Carlton. Peter was on the floor below him. The promoter kept moving rooms and wouldn't go anywhere without a bodyguard. After the first and only gig, we went back to the hotel and went to see this promoter. His armed bodyguard was standing outside his room, and you did get the feeling that something really heavy was going down. The promoter told Jeff he was really sorry, and that because it was Peter and he was loved by the Israeli people we should stay as guests of the hotel until such time as the financial hassles were sorted out.'

During the visit, the band got talking to some of the promoters who were involved with the finance. One Dutch guy told them he was into electrical installation in Africa and that he'd invested all this money in the production: 'He was hanging around to find out what had happened to it. What we gathered from him was that the organisers were groups of gun-runners who were selling arms round the international market. They had all come together to organise this festival. The contractors had done the work and erected the massive stage, the bands had arrived and suddenly there was no money up front.'

That Peter wasn't particularly surprised by these heavy business vibes is no surprise, nor was his gourmand's attack on the Tel Aviv Carlton's cuisine. But, as ever, the money was getting in the way of his playing. 'To tell you the truth,' Peter emphasises, 'why I don't play any more is because I make too many mistakes. When I played for money with Kolors, we played a lot of places like Scandinavia and Israel. All the time I was making a lot of mistakes, but when we got back to England and played for nothing at a Christian Aid charity thing I didn't make one mistake all night. So what am I meant to do? What am I meant to think?'

When they arrived back in England, some of the band members weren't too happy about not getting paid for the Tel Aviv débâcle – the line-up was then Will Bath (bass), Alfred Bannerman (of Isaac Hayes, guitar), Emmanuel Rentzos (Osibisa and Johnny Nash, keyboards), Greg Terry-Short (Ozzy Osbourne, drums), Peter and Jeff. This mealy-mouthed attitude, Jeff says, got Peter down more then anything else: 'Those guys made it clear that they were just after the money – if they didn't pick up their £100 each night, they didn't want to play.' For the first time in four years, Jeff had had enough, and as Peter didn't need much coaxing to hang up his touring boots, Kolors faded that autumn of 1984. The final gig – an on/off provisional booking at Harlesden's Mean Fiddler – never happened.

Peter retired to spend six bleak years living alone at Richmond and wrestling with his illness, the depressions, the lethargy induced by medication and intermittent voices from nowhere out to goad him into mischief.

Without a doubt this was Peter's darkest period. He still shudders when he remembers the persecution he felt from outside and from within. Children living nearby would taunt him about his scruffy, tramp-like appearance, and living alone he now says that the voices were as bad as they had ever been for him. With the exception of two guardian angels called Jan and Jill, who separately would visit him regularly, for the rest of the time he was vulnerable to life's myriad ne'er-do-wells. Sporadic bits of musical activity (eg the Enemy Within project) are thought to have taken place during those scary years, but they remain so hazy for Peter that he can't even remember participating.

In 1991/2, eldest brother Len and his wife Gloria came to the rescue and he moved out to join them – and his mother – in the East Anglian peace of their house in Great Yarmouth. And so began a long, slow process of recovery. Peter was safer in the bosom of his family, but it was also at around that time that he was put on the medication he stopped taking only several years later. Again, the benefit of hindsight does strongly suggest that the time spent so heavily sedated were lost years passed in a kind of narcotic Rip Van Winkledom. Obviously, at the time, people were doing what they thought was best. The family moved to Essex in 1993 and early the following year the author visited Peter for the first time. At first the guitarist refused to believe that tens of thousands of his fans out there wanted him back. 'Nobody's going to want to buy a book which is about me,' he said, quite seriously.

Call it strange coincidence or synchronicity, but in 1995, within months of the first edition of this book being published, in addition to Gary Moore's *Blues For Greeny*, two more album 'tributes' to the work of Peter Green were released, one by Bernie Marsden and the other a various artists compilation. Thus the seeds for his comeback were being sown.

Another strange coincidence is that virtually one year to the day after Peter first got himself off the medication, he got back onto a British stage. Together with his black Gibson Jazz semi-acoustic, he had a story to tell.

17 Peter Green Splinter Group

Peter Green returned to the British stage on 5 May 1996 at the Alexis Korner Memorial Concert at Buxton Opera House. Choosing an ebony Gibson Howard Roberts Fusion as his main guitar was a declaration of intent. He was looking forward to exploring new styles – less string bending and cleaner tones. The guitarists he was now also listening to were jazz players such as Wes Montgomery and Kenny Burrell. The Buxton opener was Otis Rush's 'It Takes Time'; on 'Black Magic Woman' Nigel Watson played Peter's well-known solo. Also in the set was The Shadows' 'Peace Pipe' with Peter playing a red Stratocaster.

His desire to play guitar again began the previous summer in the kitchen of his old friend from the early 1970s 'Heavy Heart' era. Peter in 1998: 'Nigel was playing some fingerstyle Robert Johnson – not the slide stuff that I've done in the past. And I thought, "Wow, that sounds more like the record than I've ever heard anyone do it". My dad always used to say that I hadn't got the patience to learn how to do some things properly. It's not that...it's just that if I'm not all that impressed with it – it doesn't allure me enough to want to learn. But when I saw Nigel doing so well, I thought maybe I could learn some new things too.' He told Tom Doyle for Q's August 1997 issue: 'He was playing Robert Johnson, and I said, "Blimey, that sounds just like the record. How did you work that out? I couldn't work that out". So it made me feel different. I'd been feeling pretty dead and it got my memory working again. I guess I started with the rudiments, because whatever I used to know was no good to me anymore. Something went wrong somewhere and it stopped me playing altogether.' The first blues that they practised together was Robert Johnson's 'I'm A Steady Rollin' Man'.

What can't be overemphasised is that in the early 1990s there was thought to be no chance of him playing and performing again. The initial re-learning, with trimmed fingernails, took a few weeks, according to Nigel, and then talk gradually turned to forming a band together. Peter was adamant about not reviving the original Fleetwood Mac's hits – something he later reiterated to *Guitar Player* in November 2000: 'I don't want to do *any* old things. The boys have asked me, but they don't understand how many times I've played those tunes. Although *they* might be able to do them better, I'm at the same place I was. It might be a little better, but it might not. It might be worse. I've got to work a little further.'

Soon after the Splinter Group gigs began in summer 1996, he wanted 'Who's That Knocking' from his Katmandu hook-up with Ray Dorset in the band's set as well as Duane Eddy's 'Trambone'. Meanwhile, Nigel saw the band as a way to bring Peter back to the stage, and also as an outlet for his own song-writing. Of course, in order to attract and please audiences, having Peter's well-known songs in the set list was a must. And so, reluctantly, he performed his classic hits as well as signature tracks from Bluesbreakers days like 'The Supernatural' and 'The Stumble'.

After Buxton, the Peter Green Splinter Group's first high-profile UK gig was at the Guildford Festival of Folk and Blues on 17 August, having played blues festivals in Switzerland and Italy during July. By then Spike Edney (ex-Queen) on keyboards had joined Peter, Nigel, drummer Cozy Powell and bassist Neil Murray (ex-Whitesnake). Eric Clapton was in the 6,000-strong crowd and called by the band's marquee after the gig. His verdict on Peter's playing gave cause for optimism: 'It was better than I was expecting.'

After Guildford and other blues festival appearances in Helle, Norway and in Kendal, the early autumn saw the band embark on a UK tour of larger club venues. The tour was a sell-out with fans eager to see Peter play again. And the good news was that he had got his life back – that on-the-road daily rhythm of pre-gig visits to guitar and fishing tackle shops, the performance, and then post-gig hotel lounge banter proved to be the best therapy of all. Original Mac bassist, Bob Brunning, met him backstage at Birmingham and recalled: 'Peter said, "I'm enjoying this. They're paying me good money and I'm having a laugh".'

Less good, though, was an issue with the band's live sound. From the outset Nigel played many of the solos, and the first splintering within Splinter Group came soon because the band and crew felt that he was playing too loudly. His response was that it was only at that volume that he could get off on his playing. The fact that Peter tended to dial down his volume only worsened this live imbalance. Naturally, audiences had come to see and hear Peter and so were not best pleased.

Peter didn't confront him but in an interview with the author soon after Guildford for the *Sunday Telegraph* (25 August 1996) with Nigel also present, Peter remarked: 'I'm learning the fingerboard from scratch and we're studying the balance of sound in the band. We're not a guitar-crazy band – we've only just started learning how to achieve an overall sound with no single instrument sticking out too much and letting down the others. Trad jazz players and jazz bands are marvellous at that – Acker Bilk's perfected it… The sound of the band has to be right and then it could be…a walkover.' Splinter's co-managers Stuart Taylor and Mich Reynolds did then confront Nigel but without success.

Snowy White, who saw Peter and the band play in Sardinia in the summer, saw a noticeable boost in Peter's confidence on stage by the end of the year: 'I'd already noticed he was far more confident as a person at the end of the summer compared to that Sardinia gig but his playing was much, much stronger in Brighton [21 December].'

In early May 1997, the band returned to Ireland, playing mainly large clubs and culminating at a sold-out Cork Opera House. The vibe in the band was sometimes tense. Nigel's loudness issue continued. Spike then left in late September ahead of the Rory Gallagher Memorial Concert at Buxton Opera House on 5 October. Roger Cotton (ex-Johnny Johnson and Larry Garner) replaced him. Buxton was Cozy's final gig. Tragically, seven months on he died in a car crash on the night of 5 April, when the new Splinter line-up played London's Ronnie Scott's, where the *Soho Session* live album was recorded.

1997 also took the band to Greece, Denmark, Finland, Estonia and Spain, as well as more UK dates.

In Splinter Group's live set Robert Johnson's 'From Four Till Late', 'I'm A Steady Rollin' Man' and 'Traveling Riverside Blues' performed by Peter and Nigel on acoustic and steel guitars and harmonica went down well. So in September they started work on *The Robert Johnson Songbook* album.

Replacement drummer Larry Tolfree (ex-Joe Jackson) was gig-fit for the early November 1997 six-date UK tour in which Splinter Group were support for BB King. Around that time, the record company Snapper suggested that the Robert Johnson project would benefit from Neil, Roger and Larry playing on several tracks. Arrangements were given a sweeter 'jazz lounge' feel as on 'Honeymoon Blues'. Paul Rogers sings on the final track 'Sweet Home Chicago' and in the fade Peter's percussive and melodic harp playing brings to a close the *Songbook*, which in 1999 won the WC Handy award for Best Comeback Album Of The Year.

The original band released one live album, *Peter Green Splinter Group*, on the Artisan (Snapper) label recorded at

December 1996 gigs in Cambridge, Wolverhampton and Shepherd's Bush Empire, London. Peter introduces 'The Stumble', '...and I did this one called 'The Stumble'...and I'm still trying to get it right.' And he does. The tempo now is close to Freddie King's original and slower than the Bluesbreakers' version. This grants him the time and space for more relaxed string-bends and to play some phrases slight behind – he called this 'dragging it'.

At the end of 1997, Neil Murray left to tour with Brian May. Pete Stroud joined in January 1998 on fretless bass and that line-up remained for the final six years. The band's late summer 1998 short American tour took in Cleveland, Michigan, New York, Chicago, Minneapolis and Seattle before heading to the West Coast. While in Cleveland Peter and Nigel performed at the Robert Johnson Convention held at the Rock & Roll Hall of Fame.

The band then played the Long Beach Blues Festival on Saturday 5 September. Pete Stroud: 'We played on the British blues day – John Mayall was on, The Yardbirds...we saw Kim Wilson [Fabulous Thunderbirds]. I'd never toured America, nor had Roger, so we had a great time.' Natalie Nichols reviewed Splinter Group's set for the *Los Angeles Times* (8 September 1998): 'The most anticipated appearance was that of singer-guitarist Peter Green, the Fleetwood Mac co-founder who recently returned to performing after decades of mental illness. In the '60s he succeeded Eric Clapton in the Bluesbreakers, with a slow-blues style that was both powerful and particularly lovely. On Saturday with his Splinter Group, the 51-year-old played traditional numbers and his own early tunes, such as 'Black Magic Woman'. Green appeared distant at times, and his singing voice, never more than serviceable, sounded froggy. But his musical voice rang true, especially on the spooky, moody instrumentals 'Albatross' and 'Supernatural' in which his signature style emerged intact. Filling the air with sweet, sad, beautiful sounds, Green not only reminded us of what he had been, but showed us what he could yet be again.' Posted on YouTube is another gig during this tour: Peter Green And The Splinter Group @ The Fillmore, San Francisco, CA on 4 September.

In January 1999 the band began working on the all-important first studio album, *Destiny Road*, produced by Pete Brown. Over two weeks some 40 demos were taped as possibles. Then in March the band stayed at Jacobs Studio in Farnham to record the chosen 12 tracks for the album. Peter said at the time: 'After this band played so well in America I think it would have been wrong for me or anyone else to hog the album – it's down to us all now to develop each other's playing and material.' Interestingly, the track list includes Peter's 'Tribal Dance' from his *In The Skies* album but with longer percussion breaks. Pete Brown's Pete Brown's songwriting skills, developed since the 1960s with Cream's Jack Bruce, were put to good use in shaping *Destiny Road*. Pete: 'There were a couple of Nigel's things that were all right and we did then work on them quite a lot, arrangement-wise, and they came out well. But I did feel that there were times when Nigel was repressing Peter…he came up with some stuff and Nigel would say, "No, you don't want to do that…that's a bit too jazzy". It could have been a far better record. But I was very impressed with Peter's singing on *Destiny Road* and later on when he did 'Cruel Contradictions' for Dick Heckstall-Smith. And he was playing really good harp as well. But there wasn't enough of him on that album.' His interpretation of "Cruel Contradictions" found Pete Brown and Dick close to tears. Pete: 'It was a song that was new to him and yet he invested in it a feeling like he was really living it. That was another side to him that was mightily impressive. He had a very, very musical sensibility.'

Peter really enjoyed being back in the studio again. Looking back, did he have a favourite Splinter album?: 'They were all kind of interesting, I like little bits of all of them. Nigel's

"Burglar", that was good...that was an interesting time. I've got a version of him singing it – he wouldn't have that one released, I had to sing it. I wanted him to sing it – his version was absolutely...was great...it was a hit – a massive hit it would have been to me...an outstanding thing. But he said, "No... would I sing it?" So I did, but it didn't really mean much to me. I had to try and make it mean something to me and find out what he meant...' Pete Stroud also noticed this with his first song for the *Destiny Road* album, 'Say That You Want To': 'It started as a bluesy jam, then I rearranged it, put a middle-eight in and put lyrics to it and Pete just sang it. He had a way of taking lyrics, asking you what that line means, and I'd explain about the third rhyming line, and he'd say "Yeah, yeah, I've got it now..." And then he'd sing it in a way that you'd never thought possible – now that is a great singer.' On 'Madison Blues' nephew Joe Green gives a strong sax solo and backing for Peter.

With three active songwriters, choosing album tracks was not always easy. Pete Stroud: 'I really enjoyed the gigs when I joined because we were doing the old blues set, as I call it, and I thought, "Great this is what I really like" and there was some new stuff in it. When it started becoming more of a songwriting band it got a little bit fussy. But it was okay, you know. But doing the bluesy stuff seemed more relaxed.'

In October 1999 Peter and Nigel started work on the second Robert Johnson tribute album *Hot Foot Powder* with Roger as producer. Pete Stroud played upright bass: 'All the basic tracks were recorded at Roger's Roundel Studio in Kent and then they took those across to the States and recorded the rest of it in New York, Chicago and San Francisco. It felt less like a Splinter Group thing for me and Larry – we would put down the basic tracks and then we weren't having to hang around to the end of the session.' Learning his parts for both Johnson albums Peter did feel some pressure of time: '[It was] a bit of a crush

– rush crush…learning it, you know, sort of steadily and have a go at it…you know, while you're still learning.'

The second American trip that December was a special time when he met his own blues greats – Buddy Guy, Otis Rush, Hubert Sumlin, Joe Louis Walker, Dr John and David 'Honeyboy' Edwards.

The different songwriting styles on *Time Traders* on Eagle Rock, worked well in creating a polished, stylistically wide-ranging track list. What made a real difference was playing the original material live in the UK and Europe before going into the studio in May–June 2001. Peter's talk-sing vocals add to Roger's cleverly arranged 'Real World'. Another standout is the atmospheric reworking of Nigel's 1972 release 'Uganda Woman'. Around the millennium they both flew out to Africa for a fishing trip and returned enthusing about the continent's vast openness.

Pete Stroud recalls the mood in the studio: 'It was okay…but I've got to admit it was also fraught at times. It was just the usual panic for me and Larry to get the rhythm tracks down so they could get on with everything else. I like hearing what every-body else has done and then sometimes go back and redo the bass track – it makes a big difference. But they didn't want to work like that. It was one take and get on with stuff.' The album also features a guest appearance by Snowy White on a Mac favourite of Peter's – 'Underway'. Snowy: 'They were recording in Jacobs Studio near Farnham and I just went down – it's just around the corner – and just sat in really. It's got a nice mood. Pete played the rhythm and Nigel and I did the lead bits.'

In September 2001 the band recorded a tribute to the Chicago greats – *Blues Don't Change*. Pete: 'Peter was listening to all those old blues and it was just a natural thing came round, "Why don't we do a bunch of covers?" All along I thought the band was at its best along those lines, the old blues songs, because people really enjoyed that – but the songwriting took over.'

Wedged in between their own gigs and recording, Splinter Group went on two month-long, sell-out co-headlining UK tours with John Mayall And The Bluesbreakers in 2000 and late 2002. Earlier, in spring 2002, the band returned to America before heading for Japan and Australia.

Recorded between August and October 2002 at Roundel, the final album's title, *Reaching The Cold 100*, is a line from Robert Johnson's 'Terraplane Blues'. Starting in early February ahead of its 24 February 2003 release, the band played 42 dates across the UK and one in Germany promoting the new album. Peter spoke to *Guitarist* backstage in Barnstaple on 20 February: 'I'm very pleased with the new album and hopefully it'll help to make us a mainline act. Nigel suggested the title – I was going to call it 'Greenstuff' or something like that. It took us about ten weeks to record, most of the work being done at Roger Cotton's studio, before we mixed the tracks at Sarm West Studio near Portobello Road. I think there's a very "live" feel to the album because we usually lay down all the rhythm tracks first before we do any fiddling around on top. With most of the songs we would usually get together at Nigel's house and see what we could make out of an idea, then if it worked we'd take it to the studio. I'd like to think that it sounds as up to date as life gets – it's not ultra modern but it's within the realms of what we feel comfortable about playing.' The album features four bonus tracks: 'Black Magic Woman', 'It Takes Time', 'Green Manalishi' and 'Albatross'.

The set was now two hours long and began with an acoustic 'unplugged' session in which the band were seated with an impressive street scene backdrop: Larry on brushes, Pete on acoustic bass, Roger on electric piano or guitar, Nigel and Peter on acoustic and resonator guitars and harp.

A second UK concert hall tour began in October through to Christmas. After the final gig at the Medina Theatre on the Isle of Wight on 11 December the band went their separate ways for Christmas and, as it turned out, for good. Very suddenly the Splinter Group era was over.

Why? From when he first formed the band, Nigel was over-protective. In the late 1990s he once told the author that, having got his friend playing and performing again, he wasn't going to let anybody else 'nobble' him. The following story from Clifford Chewaluza – who played floor drums on Peter's 1971 solo single 'Heavy Heart' – illustrates this: 'The last time I saw Peter was at the Jazz Cafe. I got there and they were on stage. I fought my way to the front and then beautiful Peter spotted me and started pointing at me to Nigel. Afterwards I went to the dressing room and it was a most beautiful reunion – it was like lost brothers. When I asked for Peter's number Nigel gave me his number. When I called the number afterwards I spoke to Nigel and not Peter. I tried other times and could never speak to Peter and basically gave up in the end. You could say I was blocked.' Other musician friends had similar stories to tell. This being so, some old and dear friendships were not renewed and potentially interesting musical hook-ups never happened. In Splinter's later years Peter enjoyed working with Dick Heckstall-Smith, Peter Gabriel, Chris Coco and Debbie Davies. Legal action against Nigel followed in 2004/5 by which time Peter had moved to Sweden.

Ending this chapter on a happier note, towards the end of the Splinter era Peter revealed a talent for stand-up comedy, as Pete Stroud recalled: 'He did a two or three minute thing on stage once in England – it was hilarious. He started telling the audience this story about Moses going up the mountain...then when he came back down somebody asked him, "So, what did God say to you?" ... "Oh, he told me to keep taking the tablets..." The way he put together the biblical story about the tablets with the commandments, and Peter himself and the tablets. It was just a knockout. And I thought to myself, "Well, there is the real Peter Green and it's there all the time".'

Andy Silvester witnessed Peter's fearless sense of humour when Splinter Group played at Ronnie Scott's in Birmingham: 'After the gig Peter and me sat down in the seats at the front and he said, "Do you want a coffee?" So he ordered some coffees for us, which was nice. We were chatting and then Tony Iommi came up to say hello. And he was being very respectful and saying how much he'd always liked Peter's playing and songs. Then Peter said, "What group are you in then?" and Tony replied, "Black Sabbath" to which Peter replied, "Black Sabbath? Why do you call your band Black Sabbath? There's nothing black about the Sabbath!" I couldn't tell you what Tony said because I was so impressed with how fearless Peter was about saying anything to anybody. It was all a bit bizarre but also funny at the same time.'

Similarly, Peter once told the author about meeting George Harrison in summer 1969 around the time the Apple label had shown interest in signing Mac. The Beatle's opening gambit was, 'I hear you're coming on board with us...' to which Peter replied, 'Why, are we going on a boat trip?'

Lastly, Pete Stroud noticed the importance that Peter always placed on soundchecks: 'He would always get changed from what he'd been wearing that day. He'd come out with a different hat or top or something and he'd be dancing around the stage with a little smile on his face. And then he'd change into his stage clothes for the gig. He loved soundchecks...he always wanted to jam.'

Evidently his comeback had worked for him: interviewed for *Guitar Player* in November 2003 when told how delighted his fans were to see him back on stage Peter said, 'Well, when I first started doing shows again, it felt really strange, but I've since experienced the joy of feeling what it's like playing with other people again.' This joy goes back to his early semi-pro years in covers bands like The Tridents. Being in a band, for him, was all about friendship and it was that which made for good music. During his time over in Sweden he did perform with the British Blues All Stars at the Notodden Blues Festival in 2004 and Orkney Blues Festival in 2005.

It would be some four years before he returned to the stage fronting Peter Green And Friends. With this, his last band, Peter chose almost all of the songs they performed. That freedom possibly helped to take his playing to the next, more wide-ranging, level, which partly was reflected in the different guitars he used: an Epiphone Granada for slide, an Italia Maranello, a Tanglewood and a new sky blue Hagstrom F300 Futura. There would be much that was new in the Peter Green And Friends era.

18 Peter Green And Friends

Whereas it took Splinter Group only a few months from inception to hitting the stage, Peter Green And Friends, formed by guitarist Mike Dodd, came together over a couple of years. This was a good thing both for Peter and the band.

Mike is a guitar coach and music researcher. He played in 1990s pop-rock band, Junior Cottonmouth, signed to Atlantic. He first met Peter in 2006 in his role as researcher/interviewer for the *Man Of The World* documentary. Then still living near Kristianstad in Sweden, Peter and Mike hit it off. He told Mike that he didn't play too often, instead devoting much time to his other passion, fishing. Peter returned to England and his family in autumn 2006, in time for his 60th birthday celebrations.

Soon after, he and Mike got together regularly at Peter's new home. Mike: 'I started to visit Peter at Canvey. Obviously it was a huge honour to sit down and play a bit of guitar with him. He'd say, "I like this Roy Orbison song" so we'd play that and we had a lot of fun.' Then, gradually they talked about the possibility of forming a band. Mike: 'The ball really started rolling with the idea of going away somewhere, renting a cottage and doing a bit of fishing and a bit of playing. So we spent a week in Devon fishing and going on boat trips. Then we'd have an early dinner and play music until the early hours of the morning. He'd say, "I like Billy Eckstein" and we'd play some...

then he'd suggest Jo Stafford or The Blind Boys Of Alabama and we'd go on like that.'

Back in Canvey, these sessions continued every week or so. During that time, July 2008, *The Canvey Island Sessions promo* for the 4CD box set *Peter Green: The Anthology* was filmed featuring Peter performing 'Need Your Love So Bad' and 'The Thrill Is Gone', with Mike on second guitar.

Mike's friend, drummer Andrew Flude, was living in Spain near Granada. He had a house there with a drumkit. Peter liked the idea of playing music over in Spain and so a week was booked for him, Mike and Andrew to get together and play. Mike: 'Jolena [Peter's then girlfriend] was also with us and I said, "Look, you're around, just pick up a bass". And so I taught her some simple bass lines and she did really well and we had a lot of fun.' When the author visited Peter in summer 2008 he soon put on an instrumental recorded in Spain called 'Blues Groove Jam', which featured some Wes Montgomery octave-style playing by him. While drawing or reading at home he often did this – repeatedly listen to work-in-progress by the band, thinking how it might be developed. When asked by *Guitar Player* in November 2003 if it was harder now coming up with the inspiration for new songs he replied: 'Not harder, but I'm always studying the development or lack of development in the old songs that I do. Always studying. That's where my sort of creative forces of energies would be applying themselves to. It can be found on the old songs we do – see if we can improve on them in any way.'

Another music-making trip to Spain followed, but soon after that Jolena went back to Sweden, so the search was now on for a bass player. Mike: 'Outside the Ain't Nothin' But the Blues Bar in Kingly Street, London I bumped into a couple of musicians and I just asked them if they knew any good bass players looking for a gig. "Not really" was their somewhat unhelpful response. But then their attitude changed completely when I said it was for Peter Green's band! They suggested a double-bass player called Matt Radford who used to play there. One of them gave me his number and I called Matt on my carphone. Matt told me that he'd quite recently been playing with Nick Lowe on his latest album. And, would you believe it, just before making the call I'd had that album on my car stereo! A couple of sessions with Matt then took place at a rehearsal studio in Hackney and because at that point Peter wasn't wildly into soloing I thought it would be nice to have other solo instruments. Matt had been working with Geraint Watkins on the Nick Lowe album and then there was Martin Winning who had also played with Nick.' Some 30 years previously Geraint and Peter both guested on Brian Knight's 1981 *A Dark Horse* album.

With Geraint and Martin in the band more sessions took place but no gigs were planned. Mike: 'We were happily playing and getting to know each other but the question kept on coming up, "Are we going to do any gigs?" And it was a struggle to get Peter to say yes. I contacted a friend who was a booking agent and he got back to me saying there was a promoter in Amsterdam who was interested. So one day I casually, kind of by-the-by, said, "Oh yeah, Peter...there's this guy who wonders if we fancy doing some gigs in Amsterdam." Then I think he said, "Yeah, I wouldn't mind that...".' That Amsterdam gig formed part of the first 2009 European tour which began in February in Zeebrugge. 'Gig number one was not entirely successful and I thought, "Oh my God...maybe we're doing this too soon." Maybe the crowd was expecting a kind of full-on rock show and we were playing quite gently. But then when we played the Amsterdam Paradiso in the small acoustic room, it was bloody brilliant. And so that's when it all really started. Then, when we weren't gigging I was taking Peter on fishing trips on a live-aboard boat.' Having tenor sax player Martin Winning in the band meant that the set list could include the kind of late 1950s/early 1960s soul and R&B that Peter liked, such as Bobby Parker's 'Blues Get Off My Shoulder', Bobby Bland's 'Ain't Nothing You Can Do' and Wilson Pickett's 'Barefootin". Martin and Geraint's soloing added to the band's overall live mix which was rootsy and basic. Classics from the Mayall and Mac eras included 'The Stumble', 'Rattlesnake Shake', 'Oh Well' ending with a bit of 'Part 2' and which then neatly blended into 'Albatross'. But Peter would not perform one hit. Mike: 'We rehearsed a heavy rock version of "Green Manalishi" and we all thought that it would work really well live...but Peter just wouldn't do it.' During 2009–10 the band played every major European city, many UK clubs and concert halls and also flew out to Australia to play the Byron Bay Bluesfest in early April 2010.

A story which says a lot about the band's attitude happened after a gig in Verviers, Belgium. Mike: 'We were staying in this hotel that was like something from that film *The Shining* – an old hotel with seemingly nobody else in it other than us. There was a great big room with a snooker table and grand piano. So we just got the instruments out and played for hours – it was fantastic. Peter played acoustic guitar with Geraint playing that piano. We got Matt's double bass out of the van and just played – interspersed with a few games of snooker – it was great fun.' The author noticed another revealing thing about Peter's attitude in this band at a 12 March 2010 gig in the Nottingham Rescue Rooms. With the soundcheck over, he stayed on the stage alone, guitar unplugged, music stand with lyrics in front of him. Then for some 20 minutes he kept working on one song from that night's set.

Andy Silvester saw the band at Huntingdon Hall Worcester, 23 February 2010: 'It was lovely to see him play and the musicians were doing the best they could. He'd got Geraint Watkins and Martin Winning on there who I thought were both very attuned to Peter's playing. And Matt Radford is a good double-bass player. It was much better than the Splinter arrangement – there he was, grateful to be playing again...he told me. But Splinter were rock musicians – Cozy Powell was a brilliant drummer but not for Greenie. But the band at Huntingdon Hall were much more like it.'

So, at that point nobody could have predicted that some four months on, Peter would decide to stop performing. Mike: 'Our very last gig was a blues festival in Italy, Narcao Bluesfest (23 July 2010), and he'd gone from sitting down to standing up and he was digging into the guitar and getting more dynamic range out of it. It was like he was back, digging it...he was "Whooo!" and smiling...and then that was it. He disappeared again.'

The end of the Peter Green And Friends era came in late July 2010. Mike: 'I was in Canvey Island when he told me he didn't want to gig anymore and it was a shock. I did try my best to persuade him to just do those last remaining gigs but he just wouldn't change his mind.' When the author asked why he stopped, he gave two reasons: travelling through Italy in the tour bus sometimes left him feeling too tired to perform. Secondly, he said, 'audience expectations'.

The Peter Green And Friends era was a musically rewarding and enjoyable time for him. His relaxed onstage demeanour was proof of that. And his playing continued to be different and adventurous – for instance, neat solo phrases in place of the original twin-guitar harmony parts on 'Albatross'.

Here's how Andrew Flude remembers Peter back then: 'If he wanted to, he could tell a good story, and they inevitably involved him playing with some other legend, or being somewhere I'd only read about. He told them in a very humble matter-of-fact way, but you could see he had a solid and happy memory of it. His youthful, confident self was still with him occasionally and that was nice to see and hear.' Peter did consider playing one-off concerts and, after 2010, from time to time the band would still get together at a rehearsal room in Canvey

Island. Speaking to *Uncut* magazine in March 2020 Mike Dodd detailed recording sessions that took place until about 2017: 'We did a couple of Otis Rush songs, "Double Trouble" and "You're Killing My Love", Bobby Parker's "Blues Get Off My Shoulder" and "Steal Your Heart Away", Freddie King's "Help Me Through The Day". Willie Dixon's "When The Lights Go Out" and "Many Rivers To Cross" by Jimmy Cliff and Eric Bibb's "Don't Ever Let Nobody Drag Your Spirit Down". I imagine those recordings will see the light of day at some point. And hopefully it'll show people that he was still capable of doing some really great stuff. They might not be original tracks, but nevertheless it's, "Wow, that's Peter Green!" You can't mistake that voice or that playing.'

To summarise his 1996 and 2009 comebacks, since taking up guitar again in 1995, Peter did develop a new approach that he was happy with. When asked, for the *Guitar* September 1981 issue, if he practised a lot he replied: 'I never practised runs and licks. I never looked at it that way. I still can't play a scale.' Then asked if he hears in his head what he's going to play: 'Usually.' Guitarist Kevin Winlove-Smith regularly saw the early Mac and in 1994 recalled: '[Peter] would often stand there, just playing along with what he was singing, and it was obvious he could play note-for-note whatever tune came into his head...as it came into his head.'

That ability always to find the note he heard in his head probably faded in the late 1980s when he gave up playing, and for some five years was on strong medication. In 1995 he came off that medication and when he then took up guitar again he chose the more formal approach of learning scales. Peter in 2008: 'Back then I didn't play scales, I didn't use scales. But now I do play more or less what comes under the scale of the octave. But then I was pretty loose – playing phrasing from records. I seemed to be lost for it...and now I'm not lost for it and it sounds much more individualistic, and not like the blues [approach] or the Eric Clapton approach, or whatever it would be.'

In his final years he kept on playing for pleasure, and collecting guitars. His collection is listed in *The Albatross Man*, Rufus Publications' impressive large-format photographic retrospective and biography of Peter Green's life.

He listened to a wide range of music: one CD wish-list comprised Eric Clapton's 2013 *Old Sock* album and anything by South African Afro-jazz/reggae band Bayete. When drawing his artworks, the radio was often tuned to a Chinese music station: he told *Guitarist* magazine in 2003 that Chinese was his favourite of all world music, followed by Arabic, Greek bouzouki and belly-dancing music.

And he enjoyed fishing trips with friend Paul Hoenderkamp, and their practice sessions at his home. Paul: 'We'd play my versions of the old hits like "Hey Joe", "House Of The Rising Sun" and "Runaway", and also bluesy things like "Hide Away" and "Stormy Monday". We had a lot in common. I don't mean back in the Orange Amps days, but when we met up again we just clicked...maybe something to do with us both growing up in the East End after the war.' Bernie Marsden visited him and Mick Fleetwood spent an afternoon at his home a couple of years before the All-Star Palladium Tribute concert.

Cathy Fehler became Peter's lawyer in the late 1990s. The approach taken by her and associates also looking after Peter was legal representation combined with holistic care. This was welcomed and appreciated by him and his family.

Since returning from Sweden, in his home life in Canvey Island he was lovingly cared for by sister-in-law Gloria, nieces Belinda and Rachel, and nephew Joe who took him on outings and visits to guitar and angling shops. He liked to visit and stay with brother Michael and his wife Irene. Each year on Peter's birthday the whole family would gather for a celebratory lunch. In his final years he was happy.

19 The Songwriter

A *Disc* feature published on 25 October 1969 about Peter, Danny and Jeremy's songwriting stated: 'Peter Green writes around a particular phrase that comes into his head like – "Baby Stop Messing Around" – and waits until he feels it's so right for the song he can build the rest round it. "It's like recognising a feeling you've been waiting for. You suddenly go – "yeah!" – and you know it'll all come from that. I can't write about anything that hasn't actually happened to me. This can be rather dangerous. You have to keep double checking your own material and try to dissociate yourself from it. For instance, I could be really sad about something one day and pour it all out on the lyrics. Then the next day I, or someone else, might read it and think it was a load of rubbish. You've got to be sure what you're actually feeling is going to communicate itself to people." He said he got a buzz from listening to "Closing My Eyes", "Albatross" and "Man Of The World", but regretted not having a music degree.'

The Albatross Man book includes handwritten lyrics for 'Man Of The World', 'Rattlesnake Shake' and also 'Closing My Eyes', which evidently was written on five pieces of paper. These provide some insight into how Peter wrote and developed his work. The song recalls a brief time – early spring 1969 – when he had such great faith in Jesus that he felt that he was walking and talking with God. He then evangelised on the streets but gave up, he told the author in 2019, simply because most people weren't interested.

Two pieces of paper – headed Strand Hotel Thulegatan 2, a street in Stockholm, possibly date them as 1 April 1969 while he was on tour. The other three are on lined paper with lyrics closer to the actual song which was recorded on 31 May. There are two opening lines: 'Now it's the same as before without you' then 'Now it's the same as before and I'm alone again'. He tried adding place: 'From the room where I sit I know you're there watching me' and 'From the room where I sit I can see you and if I close my eyes I can almost feel you with me again' but he also had the idea of wishing to see God. 'What should we do if we could only see you' or 'If they could only see you'. What became the song's penultimate line came to him early on: 'Seems I know nothing now except my love for you'. And apparently he tried lines with different meanings: 'Looking back through the years how I wasted my time' became 'As now I'm back to the time when I would search for a dream.' Word changes made the song less mournful: 'No use to cry anymore as before – I'd rather die just to be with you' or 'If I could cry any more as I have (done) the times before I think I'd die just so I could be with you' then became 'But no use to try any more as before someday I'll die maybe then I'll be with you.' There are other word changes: 'You washed me with your love', 'You filled me with your love' and finally 'You touched me with your love'; 'For they're all alone' became 'For they're all aglow...'. Initially the last verse began 'So I'm closing my eyes and still the people laugh' and became '...to hear the people laugh.' The last line reveals an interesting change. Initially, he wrote 'I can almost feel the warmth of your smile'. An alternative last line has two words crossed out but could be 'But while there's blood [?] in my [?] I'll go on *feeding* your smile' which became 'But while there's strength in my hands I'll go on feeding your smile' and then finally 'And with the strength in my hands to go on feeding your smile'. So, the song ends with his faith still strong.

Discussing 'Man Of The World' Peter told *NME* (26 April 1969): 'The beginning goes a long way back, nearly a year and a half. I got the phrase 'Shall I tell you about my life?' in my mind. Then at a different time I wrote the bit in the middle. All the bits came together. That's the way I write.'

Which means that while writing the song he was in a deep relationship with Sandra Elsdon. He *was* in love – not wishing he was – and he did have a good woman to make him feel like a good man should. Surprisingly, in the mid-1990s he described the words as 'corny' even 'far-fetched'. Why? Maybe because people had taken the lyrics far too literally, some thinking it was almost a suicide note.

The song is a beautifully composed portrayal of sadness – an autobiography-based story. But it was also prescient, as writer Ed Vulliamy noted in his tribute: 'Green's departure from what we call "normal" consciousness was announced by one of the most poignant songs of the age: "Man Of The World", of 1969: a searing, lonely but lyrical musical-poetic departure, which Green himself then followed in person.' That being so, could it be that 'Man Of The World' was written by a man from the other-worldly?

20 Late 1960s Spiritual Quest

Interviewed by Keith Altham ahead of Mac's third US tour (published in *Rave* in February 1970), Peter said: 'I will say that it was Christianity that really got me together. But then I also happen to think that Buddhism is a very good thing – there are so many different religions but only one true path when you get down to it.' He also spoke about his 'very rough childhood'. And about fights: 'I'd be too proud to go home and complain to my dad or elder brother that someone bigger than me had beaten me up.' And about the tough area he grew up in: '...the "Dads" used to go down to the school playground and fight out their son's battles and you got large-scale family feuds going.' And about unfairness: 'I felt the world was full of injustices and false values, and later as a musician and adult those reactions came out.' About his music early on: 'My music then seemed to be a very private thing which I was not prepared to share lightly with anyone else. I've always written what I believed and the blues to me was another way of saying the "Truth" and no one was going to question my deepest beliefs.' But he then pointed out: 'I think I have changed because I've realised that you just cannot change the world to your own ideals. You can try but the world generally ends up changing you. Perfection is just not possible. I'm still sad about so many things and you can still hear it in my writing on *Then Play On*, and even on singles like "*Oh Well*". The blues have never been rocking, raving things to me, they've always been a sad song and that's at the root of my work.'

Sandra Elsdon-Vigon said in 1994: 'And to me those are Peter's blues: the blues for him are Jewish blues.' He once sobbed, recalling the pain he felt as a little boy being Jewish and being teased and taunted. Maybe it was that which later led him to look to other faiths. Before Christianity in 1969 came a long-held interest in Buddhism, shared with Sandra, and *Then Play On*'s 'Before The Beginning' reflects that. It was the opener at Mac gigs for a while and then with Splinter Group he wanted to perform the song again. In 2008 he recalled: 'I was reading about Buddhism at the time, and about the supposed circle of life – and some of the song is about that. The Buddhism belief – that a life is suffering and you keep coming back again – the circle of life – you keep coming back until you perfect yourself in life and you reach Nirvana. A place I've never reached is what it means!' But how do the lyrics relate to the circle of life?

Directly, in the first part of the chorus: 'And/But how many times must I be *the fool* before I can make it…oh…make it on *home*'. One simplified take on the Buddhist path to enlightenment in this life is firstly to realise that you are a fool. Then you make more mistakes – such as jealousy breaking up a relationship – you suffer, learn, and become a wiser fool. Eventually, having learned completely from your mistakes and suffering, you attain enlightenment or Nirvana, which some Buddhists do refer to as home.

An instrumental version – called 'Blues In B Flat Minor' and included in *The Vaudeville Years* double CD – was taped on 8 January 1969 in New York. Then at LA's Shrine Auditorium on 25 January Peter performed it with lyrics. Five days on at the Warehouse in New Orleans an effective drum break was added before and after the guitar solo – a variation on the mallets drum pattern throughout the song. Then at the

18 April session when the final version was taped, Peter told *Record Mirror's* Derek Boltwood: 'That's what [the song title] is called at the moment, but I really don't like that name 'Before The Beginning'. It's what it's about, but it sounds a bit pretentious.' American keyboardist Nick Buck played on Peter's first solo album, *The End Of The Game*, and in summer 1970 they played gigs as a duo. Nick: 'I think the "Beginning" alludes to the start of life as an enlightened soul, and the "Before" bit is life as a fool.' The lyrics about love are perplexing: in verse one he's maybe thinking about a woman he used to love, then in the last verse he's completely lost in his search for love. Are these two different kinds of love, the latter being wholly spiritual?

In 1994 when talking about *The End Of The Game* album's title Peter said: 'The jungle idea wasn't mine – I'd already written about that with "Before The Beginning". My idea of a jungle is the Indian jungle where the elephants quietly work – in the African jungle they run around screaming.' How does the jungle relate to the song? Nick Buck: 'Maybe he was alluding to the musical idiom – the jungle rhythm of the mallets and tranquil mood of the song, with staccato guitar breaks interspersed.'

Although he would return to Judaism in the 1970s, his conversion to Christianity was largely thanks to Jeremy Spencer, who gifted him the large cross he wore on stage. Then with 'Oh Well Parts 1 & 2' he combined his new faith and his interest in classical music. In summer 1969 Peter and Sandra attended the Albert Hall Proms concerts. Peter: 'Rachmaninoff came through...and Paganini came through.' But he only liked tuneful classical music: 'Those other things don't get through to me at all...so what can that be? I suppose it's getting away from feeling lonesome or blue or destroyed – trying to resurrect yourself from destruction!' As shown in *The Albatross Man*, he studied and wrote detailed notes about Franz Joseph Haydn.

'Oh Well Part 2' started with the Spanish guitar solo which came to him at Marble Arch. Then it grew into a classical piece with Peter (guitars, cello, tympani and cymbals), Sandra (alto and tenor recorders) and Jeremy's short piano part.

'Oh Well Part 1' was *the* original rap song that inspired Led Zeppelin's a cappella call-and-guitar riff response idea on 'Black Dog'. 'Oh Well''s lyrics were inspired by the composer's Bible studies. In the *Man Of The World* film he cited a well-known verse from the Bible – from Romans 3:23: 'We have all sinned. We have all fallen short of the glory of God...that's what that bit means. It's quite good. It's nice to revisit yourself.'

Verse two is sending out a serious message, as he told Colin Simmonds in *Rave*'s June 1970 issue: 'If you were to come face to face with God would you be able to say that what you are doing is right?'...'A lot of people thought they were nonsense words, which is sad, but I hope if they keep playing the record it will get through to them in time.'

But earlier that spring a news item linked to Peter and Jeremy's Bible studies got Jeremy into trouble with the band. Headlined 'Fleetwoods Plan Story Of Jesus' (*NME* 24 May) it reported that Peter and him were thinking of making an orchestral-choral album about the life of Jesus, and that Mac's leader had written three songs for the project. In 2001 Jeremy told the author: 'We just talked about it in passing, "Oh, it would be good to do something like that". But then it came out – headlines in the next *NME*. The rest of the band, they freaked out. Pete said, "We haven't even got anything...we're not gonna do this!" That came from Nick Logan asking me, "Well, do you have anything?" I said "no – well, maybe – I think Pete might have a couple of things". But then it got blown up, "Yes, we have material ready"...which is *not* what I said! The band figured that would put our profile, you know, very dangerous like.'

This does flag the band's natural concern about their image, which during 1969 would change somewhat as Peter sometimes wore flowing robes and his cross on stage. He did so to help to get his religious message across – Peter said he wrote 'Part 1' to get everybody on it, so it's ironic that the single then proved to be divisive within the band in late summer. It was around then that he first began to think about leaving.

The single having been released on 26 September, a week later *NME*'s Nick Logan spoke to Peter at London's Lyceum: 'I asked if he'd had any second thoughts about "Oh Well" which hadn't then made an appearance in the *NME* chart, "No, I don't think it could have been better. Mick and John didn't want it released as a single but we don't go on what they say. We'd have put out "When You Say" (a Danny Kirwan song on the new LP) but for them. I don't know what they feel about it now".' Mac's rhythm section then grew to like it. 'Oh Well' rose to Number Two in the UK and became a million-seller worldwide.

Despite the frustration expressed in 'Before The Beginning' Peter's interest in Buddhism remained: in early June 1970, Sandra, Nick and he stayed at a Tibetan Monastery in Eskdalemuir, Scotland. Nick also recalls attending meetings about UFOs and astrology – and them reading *Clothed With The Sun* by Anna Kingsford, a 19th century writer, theosophist, anti-vivisectionist, feminist and vegetarian also interested in Buddhism.

At the end of his 27 April 1970 final BBC Radio 1 session with Mac, on impulse Peter asked violinist Nick Pickett to join him on a slow, melancholy take of his 'Leaving Town Blues', which they had practised. But two words were changed: he was leaving this world, not town – and going back to the Good Spirit, not Chicago. Talking to *Beat Instrumental* in June 1970 he said: 'A lot of people are afraid to say it, but I feel I am guided by the Good Spirit, or God if you like.' So, by the age of 23 Peter had studied religion and spirituality in his own way, and decided that there was only one true path to follow, which to him was the Good Spirit.

21 Mythic Munich

Much newsprint and many hours of rock-doc airtime have been devoted to the 'Munich Incident' on 22 March 1970 and its alleged dark consequences: Mac's leader lured to a mansion for three days and recruited by a rich Munich jet set who spiked him with bad acid that destroyed his massive talent.

And yet live recordings of gigs straight after the party reveal him playing at the top of his game, and at times exploring new uncharted sonic territory. For Peter Green, Munich was a musical and lifestyle lightbulb moment. And yet the accepted negative narrative still remains.

For instance, *The Times Of Israel* tribute published on 22 August 2020, among others, recycled and embellished the Munich myth. Here is an extract from a long feature by Amir Ben-David also detailing Peter's 25 December 1980 studio jam at Eshel Studios in Tel Aviv: 'Greenbaum, the haunted Jew, did not feel comfortable in Green's guitar hero suit. Three days of wild partying at a posh villa in a German forest, during which he consumed surreal quantities of LSD and played for hours on end for tripped-out bourgeois Germans who urged him on, finished him. It was the journey from which he did not return. He turned his back on the ego trip and gave himself to the acid trip.'

Mark Blake, in his insightful essay for *The Albatross Man*, also writes that Peter was there for three days with 'left-wing libertarians', spiked, and that Mac had to persuade him to leave. He then adds that 'One morning soon after Munich' he had the drug-induced nightmare that inspired 'Green Manalishi'. This timeline is wrong: Mac began performing an extended 'Manalishi' on the third US tour in late November 1969. He probably wrote it that autumn. In *Rough Notes* Bruce Thomas also buys into the Munich mythos – 'abducted, drugged and locked in a basement for a weekend'. Peter has always said that he took the LSD willingly.

The author interviewed three people who were at the party: Rainer Langhans and Margret Greenman who lived in the Highfish commune's large flat in Munich's Giselastrasse, and Amon Düül II's guitarist John Weinzierl – his band rented the country mansion in Kronwinkl and rehearsed there. These interviews revealed several things that debunk the myth. Highfish was a media artists' commune and far from being moneyed. They took great care when sourcing and experimenting with LSD – a trip was a 'holy thing' which took preparation, care and chill-out afterwards. Some young commune members were still coming to terms with their parents' generation's Nazi war crimes. Lastly, sensational tales linking Highfish, Peter's so-called abduction and far-left militant group the Red Army Faction (aka RAF and Baader-Meinhof Gang) are unfounded: Baader-Meinhof/RAF reportedly only became operational in mid-May 1970. Highfish was a peacenik commune.

One strand of the myth which remains unanswered, though, relates to which members of Mac attended the party. Commune member Rainer Langhans, an actor and promoter back then, told the author that it was just 'Peter and the roadie [Dennis Keane]'. This matches Dennis and Peter's recollections in 1994. But then in a YouTube German *Guitar Magazin* podcast Langhans said that he and his girlfriend, model Uschi Obermaier, met the band at the airport and only Peter and Jeremy 'were in' on his invitation to make music and party.

Artist Margret Greenman said just Peter and 'a blond roadie' were there. Third interviewee prog/krautrock Amon Düül II's guitarist John Weinzierl remembers admiring Peter and Danny Kirwan's Les Paul guitars at the jams, which then continued the next day. In a 1974 *NME* Steve Clarke interview, Jeremy Spencer remembered being there – and more recently, Mick Fleetwood did too.

Case unsolved forever and, in one sense, it doesn't much matter. Munich is really about Peter's new musical direction and lifestyle prompted by his one-night stay. But another mystery centres on why the 'Munich Incident' story took so long to break in the first place. In June 1970 Mick Fleetwood told *NME*'s Nick Logan: 'If we could have come down here and had this rest a month ago I think Peter wouldn't have felt the need to go. But three months in America, then a month on the Continent...living in hotels out of suitcases...it is just too much. It was affecting all of us but Peter was the first one to snap.' No mention was made of Munich – he left simply because he'd had enough of long, exhausting tours.

What was Peter's musical lightbulb moment? Recalling the jam in 2008, he said: 'I was down in the cellar of this country house playing music with some other people. I had taken LSD and was playing guitar with a wah-wah pedal...it felt as though I was breaking through the blues notation I'd been playing for years into something new. The drummer [Amon Düül II's Peter Leopold] was playing a rhythm which was very different to any blues rhythm. The people I stayed with gave me a tape of some of my playing that day and I kept listening to it from time to time afterwards. I wish I could hear it again today but I accidentally left it in America a few years later.' Then in the 2009 BBC4 *Man Of The World* documentary he said: 'I did some great stuff on LSD in Munich...some fabulous stuff which I liked.' ... '[We got] the sound, interesting curious sound. I had a good play – it was great. Someone recorded that and they gave me a tape. There were other people playing along and playing with a few of us, just fooling around and it was, er, yeah, it was great'. In contrast, in that film Jeremy Spencer described the music coming from the basement as 'the pits', and then also as 'repetitive drivel' (reported in *Uncut* in March 2020).

'Chaotic' is how Margret Greenman found the music. She was instantly attracted to Peter: 'He was a very beautiful man... so maybe I imposed myself on him! Amon Düül were my friends so I was there in the basement when they were playing. It was Amon Düül-type music you know...chaotic.'

Shortly before leaving Mac, Peter revealed more about Munich's lifestyle lightbulb moment to *Beat Instrumental* in their June 1970 issue: 'Mainly, as I say, I want to jam and that is what I am doing. If anyone calls round here [New Malden] and suggests playing then I'll go and play for the sake of enjoyment and because I can get to know other people through playing with them. I played on the commune in Germany when I stayed there, and it was then that I found out how much I've changed, through playing personally for them. When the pressure is off it all just comes out naturally.'

The basement jam gave Peter the idea of creating a musicians' commune back in England. After interviewing him, Colin Simmonds wrote in *Rave*'s June 1970 issue: 'He'd like to get his parents another home and turn the house over to a centre where musicians with common ideals can drop in any time to play and stay as they wish.'

Did the acid party adversely affect Peter's playing on the next gig? According to Rainer that gig was also in Munich at the Deutsches Museum the next day, and he said he drove Peter back to the city in his old BMW – Dennis Keane recalled that Mac drove out to collect them. The photo in the picture section of him and a smiling Peter in Munich city centre was taken then. His friend Christa Ritter, who supplied that photo taken by the late Lu Pachotta, photographer, also recalls that the next gig was at the Museum. Mick Fleetwood's verdict on Peter's playing next day was that he 'sounded mad'.

When Mac played in Copenhagen on 28 March, Mac's sound engineer Dinky Dawson, in his autobiography *Life On The Road*, recalled Peter playing directionless solos that led to the rest of the band losing momentum, and even worrying that he might at any time lose it and walk off the stage. That was the gig during which the band realised it was over, according to Dinky. But Ole John in Copenhagen's *Politiken* (31 March 1970) thought differently: 'Green's clean cut guitar playing was liberating. Fleetwood Mac has over time developed a distinct and personal blues style, built around Peter Green's virtuosic guitar, where every note shines brightly. On occasion it may sound stagnant but on Saturday the group had so much energy it saved the concert.'

One final strand of the Munich myth is that the commune recruited Peter after he returned to England. Langhans refutes this: 'Three weeks after this night we visited Peter. He met us at London Airport and drove us to our hotel in his Jaguar sports car. He said that he can introduce us to Mick Taylor and therefore to The Stones – who were in the studio recording at the time. We wanted to make a big concert in Bavaria with The Stones as the main band. Uschi and me spent a week in London. We saw It's A Beautiful Day at the Albert Hall [18 April] and Uschi spent some time with Mick Jagger. Later The Stones did send us a Letter of Intent to appear should we succeed with the organisation of this concert – but we didn't. So that week in London was the last time we met Peter.'

So Munich's significance is about the music which came afterwards. At the jam, Peter was inspired by playing to 'a rhythm that was very different to any blues rhythm'. In mid-June he would enjoy jamming with Little Free Rock – a trio from

Preston likened to Santana but with Afro rhythms. And his guitar playing post-Munich speaks volumes.

Take the live recording of 'Rattlesnake Shake' and 'Underway' in Gothenburg's Konserthuset on 2 April on YouTube. Peter's guitar boldly, at times wildly, explores uncharted territory, but is still weaving in the past – riffs and phrases from *Then Play On*'s 'Fighting For Madge' studio jam, and then phrases with a darker feel. He is flying forward, while his band in places do sound confused and unsure about where he's taking them.

And the night before in Stockholm there was his searing solo in 'I've Got A Mind To Give Up Living'. At 3:15 minutes into the 7:36 track on YouTube (Peter Green's Fleetwood Mac – All Over Again – Live In Stockholm) there is a phrase that augurs the darker mood of parts of his *The End Of The Game* solo album. Analysing that for this book, Reverb.com guitar tutor Jeff Massey explained: 'That lick is derived from the Dorian mode. Dorian always works well in minor blues.' John Altman added: 'Yes, his move away from the pentatonic blues soloing is very obvious there, and totally more so when we played together. One reason why he had to leave the others behind and find new musical companions.' Dorian is a darker mode – parts of The Beatles' 'Eleanor Rigby' are in Dorian. He probably played it intuitively, and he played variations of it in parts of the Stockholm 'Rattlesnake'/'Underway' jam.

Three weeks later, 24 April, at the Roundhouse that darker feel is there near the end of 'Black Magic Woman''s outro shuffle. And on the 'Rattlesnake Shake'/'Underway'/'Fighting For Madge' section, again he flits effortlessly between the very new and old. Naturally, it didn't all suddenly just start in the basement jam. But the Munich jam maybe led to the development of it.

That 'breaking through into something new' would be captured on vinyl with his first solo album *The End Of The Game*.

The next two chapters, 1970: Free Form – Free Festivals and 1970: Studio Time, take a closer look closer at this new-found musical and personal freedom.

22 1970: Free Form – Free Festivals

It is Sunday 3 May – a balmy late evening on England's north-east coast. Half an hour ago a three-hour Mac-on-fire set had ended at Redcar Jazz Club. One of many highlights was Peter, Danny and Mick's percussion break during 'Coming Your Way'. Peter now saunters out of the Coatham Hotel venue, still tapping away on the talking drum he played on stage. He happily chats to a small group of fans and jokes about some hash they'd recently been offered, 'It looked like Christmas cake!'

Some three weeks later he would leave Mac, intent on playing free festivals and jamming with many different musicians. His former bandmates were in shock, and, according to Colin Simmonds in *Rave* June 1970, his friends were worried: 'The coming months will be a testing time for Peter's faith and for the loyalty of his new friends. With the hope that he will succeed with his ideals there is also the fear that they may have served to cloud his view of reality. More than one of his friends and fellow musicians has put forward the view that if Peter's going to find out he was wrong it is best he finds out for himself.' By 'new friends' Simmonds may well have been referring to the Munich commune – which turned out not to be the case.

But three friends who did figure in Peter's new life attended an earlier Fleetwood Mac And Friends Sunday Lyceum charity concert on 12 April: guitarist/violinist Nick Pickett, singer Danny Da Costa and saxophonist John Altman. Nick by then was a good friend. Danny was introduced to Peter after the gig. The year before, aged 17, he released a cover of Cream's 'White Room' on Fly Records. Also Jewish, he remained a supportive friend through future good times and bad. John was a familiar face to Peter from Mac gigs. A fourth notable friend, Nick Buck – keyboardist on Peter's *The End Of The Game* solo album – flew in from America at the end of April.

Nick Pickett walked to the Lyceum gig with Danny Kirwan and Mac's fan club secretary Jane Honeycombe. Nick: 'I met up with Jane and Danny on the south side of the Thames, and the three of us walked north across Waterloo Bridge on the right-hand side. As we neared the Strand end of the bridge Danny held his Gibson Les Paul guitar at arm's length out over the River Thames and said he was going to drop it into the water. Jane and I pleaded with him not to do it, at which point he laughed and pulled his arm back. Was it just a foolish joke, or a sign that he was beginning to feel the strain of working at such high pressure? As the three of us arrived at the Lyceum's front entrance, Peter was pulling up on the opposite side of the road in his two-seater sports car. He stepped out, dressed in a long white robe and no trousers! With his long black hair and beard he looked like a strange prophet.' At the gig Nick and Peter played as a duo called Masterpiece, with Nick on violin. John Altman recalls: 'I had a quick chat with Peter about playing together in the future, and then enjoyed the Mac show.'

Nick Buck flew in from New Orleans on 27 April and stayed at Peter's parents' house in New Malden during the summer. The author interviewed him in summer 2021. He had attended a Jesuit public school in Bournemouth and would head for London and the Marquee to see John Mayall's Bluesbreakers with Peter. Then when Mac played the Whiskey A Go Go in LA in early January 1970, Peter and Nick, who'd met before at the Miami Pop Festival, chatted backstage and the guitarist invited him over to England and later organised a work permit for him. As well as playing on *The End Of The Game* sessions, they gigged as a guitar/keyboards duo, or with other musicians at free festivals and charity events, mostly billed as Peter Green And Friends. Nick, who joined Hot Tuna in 1976, kept a diary of those gigs and *The End Of The Game* studio sessions at De Lane Lea.

Accepting John Altman's earlier invitation, on Saturday 6 June Peter drove Nick Buck and Danny Da Costa down to Brighton to take part in a benefit *happening* being held at Sussex University in Brighton, where John was a student. The benefit was for psychologist, writer and counter-culturist, Dr Timothy 'turn on, tune in, drop out' Leary. John: 'It took place in the debating chamber which was like a Roman amphitheatre in mini. From about six o'clock that evening a whole bunch of people were in there playing bongos and banging beer bottles creating a sort of rhythm section noise. Peter arrived in the afternoon and then we went in and set up, with this farrago of banging, which was quite hypnotic by then because it had been going on for about an hour. Suddenly Jim Capaldi showed up with a drumkit, and bottleneck guitarist Sammy Mitchell played second guitar and we had another student who played bass. We started playing – no tunes were called, it was a bit like *End Of The Game*...Peter started, Sammy would play a solo, I would play a solo and so it went on for eight hours.' Danny also joined in, mostly scatting: 'It was unlike any other gig Peter ever did...like a tribal ceremony...the atmosphere was trance-like.' As John already described in the Introduction, for him and Peter it was a continuous transcendental ideas-exchanging jam – no drinks breaks or musical brakes. And it was only halted by a college porter. John: 'Peter was like, "Oh, let's do this again – give me your number."'

The following Saturday, 13 June, saw Peter join Little Free Rock and Ginger Johnson And His African Drummers for a gig at the Night Angel venue in central London. LFR's guitarist,

Peter Illingworth, recalls the gig: 'Peter at the time was looking into experimenting with different rhythms. The music was much like the LFR set in which we had a basic beginning and end to the songs which left lots of room for improvisation and percussion in the middle. The Drummers was usually Ginger on talking drum, Lord Eric Sugumugu on congas and Shamsi Surami [ex-Alex Harvey Band]. Peter gave me room to play. I rather expected him to take over in some way, yet he was very genteel and we shared guitar licks. He appeared to be in good spirits... he was very enthusiastic about the music we were creating.' Two more gigs – at the Marquee and Lyceum – were planned but then didn't happen. Ginger Johnson's Drummers had joined The Rolling Stones at their 1969 Hyde Park free concert to perform 'Sympathy For The Devil'. Lord Eric Carboo, aka Sugumugu, took part. Lord Eric helped to create the crossover Afro-rock sound when he had the idea of amplifying a marimba and talking drum. Peter did own a drumkit and had been into percussion and African rhythms going way back.

The night after the Night Angel was Peter and Nick's debut as a duo, headlining at the Salisbury Hotel in Barnet, north London, with Peter 'playing from the heart and quite brilliantly at times' (NME 20 June). Nick explained how they improvised: 'A key component is listening, engaging and shaping...really listening to each other and then helping to shape and form and push to another direction and then try to find areas together. This was a time of deep spiritual quest for both of us...that's kind of what it was. And we didn't rehearse – he decided that we should just go out and play.'

But the gig ended with 11 musicians from other bands on the bill joining him for a free-for-all jam. Quiver was one, and the band's then bassist, Bruce Thomas, did not take part – reportedly, he watched in dismay from the back and left after a minute. In his book Rough Notes he recalls subsequently these summer Friends jams had as many as 35–40 musicians playing alongside Peter. Peter Green And Friends then played Kingston Polytechnic on Friday 19 June and then on midsummer Sunday 21 June – a benefit gig for the artists' commune that lived next door to that iconic 1960s R&B hotel venue Eel Pie Island on the River Thames, near Twickenham. Danny Da Costa and Nick Pickett joined Peter and Nick Buck.

The 27 June Bath Festival of Blues and Progressive Music saw Peter back on stage with former bandmates John Mayall and Aynsley Dunbar, and also Ric Grech. In his autobiography *My Life As A Bluesman*, Mayall quotes his publicist, Mike Housego, recalling how just 24 hours before the gig he didn't have a band. He rang Peter who agreed to play, and reportedly Aynsley was recruited at the festival itself – borrowed from Frank Zappa. Changeover delays meant that the band actually got to perform at 5am on the Sunday. Nick Buck: 'Peter and I had planned to play as a duo at night as people were bedding down. But the multiple delays had the show run into dawn and so we didn't get to play. At the festival we talked to many of Peter's fans and you can imagine how excited people were to see him among them. We also chatted with members of Santana and others.' There is a recording of the band's set on YouTube and Peter's solo on 'No Place To Go' (Mayall's song, not Howlin' Wolf's) timeshifts – mostly mid-late 1960s classic bluesman Willie Green but then at times, screamingly, but briefly, he declares his new free-form style.

Peter, Nick and Danny Da Costa then played a free festival in Bromley on 4 July and top of the bill was none other than David Bowie with his short-lived band Hype – an early line-up of The Spiders. The weekend of 10–12 July, Peter and Nick gigged at Lewes Priory, Midland Art Centre and Argyll Hotel, Godalming. The next weekend he played at a free festival in Sheffield Park.

He was then asked to put a band together for the 100 Club benefit night for The National Blues Federation on 24 August. Billed as 'Peter Green, Duster Bennett And Friends', friends included John Altman, The Brunning Sunflower Blues Band, Dave Kelly, Danny Da Costa, and singer Errol Dixon. Danny recalled: 'I improvised melodies and lyrics depending on the flow of the music. I remember John Altman played sax more in a jazz style. We could all join in when we thought it felt right. Peter only gave us signals to end a number.'

Also around then Clifford Davis, who remained Peter's manager, told *Disc* in the 22 August 1970 issue: 'Peter says he plans no more appearances until he's officially formed a new band... In fact he's tired of people claiming he's playing with them or for them.' Curiously he then added: 'He's put down tracks with other people, but won't be using them now. He's very keen to work in public again, but won't be pushed into it.' To boost ticket sales, some festivals did spread false rumours that Peter would be appearing.

In mid September, Peter flew out to the States where he hooked up with Andrew Kastner and his band The Act in South Berwick, Maine. One gig at the Boston Tea Party venue on 12 October was recorded and features Peter often playing in his new free-form style. After that came some meditative chill-out time at Goddard College in Vermont and then on to Los Angeles and, reportedly, seeing Gary Moore's Skid Row at the Whiskey A Go Go.

Then he visited Nick Buck in New Orleans who recalls one evening which may relate to Peter's memory in 1994 about the warlock who played dark mind games with him. Nick: 'Peter, his ladyfriend and me went to visit a friend of hers, Mary Matthews, a descendant of Tabasco inventor Edmund McIlhenny. It was supposed to be an intimate gathering but somebody let slip that Peter would be there. When we arrived there were a lot of people there all wanting to meet him. We smoked and there was some jamming. One guy, not known to any of us and who had "bad energy", glommed onto Peter.' The ladyfriend recalled that on 6 November all three attended an Allman Brothers concert at Tulane University in the city. The next night the band played at the Warehouse during which Peter joined Duane Allman and Dickey Betts on stage for a jam.

Back from America in late November, Peter looked to forming a more permanent band. Initially, this might have been Andy Silvester on bass and drummer Dave Bidwell who both then left Chicken Shack in 1971. But the trio had just one rehearsal at Mac's country house, Benifold. The band he then formed was Alex Dmochowski, Ray Warleigh on sax (who played in Mayall's band on *A Hard Road*), drummer Keith Bailey (ex-Graham Bond Initiation) and singer Charlene Collins. John Altman recalls that they rehearsed for the two gigs booked: the last one of 1970 was at Hampstead's Country Club on 18 December. In 1966 Keith reportedly had turned down Noel Redding's offer to join The Jimi Hendrix Experience. Sadly it was that line-up's last gig together.

Before that on Sunday 13 December was the 'Christmas Spaced' party held by three underground papers, *Oz*, *Friends* and *IT (International Times)* at the Roundhouse, Chalk Farm, when John stood in for Ray Warleigh but was soon thrown off the stage by a Hell's Angel. In his *Altmania* column for student paper *Martlet* he wrote: 'Peter arrives fresh from the States with haircut and shave and looking like he's just stepped off the cover of *A Hard Road*. He's hoping to try out some rehearsed numbers with Alex Dmochowski but only Kwasi "Rocky" Dzidzornu have made it and his set soon becomes a frenzied jam, the stage cluttered with dancers and drummers [Ginger Johnson]. The Angels move in to clear the stage... I deposit my sax and flute back in their cases and venture out front to catch some of Green's guitar, but it's drowned by the sheer density of the drums and Alex Dmochowski's powerful bass. His set is over and he himself is not very happy with how it's gone.' After the gig John recalls having a long conversation with Peter: 'We all went to the bar and spent the evening chatting. Peter was completely normal and very funny at times. This is somebody who was supposedly wiped out in Munich earlier in March... no way!'

It is a pity that the Country Club line-up folded – Dmochowski and Bailey might well have been a great rhythm section for Peter's new style. Bailey went on to focus on jazz drumming and earlier that summer Peter and Alex played so well together on *The End Of The Game*, as detailed in the next chapter.

23 1970: Studio Time

From June through to September 1970 Peter played on sessions for blues pianist Memphis Slim, Peter Bardens, Country Joe McDonald, Dave Kelly, Cliff Bennett's band Toe Fat, and Gass (see Discography). He also played all instruments on manager Clifford Davis's single 'Come On Down And Follow Me' combined with 'Homework', released on 17 July.

While still with Mac, he said his first solo album would feature songs including 'Sandy Mary', and then *NME* reported it might be a double album. A week before he left, *NME* wrote (16 May 1970): 'Between now and 9 June he will be busy in the recording studio completing his own solo album on which he is playing virtually all of the instruments.'

Nick Buck did not recall that being so. According to his diary Peter's first session was on Friday 5 June for the free-form *The End Of The Game* album. The remaining sessions took place on 7 June, 21–22 July, 24–25 July when the actual album was taped, and 30 July. Editing and mixing took place on 27–29 July and 8–9 August.

Peter's views about *The End Of The Game* have changed over time. Harry Shapiro wrote in a career retrospective published in *Record Collector* in August 1993: 'Peter's long-time friend, Snowy White, believes that Peter "…was going in a really interesting direction. I thought his playing was superb on that album. He actually said to me, 'I thought I was getting somewhere', so I said, 'Well, why did you stop?' 'Ah well, this and that...'".'

But in 1994 he said: 'There wasn't enough there. When I was editing it I found out that there wasn't enough to make up a record: it was only free-form.'

Then in 1997 he explained to Cliff Jones for *The Guitar Magazine*'s January 1997 issue: '*End Of The Game* helped a little. It taught me what was and what wasn't possible. I made it as an experiment because I felt restricted. I'm still restricted and I can't learn fast enough to say what I have inside...but I'm learning again. That was the problem in the beginning, I couldn't play the things I heard in my head. It makes you want to give up sometimes. I thought maybe I could get closer to it by doing it that way. I don't think it worked too well.'

But after Splinter Group formed in 1996 he tried to locate the master tapes, and also borrowed the author's copy of his 'Heavy Heart' single. Then from the late 1990s he talked about making another free-form album – or 'form-free' as he often called it. Then in 2008 Peter said: 'I spent a long time afterwards trying to edit those sessions and I'm not sure that I chose the best bits for the finished album. I'd really like to hear all the tapes we recorded again someday.'

The other musicians featured were Nick Buck (electric piano, Hammond organ), Zoot Money (grand piano), Alex Dmochowski (bass) and Godfrey Maclean (drums).

Previously, the timeline for *The End Of The Game* was thought to be a five-hour long into-the-night jam. This came from the Zoot Money interview for this book in 1994. Peter rang him one evening and invited him to the studio later on to have some free-form fun on the grand piano. The date, not then known, was between May and June. He arrived at 10pm, and left around 3am. The 2019 remastered edition's liner notes also mention just a single five-hour session but don't list which musicians played on each of the six tracks. In fact, Zoot Money is on two – 'Descending Scale' and 'Hidden Depth'. Respectively, 8:07 and 4:54 minutes long, and assuming about four hours of jamming, allowing for refreshment breaks, this gives some idea of the editing task involved.

Evidently, Peter tried three free-form approaches. First, percussion and chants together with his guitar – Ginger Johnson And His African Messengers were on the second and final sessions. Nick recalls that on 7 June they played with Peter and possibly Alex, then with the whole band on 30 July.

The second approach was just Peter with Nick on Hammond organ jamming together (21–22 July). The third led to the album and was recorded on 24 July featuring Peter, Nick, Alex and Godfrey, and 25 July night with Zoot. Earlier, that day Danny Kirwan and John Moorshead each played with the studio band but their contributions were not used. Nick: 'I don't remember that much about John Moorshead but Danny was an admirer and a friend of Peter's and the vibe and camaraderie was all there. It was nice.'

The first 7 June Ginger Johnson session was the day after the Brighton marathon jam. Danny Da Costa was also there and remembers bumping into Clifford Chewaluza – aka Mataya Clifford – outside De Lane Lea and they went in together. Danny: 'I was really hungover from the Brighton gig and Sandra [Elsdon] made me some green tea. The others were listening back to tapes.' Clifford was a guitarist but also percussionist who came over from Rhodesia in 1967. Soon after, he was interviewed by *Melody Maker*: 'I was talking to Richard Williams back in 1967 and I say, "I am going to play bad, man, and I don't follow no rules…"' He also played floor drums on Peter's June 1971 'Heavy Heart' single.

The studio atmosphere became far more lively later on, as Nick recalled: 'It was wild with a lot of people coming in and out – about 20 people including Ginger's drummers. I remember at one point the jam turned into a long African chant...really very good with a lot of energy.'

After the Night Angel gig Peter invited Little Free Rock and Ginger Johnson to De Lane Lea. Not listed in Nick's diary, this 15/16 June session, noted in the book *Strange Brew*, might have been for the album. LFR/Johnson gigs with Peter had also been booked for the Marquee and Lyceum later in June. LFR's guitarist Peter Illingworth: 'Peter had arranged a session at De Lane Lea – it was more or less a jam session with the tapes left running. However, on this session several more African drummers who we didn't know arrived and picked up tambourines and cowbells to play along. Naturally, these guys expected session fees. At the end Peter paid everyone and everybody seemed happy. But a day or two later we found out that Ginger was unhappy after the session and felt he should have received all the money and divided it out. Apparently Peter was then harassed for several days and he eventually contacted our manager and said that if Ginger Johnson was doing the Marquee and Lyceum gigs he would not be involved. Peter dropped out and those gigs were cancelled. The LFR relationship with Peter Green ended.'

That session with the uninvited drummers may have been what Peter was referring to back in 1994 when he remembered one Afro-rock session: 'It didn't come together. I felt they were drumming about the power of Africa and not really about the track we were doing at the time.'

Peter's free-form jamming took some getting used to for Martin Birch, according to Nick Pickett, who played violin on one session: 'I went into the control room to ask for something and there was just Martin and the tape operator. He looked at me and said, "What is going on, Nick?" and there were just little tears in the corners of his eyes. He'd recently done "Man Of The World" and "Green Manalishi" and was used to Peter doing structured revolutionary work.

Danny Da Costa was there...I remember him singing, "I hear ya...I hear ya, man".' Now hearing the echo and panning on 'Burnt Foot', for instance, Martin soon adjusted and made a real contribution.

So, of the six album tracks, two feature all five credited players – 'Descending Scale' and 'Hidden Depth' – Nick on organ, Zoot on piano. 'Bottoms Up' has Nick on electric piano with the other three. On 'Timeless Time' and 'Burnt Foot' it's Peter, plus bass and drums, and on the album's title track it's mostly Peter and Godfrey with some bass. Near the end of 'Burnt Foot' (4:28 for ten or so seconds) Godfrey can be heard yelling – Nick Buck said that he did this occasionally. He also said that Peter thought of the track titles.

Released on 20 November, *The End Of The Game* did not chart. Critics were divided – a good indicator of how cutting-edge it was. *Melody Maker*'s Roy Hollingworth (14 November): '...for this is twice as good as anything he ever did with Fleetwood Mac...it's a delight to hear Pete's excellent playing again.' *Record Mirror* (28 November): '...almost jungle rhythmic patterns overlaid by some of the best guitar-playing Peter has ever recorded.' But *Disc* (21 November) thought otherwise: 'Green is undoubtedly a fine guitarist but here seems to be in a void neither advancing nor deteriorating.' December's *Beat Instrumental* stated: 'Sometimes going independent can be a mistake; as far as Green's music is concerned it was a major catastrophe...Even Mr Green's famous guitar technique is not very much in evidence, although it must be said if one takes each individual riff on its own merit then there are one or two nice pieces.' Bruce Thomas in *Rough Notes* described it as, 'heartaching, meandering and lost – speaking of hurt, but punctuated by the occasional explosion of intense luminosity.'

Years later the album impressed and inspired Alabama 3 and their fusion of country, blues, hip hop, electronica and acid rock. The band – whose 1997 track 'Woke Up This Morning' was played during the opening credits of the 1990s TV series *The Sopranos* – listened to it on their tour bus, as Rob Spragg (aka Larry Love) recalled: 'Jake Black and me were discussing Miles Davis's album *In A Silent Way* [1969], and Jake said, "Have you heard Peter Green's *The End Of The Game*?" When I listened to it I thought what he was doing sonically and experimentally wasn't that far off what Miles Davis was doing with *Silent Way*. The sonics on it are wicked.' In 1994, Rob called 'Bottoms Up' prototype techno. 'Rattlesnake Woman' from Alabama 3's 2016 *Blues* album was inspired by 'Rattlesnake Shake'.

One mystery about the sessions is why, after their falling out, Peter invited Ginger Johnson back for the 30 July session.

Regarding his mood in the studio, in 1994 John Moorshead said: 'He was in a corner by himself, very much in his own world. There was hardly any talking, just jamming. Some of it was really good and other bits were not. When I heard the actual album I remember thinking that some of the good stuff had been left off.' Parisian photographer Bruno Ducourant took studio shots on 25 July: 'Peter was friendly and very concerned about what he was doing. He was happy and there was no bad atmosphere.' Zoot Money and Danny Da Costa thought similarly. These good recollections do therefore cast doubt over Nigel Watson's point made in 1994 that Alex put heavy pressure on Peter throughout the making of the album.

That said, the project itself may have put pressure on him: at the mid-July Sheffield Park free festival reportedly he was not in a good frame of mind. And then he did pull out of the National Jazz and Blues Festival at Plumpton on 6–9 August, although a date clash with the second editing session may have had some bearing on this. Towards the end of September he flew out to the States for what was probably a much-needed break.

And judging by a letter Peter wrote to Nick Buck on his return, dated 4 December 1970, that break did him a lot of good. It ends: 'Everyone here has been asking about you and wishing you love. So how are things, Nick? I am slowly finding myself again and feeling much older for my US trip! Hoping to get to work soon, though, duty calls, you know, got to make use of useful things. Peace or War, Peter.'

So, looking to 1971, his mindset was positive and he wanted to make much more music.

24 1971: Turning Points

Had things gone according to plan 1971 might have continued to see changes for the better and more new music – but they did not. On 30 January *NME* reported: 'Peter has scrapped earlier plans for the formation of his new group which did not work out as he had hoped. He is now starting again from scratch and expects to get a new band together in the next few weeks.' That new band might have been Snowy White, Chris Kelly, Nigel or Alex, and Clifford Chewaluza or Rocky Dzidzornu adding percussion.

Ironically, his new band was his old band because, reluctantly, he agreed to help Mac out on their US tour after Jeremy Spencer went AWOL with the Children of God. On 19 February he flew out to LA with travel companion Nigel Watson to join the tour at the Swing Auditorium in San Bernardino.

Peter saved the day and the tour was a success. The band returned to the UK at the end of March. Then Danny Kirwan later told a music weekly on 1 May 1971: 'The dates we did with him were incredible especially after all that time when we weren't playing with him. We changed the running order of numbers doing a few of ours and some of the ones we did when Peter was with us and ended up really just jamming.' They opened with Danny's 'Station Man' at San Bernadino and 'Black Magic Woman' reportedly was the jam finale on most gigs. But the infamous four-hour jam at Fillmore East near the end of the tour actually lasted about half an hour, Peter recalled more recently.

Two years on, Mick Fleetwood told *NME*'s Barbara Charone in the 16 June 1973 issue: 'When Jeremy left, Pete played the American tour with us, it did us a lot of good. Pete didn't want to play any set numbers so we'd just jam. Pete would force us into whatever style he wanted us to play and it jolted us out of our music. A whole set of jamming is quite difficult; with an audience there you've got to be entertaining and not simply self-indulgent.' In 1998 Peter told *20th Century Guitar Magazine*: 'I did not insist on jamming it just happened.' When the tour ended, Peter and Nigel holidayed during April, first staying at Michael Shrieve's Mill Valley home near San Francisco while Santana was on tour. Michael spoke to Peter over the phone from Europe: 'He sounded well and I could hear some partying going on in the background.' They then travelled on to Sacramento, then Nevada and Colorado.

Back in England Peter stayed in Surbiton with Adrian and Lynne Boot. It was through the Boots that he met 'The Lady' (see Chapter 13) – his partner for the next four years. His first solo single, 'Heavy Heart', was released on 11 June, probably taped soon after his return from the US. In the 29 May 1971 issue, Clifford Davis said to *Melody Maker*: 'He told me this is the purest thing he's ever done. It's not a commercial single, but it will mean a lot to people who can identify with it. It's a sad piece.' The article then reports that after the *Top Of The Pops* spot with percussionists Clifford Chewaluza, Chris Kelly and Nigel on bass, he had no plans of going back on the road. In mid-June Peter guested on 'Caldonia', included on the BB King *In London* album.

Friend Maria Zantkuijl from Utrecht visited Peter in early August in Surbiton: 'I was so young and in love! But I do know it was all kind of strange. Peter wasn't paying too much attention to me and my friend. He disappeared with some friends

– I don't know who they were. And he didn't talk about where he went. He was very vague. He had arranged tickets to take me to one of the Proms concerts. But when we went there he became very irritated. I later found out he got the date mixed up and we were at the wrong concert. He just didn't have things together. Despite this and Peter not wanting to stay until the end, it was the highlight of my days there.'

A music press news item in late November reported that Peter had been working in Putney as a 'gravedigger' for the past three months; if that timeline was accurate, then he started work there soon after Maria's visit. In 1994 Peter recalled how the night before he started at Mortlake cemetery he took some Sunshine LSD at the Boots' house – 'I had such a ridiculously good time all night long. When the morning came I came down off it a bit hard'. That was the first thing he mentioned to the author in the first interview back in 1994, adding that his plan back then was to buy a motorbike, visit friends, roll joints and somehow stay on the Sunshine trip. He also mentioned that trip in the *Man Of The World* film: 'I met this chap who had this apartment in Surbiton and there he offered me the famous San Francisco Sunshine – a tablet of Sunshine. I must admit it was great but it was very, very heavy.'

Another 1971 turning point was the New Forest 'adventure'. In 1994 Nigel said it was for three days and mistakenly recalled that it happened in late summer 1972. Danny Da Costa remembers taking his parents along to visit Peter and his parents that summer in 1971, when he first met Nigel. They had moved to Bournemouth to get away from fans who were disrupting home life in New Malden. Danny: 'Peter rang me and said they were catching rabbits with a knife or something like that and every day they would take something. It was hard to connect with him after that, he was very quiet and different – like something had happened to him there and he'd seen too much. His parents also told me that they'd noticed a change.' Nick Pickett was upset when he heard about them killing rabbits: 'Peter was the reason I became a vegetarian. So I was shocked to hear that.'

The late November music press news item began by saying BB King had played in London the previous week (at the Victoria Palace Theatre on 20 November – support was Duster Bennett) and then reported: 'He [BB] would be surprised to learn that Green, who has dropped from sight this year, was in De Lane Lea's new Wembley studios last week laying down material from which a single will be released. Peter is also due to go back and cut some other tracks.' A De Lane Lea studios tape box dated 23 November 1971 lists a working title, 'The Buffalo And The Dog', possibly for the follow-up single to 'Heavy Heart', which ended up being named 'Beasts Of Burden'.

These sessions may have been for a second solo album because Snowy White has one vivid memory from when he went along to a session. Understandably, though, he couldn't recall the date: 'I went to the studio for about the last half hour of the recording session. Peter, Chris Kelly and Alex or Nigel on bass...I can't remember...were having a jam in the studio and when they finished playing Pete said, "Right, that's my last album done then...". He actually mentioned that it was the final record that he owed the record company. And I'm 100 per cent sure that it wasn't *The End Of The Game* because I'd bought that before I first met Pete. That session was just a sort of jam and the record company probably didn't bother to do anything with it.'

So, had 1971 gone according to plan there might have been more focus on Peter forming a more permanent band. But joining the Mac US tour changed all that. During their West Coast holiday afterwards, Nigel and Peter stayed in Sacramento with a half-Native American, Hank, who taught them about survival out in the wild. This hook-up inspired Nigel's 'Beasts Of Burden' song but maybe also their New Forest idea.

The aforementioned late November article also included an

interview with Bob Brunning and his wife. Peter had recently visited them, arriving on his motorbike and wearing labourers' clothes. Bob: 'He's always been very kind and people have abused his good nature. He's played on so many records as a favour. For the last year, in fact, he didn't want to play with Fleetwood Mac but he did to help them out...'.

Bob's wife then remarked: 'He's questioning the validity of everything, even the spoken word. It's terribly sad because he's a very bright person. He says he can't trust anyone and he's thinking that the only thing that has real meaning is violence.' The piece ends with Bob saying he was about to quit his gardening job partly because the local authorities refused to allow him to dig graves.

It is beyond saddening to go back just one year to December 1970 and the letter Peter wrote to Nick Buck, and the positive 'duty calls' musician he was, all set to 'make use of useful things'. What happened? As described by Nigel in 1994, the New Forest escapade sounded like an adventure. But as things turned out, misadventure might be the right word to describe it.

25 1972–75: Revisited

In May 1972 there were hopes that Peter might return to performing, encouraged by his friend, ex-Mayall bassist Steve Thompson, who joined Stone The Crows in 1971. He had been friendly with Peter ever since, aged 16, he became a roadie for John Mayall's Bluesbreakers while Peter was with them. In a 2005 interview with the author, Steve recalled: 'Peter and John McVie took me and bought me my first bass. I used to sleep on Peter's floor at Porchester Road until I took over his flat. A few months after Peter left, I left [Mayall] to learn how to play bass.' They became good friends – in time Peter would gift Steve his treasured Fender VI bass, and he was best man at Peter's 4 January 1978 wedding in LA. Steve: 'I'd moved into a flat in Hampstead in 1972 and on and off he used to come and stay for a couple of weeks and sleep on the couch and then disappear and then come back again. I lived there for six years, you see.'

After STC's guitarist Les Harvey's tragic death on 3 May, where he was electrocuted on stage in Swansea, Steve wondered if Peter might consider joining them in time for their May Bank Holiday gig at Lincoln's Great Western Express Festival. STC and ex-Bluesbreakers' drummer Colin Allen writes in his 2018 autobiography: 'I was thinking, "Leslie has died but Peter could be reborn".' Then in 2021 Colin told the author: 'We had all heard the stories, but didn't have any preconceptions about how he might be – we needed a guitarist and Greenie was a hell of a player.' STC singer Maggie Bell remembers Peter looking very healthy.

Rehearsals began, but then when a roadie went to pick him up for the fifth day – as Colin remembers it – Peter said he wasn't coming, telling the driver, 'This band is going to be big and I want no part of that' or words to that effect. Colin: 'We were all disappointed he backed out – he was playing really well. On reflection, I'm not sure he ever intended to join the band – as with guesting with the British Blues All-Stars at Notodden – in my opinion he wasn't so interested in playing for the public but mainly wanted to hang out with other musicians and rehearsing was one way of doing that.'

Maggie Bell then spoke to *Disc*'s Andrew Tyler for the 5 August issue: 'I don't want to carry on any bad feelings as far as Peter Green is concerned, it's just that the boy didn't feel that he wanted to play in front of an audience, but Steve Howe [who then joined] did an incredible job.' Tyler added: '...and Pete Green suddenly took off for Israel [to work on Kibbutz Mishmarot] announcing to friends that he had no intention of joining the Crows or any other band.'

Peter's parents moved back to New Malden around autumn 1972, as Nick Pickett recalls: 'Peter's parents didn't settle in Bournemouth and they came back to live in another house in New Malden near Coombe Gardens. I went to visit them – I didn't go to visit Peter. We talked for a long time. I tried not to mention him because I knew he was having a lot of difficulties. Then when it was time to go, I thought, "Well, I can't go and not mention Peter at all", so I said, "Have you seen Peter – how is he?" and his dad said, "He's upstairs – but he won't come down...". I was upset by that because I'd been sitting there for a couple of hours and the man that I loved was upstairs and couldn't face anybody.'

But in late autumn Peter was up north and staying with a friend in Leeds. While there he went to see the Bob Weston and Dave Walker Mac line-up at Leeds Polytechnic on 24 November. Fifty years on, unprompted he still recalled that gig to the author, and how embarrassed he felt when during Mac's set his impulsive friend decided to be Mac's self-appointed conga player – John McVie promptly 'escorted' him off the stage.

Health issues still prevailed and then it was his partner, The Lady, and musician friends who were there for him.

One such good friend was Andy Silvester. In 1972 Andy moved into the ground floor of a Victorian detached house in Ealing. Peter visited from time to time. Andy had joined Savoy Brown by then and remembers well one such visit when it was Peter Green, talented drummer, who impressed him: 'He often used to come over to see me from New Malden. I'd bought a drumkit off him and some amps and stuff. I'd got the drumkit set up in the large front room. I also had a Revox tape recorder in there. It was probably the first time he'd seen his kit set up for ages. First we played a guitar instrumental together – a version of Junior Walker's "Roadrunner", and then he put a hi-hat and snare on it. And then there was another instrumental track that I played him – it was a riff and chord sequence I'd recorded with a drum machine…Peter liked it and suggested overdubbing drums on it, which he did – the drumming was absolutely wonderful… so punchy and he really drove it, he did. When we started recording I got the mic quite close to the kit and he said, "No, no – put the mic further away"…so I put it further away and he said, "No, put it right back". I said we wouldn't get much of a signal, but he was right. It sounded fantastic… much more ambient, which brought the bass drum out a treat. A few days later Dave Walker came over and wrote some lyrics. He overdubbed his voice and we called the track "Hard

Headed Woman".' Peter's drumming can be heard on Clifford Davis's single 'Come On Down And Follow Me' combined with 'Homework' and also 'Crane's 'Train Boogie' – a track from the 1983 Katmandu album.

Then, in early 1973 he visited Mac at Benifold and delivered a melodic 'echoey' but uncredited first-take solo on 'Nightwatch' for the band's *Penguin* album. Steve Thompson had also kept in touch with Peter, and after Stone The Crows split in late May 1973 they holidayed together: 'I think it was just after I left Stone The Crows we went off on a trip to California and then Barbados and I tried to cheer him up there but that didn't work out either. I knew he was very ill but I just didn't know how to deal with mental illness.'

The pair evidently stopped off at Hawaii, because in the *Man Of The World* DVD bonus features Clifford Davis reads out a letter that Peter sent him from Honolulu. In it again he asked Clifford and Peter's accountant to forward all his royalties to the War On Want charity. Only then, he wrote, would he find peace of mind. He wrote about a jam session he was going to where if he was skint he could really let go. Instead he felt like a 'derelict pop money star'.

Bewilderingly, a news item in the 23 June 1973 issue of *Melody Maker*, titled 'Peter Green Returns To Recording', announced that he'd signed a recording contract with Clifford Davis Productions, Clifford Davis's company: 'Green, who was employed as a gravedigger for over a year, will record six albums over the next three years. He will pick his own musicians as necessary for the recording, rather than retain a full-time band. There are no plans for live appearances. The first album under the new contract is set for release during the summer. Titled "Out Of Reach" it is a collection of previously unreleased tracks Green recorded up to two years ago. The bulk of the material is recorded live. Danny Kirwen [sic] the guitarist who took over from Green, has signed a similar contract to put out six albums over the next three years. He is to start recording in a month's time. Both guitarists will be with Warner Bros.'

In fact, Danny would release three albums with DJM Records between 1975 and 1979 and Peter signed with PVK for four in 1977.

However, some of the mentioned 'Out Of Reach' collection might refer to the 1971 'Heavy Heart' and November 'Beasts Of Burden' Wembley De Lane Lea sessions. Are the tapes still lying somewhere in the Warner Bros. vaults? Probably not.

After the US/Hawaii/Barbados break in the summer, from 1973 through to 1977 came the ECT, hospitalisation, misinformation about the so-called 'Shotgun Incident', a court case, prison and more hospitalisation.

Interestingly, *The Albatross Man*, Mark Blake's essay, plus a letter from harmonica maestro, composer of 'Jumping At Shadows' and one-man-blues band Duster Bennett, reveal that Peter did at least try to keep making music during that difficult time.

Mark Blake writes that in autumn 1974 ex-Free and Back Street Crawler's guitarist, Paul Kossoff, had booked a rehearsal studio for three hours and invited Peter along to join in with ex-Spooky Tooth drummer Mike Kellie. In 2016 Kellie told Mark that the jamming went well but then Peter abruptly left after an hour.

Duster and Peter had been Blue Horizon label mates (see Discography Part 2). His letter is dated 18 October 1975, which was shortly after Peter's 6 September wedding to The Lady was called off. Peter apparently was looking for a new house but also looking for a drummer. Duster wrote that he could put him in touch with someone he'd been playing with – possibly, this was bassist/drummer Richard Ford from Duster's Thirty Days project with Keith Randall.

The second half of 1976 saw Peter visiting a girl in Canada. En route to the airport for his return flight he bought a pump-action .22 fairground rifle. He could not have known the bother this impulse buy would cause him in the weeks and months to come (see Chapter 14).

26 *In The Skies* & *Little Dreamer*

After his January 1977 'Shotgun Incident' court appearance and
having spent six weeks in Brixton prison under observation for
tests, Peter was again hospitalised at Epsom. A year later he
told the *News Of The World* (26 February 1978): 'I had no
hard times at the prison but it was different at the hospital. It
was fine at first. For three weeks I ate, made friends, played
table tennis and didn't have any treatment. But the staff want
to treat you. They want to see something wrong with you. So
they gave me injections of tranquillisers that made me feel
melancholy. You go about like a dead body all day. I had two
months and it was driving me round the bend. Then I trans-
ferred to a private hospital.' Danny Da Costa visited him in
prison and Horton Hospital in Epsom and found him heavily
sedated, chain-smoking and withdrawn. Danny: 'It was heart-
breaking and in the end I just couldn't take seeing him like that
just staring into space.' A loyal friend for some seven years,
Danny lost contact after that. After being moved to the Priory
private clinic Peter responded better to treatment but was still
ill. Then it was brother Michael and PVK label boss Peter
Vernon-Kell who helped and encouraged him to return to
making music.

Some tracks on *In The Skies* were the product of studio
jams, as Snowy White explained: 'On "Funky Chunk" Kuma
[Harada] came up with that bass – it's a nice bass line, I

remember that. And then we gradually worked our way into it. That's what happens with any jam. I think Reg started playing the groove and Kuma started playing the bass line. Peter then started and I came up with something that didn't get in the way. And that was the jam.' Sessions took place in autumn 1977: some were pre-production but still recorded, and then sessions where chosen tracks were completed. On 'Slabo Day' that hypnotic chord progression came to Peter, and then Snowy played lead over it. He preferred his soloing from an earlier rehearsal session – this is on his 1995 *Goldtop* album, as is an instrumental take of 'In The Skies' with Peter's rhythm guitar nicely up in the mix.

Interviewed again in 2016, producer Peter VK recalled: 'When we went over to LA for the Warner Bros. meeting, we hadn't finished the album and they hadn't heard it – they'd heard it was good though.' Steve Thompson was surprised by Peter's arrival in LA later that autumn: 'I had no idea Peter and Jane had kept in contact after meeting at my flat back in 1972. I moved to America in 1977 to play with John Mayall and, lo and behold, Peter arrives and says, "Oh, I'm marrying Jane and would you be my best man?" Jane was the wedding organiser in every respect. After that of course he stayed in LA and I took him out a lot just to cheer him up because he was so down.'

In LA Peter had joined Jane in the Jews For Jesus organisation and the words for 'Seven Stars' are based on the New Testament's *Book of Revelation*. Peter was really pleased with the end-of-verse turnaround riff and once told the author that co-writing it was a happy time for them both.

Peter VK recalls returning to the US after the wedding to finish the album: 'When I went the second time Peter had slipped back. I didn't dislike or like Jane – we got on well enough – but she did smoke and that wasn't what Peter needed.' Substances were also copiously on offer when Peter guested on 'Brown

Eyes' from Mac's 1979 *Tusk* album. This infuriated Peter VK who stepped in whenever he could.

Little Dreamer was made in Surrey in late 1979 and released in April 1980 – reaching Number 31 in the UK. In 1994 brother Michael said Peter kept humming the title track's melody and so he suggested that they record it. Staying with musician friend Kris Gray, he listened to 'Little Dreamer' a lot, slept a lot, and made weekly phone calls to America to find out how his daughter Rosebud was. The lyrics are repeated three times: 'Dear sleep... Dear sleep...A tender sleep...Tonight'. But then in the final half-minute golden slumbers are disturbed by what sounds like thunder – that inescapable morning call from harsh reality. Two questions spring to mind – first, is the track in fact a lullaby dedicated to sleep itself; and second, who was the little dreamer?

It's extraordinary how such a serene and mystical melody came to him after such a traumatic time in LA – a failed marriage and the painful separation from his daughter that followed. Even at his lowest ebb the creative spark did not abandon him.

27 1981–85: White Sky & Kolors

Spring 1981 saw Peter guesting on Mick Fleetwood's *The Visitor* solo album, recorded with musicians in Ghana and overdubs done at Jimmy Page's Sol Studios in Cookham, Surrey. Peter in 2008: 'I was happy to be recording...dubbing on Mick Fleetwood's *Visitor* album. It was a fabulous studio out in the country – there was a water wheel there. And at night you could sleep over there and we did stay for a few days I think. Mick was there most of the time and I got to develop my playing as I was there – I had time to develop my playing. I was playing with a dark red Guild guitar, not a Les Paul or Fender Stratocaster.' He played on two tracks: an instrumental, 'Super Brains', and a fresh arrangement of 'Rattlesnake Shake' featuring an Afro-chant outro that really works. His voice sounds strong and he added some new guitar ideas in between the original riffs. Mick Fleetwood: 'We had a really good time. He was objective, he was a lot better than I'd seen him for years.' Then in May his fourth PVK album, *White Sky*, was recorded at Ridge Studios in Surrey, which Peter co-produced and, as Ronnie Johnson recalled, on good days he was playing extremely well.

And yet, just six months later came those notorious London pub gigs that broke many Green devotees' hearts. Mark Ellen reviewed the 27 November Golden Lion gig for the *NME*: '[Peter] stared awkwardly at his fretboard, his scuffed fingers fiddling at the controls, as if even the most basic elements of his craft had forsaken him.' Nick Pickett recalls his guitar being totally out of tune for the opener, 'Black Magic Woman'. He left after a few minutes. Clearly this was one of Peter's bad health days, because fast-forward just six or so weeks to White Sky's London gig at The Venue and Mick Brown in *The Guardian* (18 January 1982) wrote of 'enough craftsmanship' and 'glimpses of the old skills to make one optimistic about Green's renaissance'.

George Clinton interviewed Peter at his Richmond terrace for *Guitar*'s September 1981 issue and asked him if he fancied touring or giving a concert: 'No, but if I had a good offer to join a band I wouldn't turn it down. I wouldn't mind joining a reggae band – but black music. It could be anything so long as it's different, I'd have a crack at it. A lot of people suggest I give a concert somewhere. But one gig is no good to me. I've got to be able to loosen up, get into it, build up a following: build up a rapport with the audience so that I can get to know myself again.' He then went on to mention his ongoing health problems which sometimes strained his relationships with friends and family. He was far from well. And, as Kris Gray mentioned in 1994, when he visited him in Richmond, there was a lot of smoking going on.

That summer, bassist Gregg Brown was introduced to Peter by Reg Isadore – drummer on *White Sky* and *In The Skies*. Gregg: 'He used to come over to mine and he'd pick up my guitar and have a little tinkle. We talked about the blues and listened to reggae and African music. Then he asked me to put a band together for him. That band was Peter, Peter Bardens, Reg and Gus Isadore, myself and Jeff Whittaker. We had a couple of rehearsals. We called this band The Bomb partly because it sounded like the end of Greenbaum and also "the bomb" was slang for "cool" or "it's happening". The first gig we did was in Southampton.' In the *Guitar* interview Peter mentioned Gregg: 'I've got a friend called Greg [sic], an American guy, he comes round with his bass and we have a little play if he wants to. Danny Kirwen [sic] came around the other week and the three of us were playing.' *Was that enjoyable?* 'Oh, yes.' After The Bomb's 2 October debut at the Stowaways venue, local press reported: '...most of the set consisted of uninspiring pieces of funk from the Isadore pen or from Green's latter PVK albums and what with tuning problems and clear signs of insufficient rehearsal there were plenty of low spots: "Me and my baby getting it together, yeah, hey, why aren't you clapping?"'...'There were a couple of thrills as well, in the form of Black Magic Woman and everyone's favourite Need Your Love So Bad, featuring Green actually singing and playing as everyone remembered, over a gorgeous silky Hammondesque foundation laid down by Peter Bardens.'

Bardens soon left. Here's Gregg's take on the review: 'That was Greenie's first live gig since leaving the Priory. He didn't want all the spotlight so Gus and I sang a few songs totally out of context to what Greenie was doing. As I delved more into Peter's material the song choice and the sound got better.'

Gus Isadore (ex-Marc Bolan, Camel and Seal) enjoyed the gigs: 'He [Peter] was together...together enough to play. He, like, let everybody else shine and then had his moments when he really shone. He liked me and I could just feel this warmth from him.'

The Bomb morphed into White Sky. Gregg: 'Peter's brother Michael wrote most of the songs for the *White Sky* album [released 1 June 1982]. I was asked to put a band together to do gigs playing music from it and called White Sky. That band was Jeff Whittaker (congas), Ronnie Telemaque (ex-Equals on drums), Webster Johnson (keyboards) and Carlos Morela (guitar) and one of the first gigs we played was January 1982 at The Venue in London, which got good reviews.' Photographer Julian Swainson was there: 'Peter came on with a backing group of black musicians who were very sharp and capable, and clearly well-rehearsed on the Fleetwood Mac back catalogue. Peter himself showed flashes of the emotional power that made him and Fleetwood Mac so famous originally, but he also looked bewildered and unsure of why he was there or what he was doing. The band appeared to have been primed to deal with this uncertainty.' From then on Jeff gradually became Peter's manager. Acute hearing issues led to Gregg leaving, and Jeff soon broke up White Sky. But it was Gregg who helped Peter to return to performing. They remained good friends and later did some recording together.

The first Kolors line-up reportedly was guitarist Stephan Rene, drummer Godfrey Maclean, bassist Larry Steele or Durban Laverde, keyboardist Emmanuel Rentzos, Alan Barnes on piano/vocals, Jeff and Peter. In 1994 Jeff recalled that their debut was midsummer's day 1982 on the Dom Plaza in front of Cologne Cathedral. Peter and Emmanuel became friends: 'I used to bring him down to my house. He liked wearing the African gowns, the big ones. I had a few which I didn't wear very much so I gave them to him and he was very chuffed with them. And there was one meal which he liked so much which was fried plantain with black eyed peas...and he liked his coffee. He loved my children and my wife too.' His interest in African music and culture was lifelong – his house in Canvey had several African *objet d'art* on display.

In the video for live music TV show *Rockpalast*'s 4 December 1982 gig in Germany, Peter is wearing red headgear. His singing is hit and miss but his playing is fluent despite the long fingernails. Audience reaction is good. By June 1983 Mick Weaver was on keyboards. Bela Swardmark Stephens, from Swedish blues band The Blue Pearls, attended gigs in Stockholm and Gothenburg. Bela: 'He played beautifully on his "Supernatural" though and showed that he's still got the touch. I was under the impression that he would have felt better and consequently played much better with other musicians around him.' On 28 November 1983 Kolors played London's Dominion Theatre and marked the start of the end because, according to Jeff, the band members were losing interest.

A chance meeting that Christmas between Jeff and Ray Dorset led to the Katmandu *A Case For The Blues* project in early 1984, recorded at Ray's Satellite Studios. Peter enjoyed working with Vincent Crane, the ex-Arthur Brown and Atomic Rooster keyboardist and composer of the single 'Fire'. There was even talk of Peter, Ray and Vincent forming a band: tragically, Vincent took his own life in 1989. A favourite of Peter's, 'Who's That Knocking?', took shape during a jam. Drummer Greg Terry-Short would join the last Kolors line-up, along with Ghanaian guitarist Alfred Bannerman (ex-Hugh Masekela) and keyboardist Emmanuel Rentzos.

Bassist Willie Bath's (ex-Jackie Lynton Band) first gig was in Stockholm on 22 August 1984. Alfred also joined around then. Alfred: 'At rehearsals Peter would say things like, "Don't play that off the shelf!"...meaning don't copy my old solo, do something creative. And he'd say, "Don't force it". We agreed that I would play nearly all the lead lines and Peter would play rhythm, and sing. He was always gently listening and sometimes he'd play a phrase and the feeling he put behind the notes – the sensitivity that he had. And that was a good thing for me...I liked to hear that. We did a gig in Sweden and his fans came. But at the end some of them were angry that I wore my African Ghanaian costume. They were disappointed that their hero didn't play that many solos.'

A good quality recording of a 13 December 1984 gig in Germany is posted on YouTube (Peter Green & Kolors @ Sinkkasten). Alfred, with occasional stinging vibrato, solos impressively. On 'Proud Pinto' his guitar is well-attuned to Peter's playing, and in parts they duet in unison. Oddly, Jeff introduces the band near the end by saying Peter is on lead guitar and Alfred on second guitar. 'Green Manalishi' and 'Need Your Love So Bad' find Peter's voice strong and judging by some between-numbers chat he was enjoying himself. Willie Bath: 'At this Sinkkasten place you can hear on the live recording the audience is absolutely beside themselves with joy. The band always went down really well which was why we were asked on the day of Live Aid, 13 July 1985, to play at Dingwalls in Camden, London, to do Club Aid. That night featured the bands that had proved most popular at Dingwalls and we were one of them and we went down great.' It was billed as The Alternative Live Aid Benefit.

The band toured Europe and Scandinavia during the first half of 1985 and the final gig came on their second visit to Tel Aviv on 8 August 1985 when Kolors played one of three scheduled gigs at the Ramat Gan Stadium. Willie recalls how that was not the only gig for which they didn't get paid. On their return to England the band went their separate ways.

The Kolors era will always be controversial but it is plainly wrong to typify it by those late 1981 London pub gigs or, for that matter, Jeff Whittaker's misleading perspective about band members' motives given in 1994 (see Chapter 19). One commenter on YouTube described walking out of a 1984 gig in tears. But a Green devotee who saw Kolors in 1982 remembers still hearing that signature Peter Green tone and blue feeling intact.

In 1994 Peter recalled that he was 'over-encouraged' to perform again, but in 1981 seemingly he was open to the idea. Had the last Kolors line-up stayed together, travel and being among musician friends holistically would have been far better than the isolated, bleak years that followed in Richmond in the late 1980s. Thankfully, eldest brother Len (who sadly passed in 2008) and his wife Gloria stepped in and then helped him on his gradual road to recovery: he lived with them first in Gorleston near Great Yarmouth, and then Leigh-on-Sea near Southend.

28 The London Palladium
All-Star Tribute

Luckily, fate placed the 25 February 2020 Before The Beginning All-Star Tribute To Peter Green concert very shortly before the Covid-19 pandemic and lockdown. It was also just five months before Peter's untimely passing. So, the massive task of bringing that show to the stage turned out to be Mick Fleetwood's parting thank-you gift to his old friend and mentor. Peter didn't attend but brother Michael and friend Paul Hoenderkamp did, so he got to know all about it.

The planning began some two years before the event when the house band was formed. This comprised Jonny Lang, Dave Bronze, Zak Starkey, Mick Fleetwood, Andy Fairweather Low and Ricky Peterson, who has played keyboards for the latest Fleetwood Mac and was a producer for Prince.

Andy takes up the story: 'They didn't have a list of people then. Ricky was officially MD but we all came with knowledge of the songs and what to play, and what to do. Also Rick Vito wasn't involved at that point and I said to Glyn Johns, who was the producer, "You've got to get Rick – he can do the whole thing". Glyn said, "Well you can do all those things you can do…" and I said, "No…I've seen him with Mick's Blues Band, and he's your man". Luckily, we got him – because he could do *everybody* at the rehearsals; he knew it all inside out.

'So we flew out to Hawaii and to a five-star hotel on the

beach. Mick's band there were unbelievably supportive – any gadgets we needed they got for us. At the first rehearsal up in the hills theyre saying Kirk's coming in today. And I thought, "Metallica? Heavy Metal?" and then Kirk arrives looking beamingly healthy and he arrives with Peter's Les Paul. Of course, everybody wanted to give it a play. And I remember Kirk did say that "Green Manalishi" was Metallica's "in" to Peter's music. Mick choosing Noel Gallagher was another surprise for me but Mick said, "Yeah, he's really into Peter and before every gig he sits and plays 'The World Keep On Turning'." When I heard him sing it I was impressed with him and his attitude. Dave Gilmour's name came up. Joe from Mick's Hawaii band put together an end section for "Oh Well Part 2" that we routined and sent to Dave. He then recorded his version of it and returned it, which we then learned. Jonny Lang, he took "Need Your Love So Bad" and made it his. I loved "Stop Messin' Round" with Christine – again, Rick did it so well. One time, playing "Doctor Brown" I pointed my finger at Mick and said, "King of the shuffle...". There's nobody can do that – it's that full-on commitment. Jeremy with Bill Wyman on "The Sky Is Crying" was just fabulous.

'The London rehearsals were at Music Bank in Bermondsey. John Mayall – I played on John's 70th anniversary. He turned up looking a bit frail, then I didn't see him again until I'm on stage and someone says "John Mayall!", and out bursts this man like a teenager. If you see the DVD you can see him just bounding on. Once he put the John Mayall persona on – look out...he's dropped at least 20 years. 'Station Man' wasn't on the original list but Pete wanted it and he did it really well. But that song was a nightmare for me with all the sections and changes. So we had a day off to think about it...and we still had to think about it right to the very end. I'd met Zak when he was young with his mum and dad – Ringo was a fan of *La Booga Rooga* [1975]. Zak is a true fan of Peter's. And Glyn

Johns...I called into the studio the day after the concert. Glyn is used to three mics on a drumkit but Mick has many more than that – plus all the guitars. Glyn got Ryan Ulyate in to help him and, boy, did he have a job on his hands – but the end result was fantastic.

'Looking back at that night, the rehearsals were the fabulous times – the gig was, "Be on your toes, be respectful and get on with it". Three weeks in Hawaii and three weeks in Music Bank playing Peter's music – finally getting that picture and the right amount of respect for him...an absolute joy.'

'Oh Well Part 1' featured Billy Gibbons with Steven Tyler sharing vocals and on harp. Before performing it Billy Gibbons stepped up to the microphone: 'I gotta say one of the reasons I'm up here is when I started off I learned from the best. And tonight we're definitely celebrating the best – you know what I'm sayin'? Thank you Mick Fleetwood, thank you for the early years of Fleetwood Mac.'

Epilogue

There are many telling images of Peter Green, performer, tracing his 73 years and nine-month journey in this world: The Intense Young Bluesman, The Rock God, The Ancient Prophet dressed in flowing robes, The Bearded Rasta.

But the stage image that I now keep front-of-mind is much more recent and sees him fronting Peter Green And Friends. He's sat on a high bar stool, joking with his audience and radiating a Zen-like peaceful energy. He had that same demeanour in summer 2017 in his back garden when something extraordinary happened.

Having been lucky enough to hear him practice and try out new ideas many times before, I'd noticed how phrases would sometimes come to him that perfectly echoed Pete Green back in the day.

This one time was different though. Sat out in the sun, he'd asked me to put new strings on a nylon-string classical guitar of his, while he then checked out a 1960s Framus parlour guitar I'd brought with me to show him.

While I was focusing on my task, suddenly he began to play repeatedly, fingerstyle, an original minor chord progression lasting, from memory, about ten seconds. It involved intricate picking – Davy Graham, Bert Jansch-level intricate – but each sequence mirrored *exactly* the one before. It was as if the music was on a loop tape.

By now I was transfixed and adrenaline was flowing. After a minute or so he stopped. Breaking a brief silence, I said something perfectly inadequate like, 'That was amazing, Peter,' but I was actually feeling a bit shaky. So I went indoors and sat on my own for a few minutes to reflect on what I'd just heard.

Before leaving the next day, Sunday, I enthused again about his playing the day before. Typically, on hearing my compliments at first he looked askance, but then after a short pause remarked, 'But I know what you mean...'.

His unique gift sometimes faded – especially when health issues set in – but somehow always eventually returned, and did so revealing subtle but meaningful changes.

Singer and writer Daliah Sherrington echoed this in her *Jewish Chronicle* tribute (21 August 2020) recalling a Peter Green And Friends performance at the Secret Garden Party festival in Huntingdon on 26 July 2009. The concluding part of the article serves as a fitting eulogy with which to end this book:

'Green fundamentally shaped the British Blues Explosion of the 1960s and it is no surprise that BB King claimed he was – "the only one to give me the cold sweats". Perhaps because, like his Mississippi Delta blues heroes, he was able to understand the pain of the outsider, this poor boy from Bethnal Green interpreted those mournful tones with a truthfulness that allowed emotion to pour from his fingertips. That quality was still there when I witnessed Green's festival performance. It was as if all the mental anguish he had endured only served to raise his playing. His guitar rang out with a subtle passion that seemed to override the tragedy of his wasted years.'

Peter Green is survived by daughter Rosebud from his brief marriage to Jane Samuels, and son Liam Firlej from a relationship with Liam's mother, Janina.

DISCOGRAPHY

BY MARIO PIRRONE AND RJ GREAVES

PART 1 OFFICIAL RECORDS
Solo Works

45 Singles
'Heavy Heart'/'No Way Out' (Reprise RS27012) 1971
'Beasts Of Burden'/'Uganda Woman' (Reprise K14141) 1972
'The Apostle'/'Tribal Dance' (PVK Pv 16) 1978
'In The Skies'/'Proud Pinto' (PVK Pv 24) 1979
'Walkin' The Road'/'Woman Don't' (PVK Pv 36) 1980
'Loser Two Times'/'Momma Don'tcha Cry' (PVK Pv 41) 1980
'Give Me Back My Freedom'/'Lost My Love' (PVK Pv 103) 1981
'Promised Land'/'Bizzy Lizzy' (PVK Pv 112) 1981
'The Clown'/'Time For Me To Go' (Headline Lin 2) 1982

Albums
The End Of The Game (Reprise RSLP 9006) 1970
In The Skies (PVK PVLS 101) 1979
In The Skies (PVK PVLS 101 Limited Ed. Green Vinyl) 1979
Little Dreamer (PVK PVLS 102) 1980
Whatcha Gonna Do (PVK PET 1) 1981
Blue Guitar (Creole CRX 5) 1981
Blue Guitar (Creole CRX 5 Limited Ed. Blue Vinyl) 1981
White Sky (Headline HED 1) 1982
Kolors (Headline HED 2) 1983
Katmandu/*A Case For The Blues* (Nightflite NTFL 2001) 1986
Legend (Creole CRX 12) 1988

Group Works
THE PETER B'S

45 Singles
'If You Wanna Be Happy'/'Jodrell Blues' (Columbia DB7862) 1966

JOHN MAYALL AND THE BLUESBREAKERS

45 Singles
'Looking Back'/'So Many Roads' (Decca F12506) 1966
'Sitting In The Rain'/'Out Of Reach' (Decca F12545) 1966
Bluesbreakers With Paul Butterfield EP (Decca DFe-R 8673) 1966
'Curly'/'Rubber Duck' (Decca F12588) 1967
'Double Trouble'/'It Hurts Me Too'* (Decca F12621) 1967
*An alternate mix including Mayall's piano is available on the
    compilation *Looking Back* (Decca SKL 5010) 1969

Albums
A Hard Road (Decca SKL 4853) 1967
Live At The BBC (Decca 984465-5) 2007
Live In 1967 (Forty Below FBR 008) 2015
Live In 1967 – Volume Two (Forty Below FBR 013) 2016

FLEETWOOD MAC

45 Singles
'I Believe My Time Ain't Long'/'Rambling Pony' (BH 3051) 1967
'Black Magic Woman'/'The Sun Is Shining' (BH 57-3138) 1968
'Need Your Love So Bad'/'Stop Messin' Round' (BH 57-3139) 1968
'Albatross'/'Jigsaw Puzzle Blues' (BH 57-3145) 1968
'Man Of The World'/'Somebody's Gonna Get Their Head Kicked In
    Tonite' (Earl Vince And The Valiants) (Immediate IM 080) 1969
'Need Your Love So Bad'/'No Place To Go' (BH 57-3157) 1969
'Oh Well Part 1'/'Oh Well Part 2' (Reprise RS 27000) 1969
'The Green Manalishi (With The Two Prong Crown)'/'World In
    Harmony' (Reprise RS 27007) 1970

Albums
Peter Green's Fleetwood Mac (BH 7-63200) 1968
Mr. Wonderful (BH 7-63205) 1968
English Rose (CBS 22025) 1969
Pious Bird Of Good Omen (compilation BH 7-63215) 1969
Then Play On (Reprise RS LP 9000) 1969
Blues Jam At Chess (BH 7-66227 double) 1969
The Original Fleetwood Mac (CBS 63875) 1971
Greatest Hits (compilation CBS 69011) 1971
Live In Boston (Shanghai HAI 107) 1984

Cerulean (Shanghai HAI 300 double) 1985
Live At The BBC (Castle EDF CD 297) 1995
Shrine 69 (Rykodisc RCD 10424) 1999

Splinter Group

Albums

Peter Green Splinter Group (Artisan SARCD 101) 1997
The Robert Johnson Songbook (Artisan SARCD 002) 1998
Destiny Road (Artisan SMACD 817) 1999
Soho Session Live At Ronnie Scott's (Limited Ed. Artisan SDDCD 816) 1999
Hot Foot Powder (Snapper SMACD 828) 2000
Time Traders (Eagle EAGCD 193) 2001
Blues Don't Change (Eagle EAGCD 200) 2001
The Best Of Peter Green Splinter Group (compilation Snapper SMADD 849) 2002
Reaching The Cold 100 (Eagle EAGCD224) 2003

PART 2 GUEST APPEARANCES SINGLES/ALBUMS

45 Singles

EDDIE BOYD AND HIS BLUES BAND

'Empty Arms'/'So Miserable To Be Alone' (BH 1009) 1967

JOHN MAYALL

'Jenny'/'Picture On The Wall' (Decca F 12732) 1968

EDDIE BOYD

'The Big Boat'/'Sent For You Yesterday And Here You Come Today' (BH 57-3137) 1968

OTIS SPANN

'Walkin''/'Temperature Is Rising' (98.8°F)' (BH 57-3155) 1969
'Blues For Hippies'/'Bloody Murder' – Side A only (Excello EX 2329) 1972

DUSTER BENNETT

'Bright Lights, Big City'/'Talk To Me' (BH 57-3154) 1969

CLIFFORD DAVIS

'Before The Beginning'/'Man Of The World' (Reprise RS 27003) 1969

CLIFFORD DAVIS AND FRIENDS

'Come On Down And Follow Me'/'Homework' (Reprise RS27008) 1970

CD Single

CHRIS COCO

'Albatross' (Distinct'ive Records DISNCD 99) 2002

Albums

EDDIE BOYD

Eddie Boyd And His Blues Band (Decca SKL 4872) 1967
7936 South Rhodes (BH 7-63202) 1968

GORDON SMITH

Long Overdue – 'Divin' Duck Blues' (BH 7-63211) 1968

DUSTER BENNETT

Smiling Like I'm Happy – 'Shady Little Baby'; 'My Lucky Day'; 'My Love Is Your Love'; 'Times Like These' (BH 7-63208) 1968
Bright Lights – 'Bright Lights (And More Bright Lights)'; 'Talk To Me' (BH 7-63221) 1969
Out In The Blue – 'Trying So Hard To Forget'; 'Kind Hearted Woman'; 'Coming, I'm Coming'; 'I'm Thinking About A Woman'; 'Two Harps' (Indigo IGOCD 2018) 1995

JOHN MAYALL

Blues From Laurel Canyon – 'First Time Alone' (Decca SKL 4972) 1968
Along For The Ride – 'Yo Yo Man' (Eagle EAGCD 150) 2001

OTIS SPANN

The Biggest Thing Since Colossus (BH 7-63217) 1969

BRUNNING SUNFLOWER BLUES BAND

Trackside Blues – 'Ride With Your Daddy Tonight'; 'Simple Simon'; 'It Takes Time'; 'If You Let Me Love You'; 'Ah! Soul (Uranus Pt. 1)' (SagaEros EROS 8132) 1969
I Wish You Would – 'Uranus Take 2' (SagaEros SAGA 8150) 1970

JEREMY SPENCER

Jeremy Spencer – 'String-A-Long' (Reprise RSLP 9002) 1970

PETER BARDENS

The Answer (Transatlantic TRA 222) 1970

TOE FAT

Toe Fat Two – 'There'll Be Changes'; 'A New Way' (Regal Zonophone SRLZ 1015) 1970

GASS

Juju – 'Juju'; 'Black Velvet' (Polydor Super 2383 022) 1970

MEMPHIS SLIM

Blue Memphis (Barclay 920214) 1971

COUNTRY JOE MCDONALD

Hold On, It's Coming – 'Air Algiers'; 'Only Love Is Worth This Pain'; 'Mr. Big Pig' (Vanguard VSD 79314) 1971

DAVE KELLY

Dave Kelly – 'Gotta Keep Running'; 'You Got It'; 'Green Winter' (Mercury 6310 001) 1971

BB KING

In London – 'Caldonia' (ABC ABCL 5015) 1971

RICHARD KERR

From Now Until Then – 'Be My Friend' (Warner K 46206) 1973

FLEETWOOD MAC

Penguin – 'Night Watch' (Reprise K 44235) 1973
Tusk – 'Brown Eyes' (Warner K66088) 1979

DUFFO

The Disappearing Boy – 'The Idiot'; 'Lost In My Room' (PVK 2) 1980

BRIAN KNIGHT

A Dark Horse – 'Going Down Slow'; 'Trouble In Mind'; 'Blues Is Rock And Roll'; 'Mannish Boy' (PVK BRY 1) 1981

MICK FLEETWOOD

The Visitor – 'Rattlesnake Shake'; 'Super Brains' (RCA RCALP 5044) 1981

THE ENEMY WITHIN

A Touch Of Sunburn – 'Chinese White Boy'; 'Post Modern Blues' (Red Lightnin' RL 0067) 1986

SNOWY WHITE

Goldtop: Groups & Sessions '74–'94 – 'In The Skies'; 'Slabo Day' (RPM 154) 1995

SAS BAND

SAS Band – 'That's The Way God Planned It' (Bridge BRGCD25) 1997

DICK HECKSTALL-SMITH AND FRIENDS

Blues And Beyond – 'Cruel Contradictions' (Blue Storm Music 3004-2) 2001

PETER GABRIEL

Up – 'Sky Blue' (Real World Records PGCD11) 2002
Long Walk Home – 'Ngankarrparni'; 'Cloudless' (Real World Records PGCD10) 2002

CHRIS COCO

Next Wave – 'Albatross' (Distinct'ive Records DISNCD 78) 2002

DEBBIE DAVIES

Key To Love – A Celebration Of The Music Of John Mayall – 'Nature's Disappearing' (Shanachie 9034) 2003

RUDY ROTTA AND FRIENDS

Some Of My Favourite Songs For... – 'Black Magic Woman' (Slang Records SR001) 2006

THE BRITISH BLUES ALL-STARS

At Notodden Blues Festival – 'Black Magic Woman'; 'Standing By My Window'; 'I Got My Eye On You'; 'Everyday I Have The Blues' (SPV 49692) 2007

PART 3 AA.VV. VARIOUS ARTISTS COMPILATIONS AND CD RE-RELEASES FEATURING UNRELEASED TRACKS NOT AVAILABLE ON THE ORIGINAL RECORDS

Raw Blues (Ace Of Clubs SCL 1220) 1966
History Of The British Blues – Volume One (Sire SAS 3701) 1973
The Blue Horizon Story 1965–1970 Vol.1 (Columbia 488992 2) 1997
Twang! – A Tribute To Hank Martin & The Shadows (Pangea 72438 33928 2) 1996
Knights Of The Blues Table (Viceroy 54189-2) 1997

JOHN MAYALL AND THE BLUESBREAKERS

A Hard Road – Expanded Edition (Deram B0001083-02) 2003
The First Generation 1965–1974 (Madfish SMABX1140) 2021

OTIS SPANN

The Complete Blue Horizon Sessions (Columbia 82876822902) 2006

PETER BARDENS

Write My Name In The Dust (Castle CMEDD 1070) 2005

MEMPHIS SLIM

The Blue Memphis Suite (Maison De Blues 983211-1) 2006

FLEETWOOD MAC

The Complete Blue Horizon Sessions (Columbia 494641 2) 1999
The Vaudeville Years Of Fleetwood Mac (Receiver RDPCD 14 Z)
   1998
The Boston Box (Snapper SMBCD 598) 1999
Show-Biz Blues (Receiver RDPCD 15 Z) 2001
Tusk Deluxe Edition (Warner 081227950859) 2015
Before The Beginning 1968–1970 Live & Demo Sessions (Sony
   19075923252) 2019

SOLO WORKS

Rock & Pop Legends (Disky RPCD 012) 1995
White Sky (Castle CMRCD 1155) 2005
Kolors (Castle CMRCD 1156) 2005

NB There are many interesting, obscure Peter Green recordings
to supplement this discography. Most of them are freely available
at http://tela.sugarmegs.org/ and YouTube.

Index